LABOUR INSPECTION

A guide to the profession

WOLFGANG VON RICHTHOFEN

INTERNATIONAL LABOUR OFFICE • GENEVA

Richthofen, von W.
Labour inspection: A guide to the profession
Geneva, International Labour Office, 2002

Labour inspection. 04.03.5

ISBN 92-2-112710-9

ILO Cataloguing-in-Publication Data

Printed and Bound in Great Britain by Biddles Ltd
www.biddles .co.uk

LABOUR INSPECTION

A guide to the profession

PREFACE

Effective and efficient labour inspection is an essential paradigm of any civilized government and of any successful economy. At the start of the twenty-first century, this paradigm is still as valid as when labour inspection was created at the beginning of the nineteenth century.

The goal of the International Association of Labour Inspection (IALI) is to promote cooperation among its worldwide membership, exchange information on best practices in different countries, and strengthen and develop inspection systems for the benefit of employers and workers alike.

Since its inception over 30 years ago, the IALI has enjoyed an excellent partnership with the International Labour Organization. Its work, like that of the ILO, is based on a set of common principles and values, as embodied in the international labour Conventions and Recommendations relevant to labour protection in general, and to labour inspection in particular.

It is therefore with great pleasure that I welcome and endorse the publication of this new, comprehensive and authoritative ILO work on labour inspection. It addresses the profession, and thereby underlines the indisputable fact that labour inspection is a complex, demanding occupation requiring professional training, competency and commitment.

The IALI positively wishes to help promote and disseminate this book which, some 30 years after the last comprehensive ILO publication on the subject, fills a prominent gap. The need for a guide like this has been evident for some time. I therefore wish this significant new work all the success it decidedly merits.

Gerd Albracht
President
International Association of Labour Inspection
January 2002

CONTENTS

ACKNOWLEDGEMENTS

I owe all the thanks in the world to J.D.G. Hammer (former Deputy Director General of the Health and Safety Executive (HSE), United Kingdom, and long-term former President of the International Association of Labour Inspection (IALI)), mentor, friend and editor-in-chief, for his assistance and advice; Jean Courdouan, former chief, Labour Administration Branch of the ILO, for relentlessly prodding me on; Jukka Takala for giving all-important material support; my wife, Geneviève, who did so much typing after hours, and provided coffee and encouragement throughout; Lilian Neil and Rosemary Beattie for managing the editorial side of the project; Geraldeen Fitzgerald for all the nitty-gritty and tying up the loose ends; and Jacinta Tierney for helping finalize the text. I also wish to pay thanks to my father for the inspiration he provided, without knowing it, but which has been so important to me in helping complete this book. Finally, without being able to name them all, my grateful thanks are due to numerous professional colleagues inside and outside the ILO for their invaluable advice and comments.

ABOUT THE AUTHOR

Wolfgang Freiherr von Richthofen studied law, economics, political science and Indonesian anthropology at Berlin, Bonn and Heidelberg universities in Germany, and became a Barrister-at-Law at the High Court of Berlin in 1973.

His professional career over the past 20 years has included the post of Deputy Director, Center for Socio-Economic Development, German Foundation for International Development, Berlin; and, in the ILO, Senior Labour Administration Specialist, former Labour Administration Branch, and Coordinator, Development of Inspection Systems, SafeWork – ILO InFocus Programme on Safety and Health at Work and the Environment.

Over the years he has been the author and editor of, and contributor to, numerous publications on labour inspection. He is a Member of the Jury of the StGB Work, Safety and Health Award in Germany. He is principal lecturer on labour inspection at the African Regional Labour Administration Centre (ARLAC), Harare, Zimbabwe, and also acts as visiting lecturer on comparative labour protection at Hanover University, Germany, and on labour administration at the Department for Extramural Studies (Ruskin College), Oxford University, United Kingdom.

INTRODUCTION

Labour inspection has been on the ILO agenda ever since the Organization was founded over 80 years ago. In 1919, at the very first International Labour Conference (ILC), an international labour standard on labour inspection was adopted in the form of a Recommendation. Subsequent ILCs continued to debate standards, culminating in the 1947 adoption of the fundamental ILO instrument on this subject, the Labour Inspection Convention (No. 81). Based on substantive research carried out in the late 1960s, the Labour Inspection (Agriculture) Convention (No. 129) was adopted in 1969.[1] However, this standard-setting work and the frequent general discussions on labour inspection as an issue at successive ILCs have not been reflected in a similar number of ILO publications on the subject. In 1972, a manual entitled *Labour inspection: Purposes and practice* was published, embodying the knowledge on labour inspection accumulated during the first part of the twentieth century and, in particular, developments since the Second World War. This manual has served as the standard ILO text on labour inspection for almost 30 years. Although still a useful reference work, it is now largely out of date.

Subsequent ILO publications include: *Labour inspection: General Survey by the Committee of Experts on the application of Conventions and Recommendations*, in 1985; *Labour inspection*, A workers' education manual, in 1986; *International labour standards concerned with labour inspection* in 1991; and a series by the Labour Administration Branch on such topics – often sector specific – as labour inspection in the petroleum industry, in construction and in the non-commercial services.[2] A Protocol to Convention No. 81 was adopted by the ILC in 1995 to cover the non-commercial services sector,[3] and more recently, in 1996, labour inspection in the maritime industry appeared on the agenda of a special session of the ILC aimed at the adoption of the Labour Inspection (Seafarers) Convention, 1996 (No. 178).

However, since the early 1970s (perhaps starting in the United Kingdom as a result of the ground-breaking Robens report, but also in other (then)

1

European Economic Community (EEC) countries and Organisation for Economic Cooperation and Development (OECD) member States), substantial new developments and major changes have occurred in both the policy and practice of labour inspection. As a result of the transition in Central and Eastern Europe, an entire system, as practised in the former centrally planned economy countries, disappeared. Entirely new strategies have surfaced: that of "internal control" in Norway and Sweden, or the merging of parts of social insurance (workers' compensation) with the inspection services in some states of Australia, in New Zealand and elsewhere; and the concept of occupational safety and health management systems.

With the vision of "decent work" and the ILO's response to globalization high on the agenda, labour inspection is entrusted with a whole new set of responsibilities. This is expressed in the by now familiar slogan, "Decent Work is Safe Work".

Various developments in the socio-economic context of different regions and ILO member States therefore call for a broader reflection on the changing role of labour inspection systems and services in the twenty-first century. Some of the major, foreseeable economic developments in the labour market with regard to technology and national, sectoral and enterprise social structures, which will directly affect labour inspection, include:

- the effects of globalization;
- the growth of more and more small, independent enterprise units that are more and more difficult to supervise effectively with leaner resources;
- the continuing trend of enterprises to exist for only a short time, changing their form and ownership and becoming geographically more mobile (nationally as well as internationally);
- the worldwide increase of different forms of the "shadow economy";
- the appearance of "virtual" networks of enterprises where people do what they can do best;
- virtual employers, and small and micro-employers ("dependent independents"), and how labour inspection can keep track of them and influence their working environment;
- cost and competition pressure, which is likely to increase and become dominant, to the continuing detriment of social considerations;
- changes in the labour market such as: shorter or longer working hours; increases in atypical or precarious work relationships; "employees" working for several "employers" at once; the "downgrading" of jobs; new forms of subcontracting, and their impact on traditional concepts of labour protection; insecurity of employment, leading to increased stress and reduced solidarity among employees, as well as reduced participation; and

- new forms of work organization and, consequently, new social relations structures in enterprises, creating new and unfamiliar problems in the area of labour inspection and issues arising from the partnership between tradition and technology.

However, countervailing trends are likely to impact on labour inspection. Insecurity may lead to an increasing need for protection, and demands for stronger state intervention and control. After deregulation and privatization, there may be a need for "re-regulation", if tasks abandoned by the State cannot be properly handled by market forces. The need for international compatibility, and equality of standards and levels of protection, as well as equity of enforcement, may grow. The secondary (manufacturing) sector will continue to shrink. As a result, new risks in the tertiary (services) sector may receive greater attention, and enterprises will regard good social relations and risk management as an opportunity to enable cost control and loss reduction. They will therefore seek to build productive and cooperative working relationships at the workplace and with labour inspection services.

For labour inspection services, these and other tendencies will have significant and multiple consequences, many of which are not yet readily understood. Inspection systems, in particular the managers of such services, will have to be able to broadly analyse and understand the diverse forces driving economic, social, ecological and technological change. They will have to acquire the capacity to respond rapidly, flexibly and in an anticipatory manner to these challenges. It will be necessary to abandon a rigid, narrow approach based on a single specialization (legal, technical, medical, social) in favour of a truly integrated vision, and develop an understanding of the factors that influence and contribute to improved labour protection.

This comprehensive ILO publication on labour inspection is designed to enable professional inspectors in member States to understand, anticipate and effectively cope with economic and social change in the world of work. As such, it seeks to guide the reader through four parts. Part I provides the background and discusses some major issues and challenges, and the response to these challenges from managers of high-performance inspection services. Part II presents policy issues in an international context. Part III addresses topical aspects of organization and management of inspection services.

Part IV examines some major sectoral issues facing labour inspectors worldwide. Various sectors present singular problems to labour inspection, and require special handling and different solutions. For example, how can any labour inspectorate, with finite resources, realistically and effectively oversee labour conditions in the vast number of small and medium-sized enterprises

(SMEs) which make up the great majority of workplaces and are multiplying daily in every country of the world? This is a perennial and much-debated concern at meetings and conferences. In practice, however, many effective strategies have been developed in various countries. Therefore, an analysis of the needs and concerns of SMEs and a summary of the tested experience of many different inspectorates are presented in Part IV. It goes without saying that these are not ready-made solutions; in practice, each inspectorate will need to select and tailor a strategy to fit its own institutions, culture, resources and current priorities.

Child labour calls for a particular understanding of the circumstances in which it occurs. But it needs determination to end the exploitation, mitigate the suffering and improve the lot of many millions of children. The Worst Forms of Child Labour Convention (No. 182) was adopted in 1999 with a view to eliminating the most hazardous forms of child labour. The role of labour inspection in this context has no doubt taken on a new dimension.

Likewise in agriculture, a term covering a vast range of activities world-wide, there are nevertheless similarities in terms of high risk, hazards to children and families, and the isolation of individual units. Again, these require either specialized attention, or else greater emphasis on particular policies and other, different compliance strategies.

The non-commercial services sector, brought within the ambit of Convention No. 81 by the Protocol of 1995, presents a particular challenge to labour inspectors. Government departments, universities, medical services, the armed forces or prison services have generally been unaccustomed to being subject to the inspection process. Both understanding and sustained pressure are necessary to achieve results in this sector.

Thus, the purpose of this book is to collect, analyse and make available to ILO constituents, and particularly to interested professionals worldwide, an authoritative reference work on labour inspection, its fundamental principles, the challenges it is likely to face in the dawn of the new century, and the major aspects of its role, scope, policy, organization, management and functions. Emphasis has been laid on recent global developments in the field, and the best practices adopted in different countries to meet the challenges outlined above.

To sum up, the purpose of this book is to:

- present the response of labour inspectorates to labour protection issues in a globalizing world, be they economic, social or technological;
- describe improved ways to meet old and new challenges facing labour inspectorates in respect of major policy, organizational, management and sectoral issues;

- identify and analyse best practices in some high-performance inspection systems in ILO member States;
- disseminate the results of this reflection as a source of guidance and reference to the ILO's tripartite constituency;
- underscore the overriding importance for labour inspection to develop a preventive capacity, to contribute to building a prevention culture in the world of work; and
- emphasize the need to adopt a professional approach to labour inspection, indeed, to validate labour inspection as a profession in its own right.

This guide addresses labour inspection managers throughout inspection systems. It is intended to be helpful to inspectors, labour protection specialists from government, employers' and workers' organizations and their representatives in enterprises, researchers, experts and other professionals and, finally, the public.

Jukka Takala
Director
SafeWork – InFocus Programme on Safety and Health at Work and the Environment

Notes

[1] The operative paragraphs of the major international labour standards on labour inspection are reproduced in Annex I.

[2] See the Bibliography, section III.

[3] See Annex I.

PART I

LABOUR INSPECTION:
BACKGROUND, EVOLUTION AND CONTEXT

"Labour legislation without inspection is an exercise in ethics, but not a binding social discipline."

Francis Blanchard, Director-General of the ILO, 1974–89

THE FOUNDATIONS 1

1.1 Historical origins

Labour inspection, as an indispensable institution of social policy, has its origins in the nineteenth century – a child of the Industrial Revolution, it spread from Great Britain to Europe and beyond. Like industrialization itself, labour inspection started in Britain, in 1802, when Parliament passed an act on the preservation of the health and morals of apprentices in textile and other factories. Compliance with this act was supervised by voluntary committees but proved to be ineffective. Therefore, in 1833, the Government entrusted supervision to "persons of high standing", who carried out real functions of inspection, essentially with regard to excessively long working hours, then common practice, even for children. The appointment of the first four of these "inspectors" marks the birth of modern-day labour inspection.

However, understanding the risks related to work, and the need for, and usefulness of, preventing risks is much older. Hippocrates, the father of medicine, had already established a link between rock dust and lung disease in stonecutters. At the end of the Middle Ages, the connection between different trades and specific health hazards was well known in Europe.

But it was because of the appalling conditions which prevailed, as a result of industrialization and mass labour, that labour inspection came to be considered a responsibility, indeed a necessity, of state intervention, a function of the constitutional obligation of government to protect the integrity of its working population.

This development was driven by notable nineteenth century humanists, such as Robert Owen, the Welsh industrialist, who was both successful in business while also offering workers exceptionally good conditions for the era. Schuchart, a German entrepreneur, proposed setting up a state-run factory inspectorate in Germany in 1837, but it took another 15 years before his demands became reality. In France, at the instigation of entrepreneurs such as Daniel le Grand, a first labour protection act was adopted in 1841, though a further 30 years passed before an inspectorate was actually set up. There were not only humanitarian considerations: some governments were concerned that hard labour for children ruined the health of their prospective soldiers. Thus, political and economic motives were as much a driving force for better working conditions, and for a government role in implementing relevant legislation, as were mere social ones. To this day, these considerations remain at the centre of discussions in the unending struggle to improve the safety, health and welfare of workers the world over.

During the nineteenth century, most European countries adopted, albeit slowly, legislation reflecting new developments in industry, as well as more democratic and socially aware attitudes. In 1890, representatives of 15 States attended a conference in Berlin to adopt the first international labour standards. That conference affirmed that laws in each State should be supervised by an adequate number of specially qualified officers, appointed by government and independent of both employers and workers. Again, concerns for more equitable economic conditions in international trade and competition were as much behind these reforms as were social considerations. After that, however, social progress was further accelerated. The first medical inspector of factories was appointed in Great Britain in 1898. By 1899, the first specialist engineering adviser was in office. And, in 1901, the first female factory inspector, Elsa von Richthofen, was appointed in Germany. Thus, the foundation of a modern labour inspection system, with general inspectors, both men and women, and technical and medical specialists, had been laid in a number of European countries by the beginning of the twentieth century.

1.2 Fundamental principles

The end of the First World War saw the creation of the ILO through Article XIII of the Treaty of Versailles. In its Constitution, the ILO required all member States to set up a system of labour inspection, and two of its very first international instruments were the Labour Inspection (Health Services Recommendation, 1919 (No. 5), and the Labour Inspection Recommendation, 1923 (No. 20). These initial international standards on labour inspection contained several basic principles of modern labour inspection, if only in a non-binding form. At the end of the Second World War, work had been completed on an ambitious set of standards: the Labour Inspection Convention, 1947 (No. 81), and associated Recommendations (Nos. 81, 82 and 85[1]). These new standards were comprehensive and far-sighted. The principles they laid down over 50 years ago are still valid and entirely relevant today, so much so that few ILO member States are in a position to report that they have attained and are maintaining the standards contained in this Convention and its sister instrument, the Labour Inspection (Agriculture) Convention, 1969 (No. 129).[2]

These instruments, first of all, set forth the principle that labour inspection is a public function, a responsibility of government, best organized as a system, within the larger context of a state system, in order to administer social and labour policy and to supervise compliance with legislation and standards. Therefore, labour inspectors should enjoy the status and independence of public officials exercising their powers and functions in an impartial manner compatible with their public office and free of undue pressures and constraints from outside the system. As representatives of the State in the world of work, labour inspectors are empowered with considerable rights, but also bound by a set of duties regarding the way they exercise their functions, which may extend even beyond the termination of their office. The proper exercise of these rights and duties is fundamental to the authority of inspectors and the inspection system as a whole.

A second principle concerns the need for close cooperation between labour inspection and employers and workers. This cooperation is essential. It begins with the collaboration between labour inspection, government, employers and employees' organizations in the formulation of labour protection legislation and its application in the workplace, and includes the study of problems and proposals to improve living and working conditions, and the provision of information to employers concerning their statutory obligations. Cooperation presupposes that the participation of workers' representatives is guaranteed, and that employers assume their responsibilities in full measure.

The effectiveness of labour inspection is directly linked to the interest that management takes in labour protection issues, and the resources it devotes to solving them. It is also, directly, linked to the presence and action of trade unions at the workplace (hence the difficulty of ensuring inspection in small enterprises or, more generally, in countries where the trade union movement is weak or has not realized its role to ensure the protection of workers). The purpose of inspection is to see to it that the greatest possible number of problems relating to the protection of workers are solved at the workplace, as a result, first and foremost, of dialogue and consultation between the actors directly involved (employers and workers), and with the advice of the labour inspector, regarding compliance with legislation, minimum standards and the terms of any collective agreements that contain relevant standards.

This gives rise to a number of points of relevance to labour inspection. How is this dialogue to be initiated? How can it be conducted? How much time is to be devoted to it? How can one strike a balance between the need to achieve quick concrete results on which the quality of working conditions in an establishment depends, and the equally legitimate concern to stimulate the social partners to become responsible actors, dealing directly with the problems that affect them and not having recourse uniquely to the labour inspector? As will be seen later, different inspection systems provide different answers to these questions, but all inspection systems are confronted by them.

A third principle concerns the need for effective cooperation with other institutions such as research institutes, universities, the prevention services of social security authorities, and with experts, and the need to coordinate their activities. The complexity of technical and legal problems today is such that labour inspection cannot, as a general rule, ensure effective knowledge of enterprises without external cooperation. It must have access to the aid of specialists (doctors, engineers and chemists). No inspection department can have a staff of agents covering all fields of technological competence, each versed in all relevant aspects of modern industrial technology. But it is clear that every inspector should have sufficiently general technical knowledge to understand and assess the nature of a hazard, to call in specialists, and indeed to preserve coherence in the simultaneous intervention of experts in very varied fields. In this manner, labour inspection becomes capable of conducting a "global and coherent" action.

A fourth principle relates to labour inspection's increasing orientation and emphasis on prevention. To speak of prevention in the context of labour protection implies, first of all, a determined effort to avoid incidents, disputes, accidents, conflicts and occupational diseases by assuring compliance with existing legislation. Today, a preventive orientation has, as its ultimate objective, the development of a culture of prevention in a social and labour policy paradigm. It also aims more and more at the broader goal of enabling individuals to lead a long, productive and healthy life, at the same time as reducing the exponentially growing costs of non-prevention, or loss caused by all manner of incidents to individuals, enterprises, and society as a whole. Prevention, in today's world of work, is increasingly being identified not only for its short- or medium-term advantages, but for supporting long-term economic and social policy objectives at national, sectoral and enterprise levels, sustaining working capacity, productivity and quality, motivation of employees and security of employment. Prevention is therefore seen as a decisive prerequisite both for individuals to lead a dignified life in society, and for enterprises to be successful competitors in the (global) market. It is therefore increasingly defined as a holistic, "open" or pluralistic concept, aimed at avoiding a multiplicity of technical, social, medical, psychological and economic hazards. For this reason, a recent major change in labour inspection orientation has been towards adopting a broader, multidisciplinary approach to prevention. This vision-of-the-whole approach is considered a prerequisite to dealing effectively in a preventive manner with the host of complex, interdependent problems that exist in the world of work today.

The fifth principle concerns the drive for universal coverage, the need to extend labour inspection's protective and preventive action to the largest possible number of working people in all areas of activity. In principle, society should not, and labour inspection cannot, tolerate the existence of an economy where certain categories of workers are protected and others are not. Labour inspection is also based on the notion of solidarity and respect for the collective values of society. That is why, in recent years, labour inspection systems in many countries have extended their coverage in various directions traditionally not under their responsibility such as: central government administration, the public services, the armed forces, the police, the self-employed, the "informal" sector and so on. Some even go beyond the confines of formal employment relationships (in many systems the point of departure, and basis, for labour inspection intervention) to include the protection of anyone affected by work activities, although this is by no means undisputed. What is evident is that these fundamental principles are at the heart of an ongoing, concerted dialogue with the labour inspectorate partners on the role, scope and functions of inspection, its organization, methods and resources, with a view to continuing to adapt them to economic, social and technical developments and to developing and maintaining a viable, long-term perspective.

1.3   Sources of authority

The sources of labour inspection authority are to be found in a set of relevant international labour standards.[3]

By virtue of the ILO Constitution,[4] ILO member States are urged (though not obliged) to ratify the Organization's newly adopted Conventions (and Protocols). Members must, within a year of the adoption of an instrument by the International Labour Conference, bring the new Convention before the national authority, usually a country's parliament, for "the enactment of legislation or other action".

In ratifying an international labour Convention, a member State makes a formal commitment to give effect to the provisions of that Convention. Ratification has an immediate impact on national legislation in countries where, under the constitutional system, ratified Conventions become automatically part of the law of the land and are therefore directly enforceable by the courts when they are self-executing (for example, certain social security Conventions, or the Conventions on maternity protection). In other countries, the provisions of a ratified Convention have to be transposed into national legislation before becoming effective. In many instances, such legislation is adopted prior to ratification to facilitate the application process.

There are also cases in which a Convention is ratified when national legislation is already in conformity with its provisions. Even then, ratification is important since it enables the multilateral supervisory procedures foreseen in the ILO's Constitution to function. Furthermore, it also secures for the ratifying States the international recognition of the level of their labour policy and legislation, and it gives other States an incentive to attain the same standards, providing both an example and an assurance of widespread implementation.

The concept of labour inspection, as developed by the ILO constituents, is that of a subsystem embedded in the larger system of national labour administration. Thus, the Labour Administration Convention, 1978 (No. 159), entrusts member States with the obligation to establish a system of labour administration, encompassing all aspects and institutions of national labour policy. In the Labour Administration Recommendation, 1978 (No. 158), members are urged to set up a system of labour inspection integrated into the national labour administration structures.

The ratifying member State must organize an effective system of labour administration, whose functions and responsibilities must be properly coordinated. It must secure, within this system, consultation, cooperation, and negotiation with employers' and workers' organizations.

Convention No. 150 sets out the functions of labour administration as:

- preparation (of legal instruments);
- administration;
- coordination;
- checking and reviewing national labour policy;
- preparing and implementing laws and regulations;
- tasks relating to national employment policy;
- conditions of work and working life;
- terms of employment;
- services and advice to employers and workers and their organizations; and
- representing the State in international labour affairs.

The staff of the labour administration system must be composed of people who are suitably qualified and independent of improper external influences. They should have the status, the material means and the financial resources necessary for the effective performance of their duties. Finally, the extension of labour administration services to cover workers who are not, by law, employed people is to be promoted.

Two specific Conventions and a Protocol deal exclusively with issues of labour inspection: the Labour Inspection Convention, 1947 (No. 81), covering industry and commerce as well as mining and transport, and the Labour Inspection (Agriculture) Convention, 1969 (No. 129). The Protocol of 1995 to Convention No. 81 covers the non-commercial services sector.

Convention No. 81 provides for a system of labour inspection to secure the enforcement of legal provisions relating to conditions of work and the protection of workers in industrial workplaces, as well as in commercial workplaces, if the ratifying State accepts this extension.

Convention No. 81 deals with:

- the organization and functioning of inspection services;
- the responsibilities of a central authority;
- their cooperation with other public and private services, and with employers and workers or their organizations;
- the recruitment of qualified staff in sufficient numbers (including women with appropriate status);
- material means and facilities (offices and transport);
- the thorough and regular inspection of workplaces; and
- the publication of reports and annual statistics on the work of the inspection services.

The Convention defines the functions of labour inspectors and their powers to:

- freely enter any workplace liable to inspection;
- carry out inquiries freely, and in particular to question people;
- examine documents and take samples;
- make orders with a view to remedying defects and deciding whether they are appropriate;
- give warning and advice, or institute or recommend proceedings.

In return, inspectors are required to respect certain obligations: they are prohibited from having any direct or indirect interest in the undertakings under their supervision and shall not reveal manufacturing or commercial secrets of the workplaces they inspect, or the source of any complaint.

Convention No. 129 applies to agricultural enterprises and covers employees or apprentices or – subject to a declaration by the ratifying State to this effect – tenants, share-croppers and similar categories of agricultural workers, members of a cooperative or of the family of the operator. Its provisions are to a large extent based on those of Convention No. 81 regarding the organization, the functions and the staff of the system of inspection, as well as the duties, powers and obligations of the inspectors.

The Convention contains certain innovations which take into account the special characteristics of the agricultural sector, and the experiences gained since Convention No. 81 came into force 20 years earlier. These innovations take the form of certain provisions: the organizational flexibility and structure of the inspection services; the extension to inspectors of advisory or enforcement functions regarding legal provisions relating to the living conditions of workers and their families; and the possibility of including representatives of occupational organizations in the system of labour inspection officials and of entrusting certain inspection functions at the regional or local level to other appropriate government services or public institutions.

Finally, the Protocol to Convention No. 81, which is open to ratification by all member States having ratified the Convention, reaffirms the principles of that standard and encourages its application to the non-commercial services sector, while at the same time providing the necessary element of flexibility to ensure that legitimate concerns, for example, for national security and the proper functioning of the executive, do not stand in the way of applying the Convention to that sector.

These standards provide the indispensable, universal framework for the status and functioning of labour inspection, its foundations and its basic structures. As such they are also a source of strength to the inspection system, the inspectors and the clients they are to serve.

1.4 Tripartism

Tripartism constitutes the framework in which labour inspection must operate if it is to be successful. In the ILO context, this means the interaction between government (the labour administration system), and employers and workers, their organizations and their representatives. It is an instrument for addressing common concerns, involving various means of interaction within a framework of social dialogue: sharing of information, consultations, negotiations and decision making. In the context of labour inspection, it can take place at international, national, provincial, sector or enterprise level.

Tripartite interaction has several objectives: it enables the parties to be actively involved in issues of mutual concern, thereby promoting improved understanding of their common and conflicting interests. With tripartite interaction, a balance can be found between economic, political and social concerns, as well as between the individual interests of each of the three parties and overall sectoral or national interests. Tripartite cooperation means that the specific knowledge and interests of each of the three parties can be taken into account in addressing economic and social questions. In so doing, policies, laws and specific solutions can be formulated which are acceptable to each party and which address its specific needs. Tripartite cooperation can result in a broader consensus in decision making, thereby enhancing the legitimacy of the process and the acceptability of its outcome, and ultimately easing the task of enforcement by inspectors in the field.

Effective tripartism requires that each of the social partners be represented. For workers' and employers' organizations, this implies that they speak on behalf of the majority of workers and employers in the country, or at least a sufficient number to give credibility and recognition to these organizations; that they have effective contact with the members they represent to ensure that those members' interests and ideas are considered; and that they are able to nominate whom they choose as their representatives in the tripartite consultative forum.

Just as employers' and workers' organizations must be representative, so must governments. In this context, "representative" means that the government in question is perceived as pursuing the legitimate interests of its working people.

Effective tripartism requires that workers' and employers' organizations be independent: each social partner should be operating according to its own objectives and procedures without undue influence from government authorities.

Effective tripartism and social dialogue can lead to reduced conflict, greater industrial peace, better motivation, higher productivity, improved quality, better labour protection and, in consequence, a reduced need for labour inspection intervention. It is therefore an imperative element of successful labour protection strategies, from national level down to the shop floor.

Notes

[1] See Bibliography, section IV.

[2] The operative paragraphs of the major international labour standards on labour inspection are reproduced in Annex I.

[3] See also Part II, "Inspection systems: Policy", and ILO: *International labour standards concerned with labour inspection: Main provisions* (Geneva, 1990).

[4] Article 19, para. 5.

THE FRAMEWORK

2

2.1 The socio-economic context

As the twenty-first century begins, most institutions in the field of labour and social policy (originating, as they do, in the nineteenth century) are undergoing profound, rapid and dramatic changes the world over, and labour inspection is not exempt from the socio-economic impact of these changes. This is due to a combination of various factors and transformations, both "internal" and "external" to the organizations, often a mix of a political, social, economic, administrative, cultural and technological nature. These changes have a profound impact on the role, scope and functions of the institutions concerned, their relationships with each other, with their principal "clients" and with the general public. An understanding and analysis of the nature of these changes, how they affect the performance, impact and relationships of the principal actors and the social reality in which they operate and, in particular, how they contribute to the accomplishment of the main actors' most important functions will help labour inspectorates to cope better with the pressures of change in fulfilling their mission.

Rapid change and innovation in the world of work and the working environment continue to pose major problems to labour inspectorates everywhere. In fact inspectors face two sets of issues. The first stems from evolution in the client system, such as rapid and complex technological changes, fragmentation and growing volume of labour legislation and standards, segmentation of the labour market and the increasing vulnerability of the labour force accompanied by shifting economic and social conditions, changes in the mentality and expectations of clients, an altered role for employers' organizations and trade unions, a revised view of the general role of the State in labour administration and its regulatory service, labour inspection in particular, and so on. The second set expresses the full force of pressures brought to bear upon public administrations worldwide, from which labour inspections are not exempt, and are characterized by factors and processes such as reductions in public spending, drives towards lean administration, calls for accountability and transparency, moves to privatize or outsource "non-core" functions, decentralization of responsibilities and market testing of services.

These changes compel labour inspectorates the world over to adjust, to innovate, to adopt new policies, to strengthen old partnerships and to look for new ones. In particular, inspectorates are faced with the task of improving their productivity, increasing their effectiveness and efficiency, and optimizing – and showing proof of – their impact by developing new, or revising existing policies, strategies and intervention methods. In this context, initiatives aimed at re-emphasizing labour inspection's role in and contribution to prevention, in all potential areas under its purview, are providing key elements for new strategies. However, many labour inspection systems, while continuing to enforce protective labour legislation, have yet to explore their potential as a major driving force in a comprehensive approach to implementing such new strategies.

Labour inspection operates in an environment that is neither homogeneous in its social components nor constant in its technical and economic characteristics. It is subject to the far-reaching and increasingly rapid developments affecting the economies and societies of all countries, of which globalization is the latest, but only one of many determining factors. Labour inspection thus finds itself continuously confronted with a complex set of challenges (which will be analysed in Chapters 6 and 7, and in Part IV), but can be briefly characterized as follows: technological developments; increasingly precarious labour markets; more complex labour legislation; and the overall challenge presented by developments in the economic and social context, that is, to maintain (and develop) labour inspection's ability to develop original and innovative means of achieving its specific aims in the face of economic and political pressures.

There is, in this context, a growing interpenetration of economic and social issues. The advisory and supervisory action devoted by labour inspection to the amelioration of working conditions, the prevention of accidents and ill health, and the improvement of human and labour relations is producing increasingly noticeable effects in the context of economic developments. It has been observed more and more frequently that differences in national economic trends largely reflect differences in the social climate, as economic potential depends on a close conjunction of technical and human resources. This is a development that has transformed and broadened the significance conferred on labour inspection in the government intervention machinery of many countries, although inspectorates were long considered as devoting themselves primarily to a police-type intervention, which was mistakenly judged only in the light of its constraints and burdensome consequences. If one primary objective of labour inspection has always been to promote social support measures in step with economic development, it is now contributing very directly to this development by the introduction of social measures, without which economic performance would inevitably be compromised, and by its faculty of strengthening the cohesion of all actors involved in its success. Labour inspection is thus an instrument of both social and economic development. However, few political leaders are as yet genuinely aware of this fact.

2.2   The political framework

There are few countries in which the role of labour inspection is as yet fully known, understood and recognized for its true worth. Awareness of its role and its usefulness is not, as a general rule, sufficiently established either at a political level or even among those groups directly concerned, employers and trade unions. In some countries, it is the role and place of the State that are called into question, and thus the whole role of labour administration, with all the familiar consequences for resource allocations and status. In other countries, which have moved from a bureaucratic and state-controlled system to a market economy, the role of the State, of labour inspection and of employers and employees must be explored anew, redefined and reinforced. A market economy, left to itself, cannot adequately regulate the functioning of societies, and certainly not in the field of labour protection.

In developing countries, additional political factors arise. Such countries tend to suffer even more from the effects of unemployment, underemployment, over-rapid urbanization, lack of training for industrial activities and adoption of new technologies in difficult conditions. Moreover, the transfer of polluting and dangerous industries and the absence of modern, appropriate labour legislation have brought about two coexisting labour worlds, one technologically advanced, the other using traditional working methods (in the urban as well as the rural "informal" sector). Other factors include a heterogeneous working class, implying differences in status with regard to workers' protection, a low proportion of the active population in wage-earning employment, and the natural tendency of the wage-earning population is to devote more attention to questions of employment and wages than to improving conditions of work. Workers are obviously reluctant – in a context of poverty and unemployment – to jeopardize their jobs by demanding that their social rights be respected. The "worst possible working environment" in this case is simply having no work at all. This is the political environment in which labour inspection in many countries operates, and where its proper functioning results in a daily struggle for survival.

2.3   The legal basis

Notwithstanding the authority given to labour inspection by the relevant international labour Conventions and Recommendations (and, to a lesser degree, by other international or supranational norms and standards), these instruments, as a rule, have to be ratified by special procedure, usually an act of parliament, before they can effectively enter into force at national level, creating binding legal obligations, rights and duties for labour inspection systems, inspectors, employers and workers.

By their very nature, labour inspection services, as part of the public admin-istration system, require an institutional framework based on laws or regulations. In a great many countries, the organization of the labour inspectorate is based on broader laws designed to protect workers, whether these texts be of a general nature or specific to certain issues or branches of the economy. Generally speaking, these laws outline the organization of the labour inspection service, or else contain provisions concerning (institutional) enforcement. Very often they are complemented by more detailed texts governing specific aspects of the operation of an inspectorate, although in many countries this area is governed by provisions that are generally applicable to public service organizations. Other countries may have specific regulations for the inspection services, that is, a labour inspection law or decree (often modelled closely along the lines of the Labour Inspection Convention, 1947 (No. 81).[1]

In many countries, basic legal foundations of labour protection are already found in their constitutions. As an example, the Indonesian Constitution of 1945 proclaims, in Article 27, that: "Every citizen has a right to employment under conditions appropriate to humanity". The basic function of the system of labour inspection (created in that country in 1951) is thus to fulfil a constitutional obligation of the State towards its citizens. In Germany, Article 2 of the Constitution (the "Basic Law") requires that the State ensure the right to life and physical well-being at the workplace. This is representative of a large number of ILO member States. However, such expressions of political interest are rarely in themselves directly applicable. Rather, they regularly have to be supplemented by a framework of labour protection/inspection legislation. This body of law has itself undergone dramatic change in many countries in recent years. While originally intended to protect the workers as the weaker party in an employment contract, it now frequently constitutes a charter of rights of people at work and provides a framework for the organization of relationships among all sections of the community.

This framework will usually be made up of a composite of laws, regulations, norms, standards and "softer", often negotiated conditions, as in collective agreements or codes of practice. Some countries, such as France, have consolidated the bulk of their labour protection legislation into one single labour code, essentially covering all major functional areas of labour inspection: industrial relations, general conditions of work, employment, occupational safety and health, and elements of social security. Others have more recently promulgated a separate body of legislation only for select functions, concentrating for example on occupational safety, health, welfare and the working environment. This process was started in the 1970s in several countries, first the United States Occupational Safety and Health Administration (OSHA, 1970), then the United Kingdom (1974), Norway and Sweden (1977/78), the Netherlands (1981) and, quite recently, Germany (1997). It marks a development away from a relatively narrow, prescriptive and reactive legislation towards a more flexible, proactive, "enabling" legislative base, allowing employers to adopt those measures most appropriate to the hazards associated with their enterprises. This new-type legislation is often called "goal based", as it sets protection objectives and defines the desired and required end results, but leaves employers considerable freedom as to how to attain them.

During the past decade, many governments have found it expedient to undertake in-depth reviews of their legislative base. In quite a number of countries, this is an ongoing exercise incumbent upon the labour inspectorate. It has resulted in a move towards revised, more objective-based framework legislation (e.g. Norway, 1992), complemented by specific regulations, and codes of practice. These latter are not binding, making them both flexible and easily adaptable to changing circumstances. They are usually defined in consultation with governments, workers' and employers' organizations. As they do not have legal force in a strict sense, employers may choose other solutions to deal with hazards, provided they achieve the same level of protection that the code of practice aims for. On the other hand, if employers follow the code, they can be sure of having complied with the minimum legal requirements.

One further noticeable consequence of legislative review has been a marked tendency to simplify the structure of the legal framework, and to reduce its complex content, as well as the number of texts, to eliminate overlap and contradictions, and to recast the norms and standards to be retained into clearer, more readily understandable, user-friendly language, benefiting smaller enterprises, to whose problems labour inspection systems worldwide feel a need to devote more and more time and attention.

2.4 The administrative environment

Labour inspection systems today have a considerable number of similar features concerning their policies, role, powers and methods of intervention. Indeed, one cannot but notice convergence trends in these areas even between systems traditionally considered far apart. Yet, organizational structures and the administrative environments in which they operate tend to differ widely. This is a reflection of the fact that they are part and parcel of the general civil administration of each country and thus embedded in traditions, procedures, and a political and administrative culture that usually originated long before the advent of labour inspection and, until recently, tended to develop in relative isolation from other systems and the international community. Harmonization trends that are now emerging, for instance in supranational trade blocs, and which in some cases have a very considerable impact on the development of labour protection legislation and the functioning of labour inspection, are a relatively recent phenomenon.

The international instruments on labour inspection are more or less silent on this subject. As already mentioned, the Labour Administration Convention, 1978 (No. 150), and its accompanying Recommendation No. 158, envisage that the labour inspection system be integrated into national labour administration structures (usually the Ministry of Labour and/or Social Affairs and its field services, or an equivalent body), but that is as far as it goes.

Convention No. 81 itself is no more explicit. It requires (in Article 4) that labour inspection be placed under the supervision and control of a central authority (again, as a rule, the respective Ministry of Labour), but understandably gives member States the widest possible leverage to apply this norm "so far as is compatible with the administrative practice of the Member". It does, however, stipulate (in Article 6) that "inspection staff shall be composed of public officials whose status and conditions of service are such that they are assured of stability of employment and are independent of changes of government and of improper external influences". This is an important provision which has considerable consequences in the practice of labour inspection throughout the world, but again it does not necessarily position inspection systems in the administrative environment in which they must operate.

Thus, experience in ILO member States tends to be remarkably heterogeneous, added to which the practice in federally constituted Members is often even more complex. Indeed, in some federal countries, this heterogeneity applies even internally – the system being different between one province, state or territory and another (e.g. Australia, Canada, United States). The Labour Inspection in Agriculture Convention, 1969 (No. 129) is more helpful in this respect, but really only with regard to the sector it covers. Here, it specifically lists four possibilities whereby effect might be given to the general principle of placing the inspection services under a central authority:[2]

- "a single labour inspection agency responsible for all sectors of economic activity"; this tends to work well in small countries or in countries where the civil service is still more or less in a state of development;
- a single labour inspection agency which would, as the Convention puts it, "arrange for internal functional specialization through the appropriate training of inspectors called upon to exercise their functions in agriculture"; this system has been adopted in certain Latin American countries where there is a single central inspection authority (again, the Ministry of Labour), but where agriculture is considered so important that inspectors are specially trained for agricultural inspection;
- a single labour inspection agency which (in the language of the Convention) "would arrange for internal institutional specialization by creating a technically qualified service, the officers of which would perform their functions in agriculture"; or
- "a specialized agricultural inspection service, the activity of which would be supervised by a central body vested with the same prerogatives in respect of labour inspection in other fields, such as industry, transport, and commerce" (although Convention No. 129 clearly does not imply the establishment of a separate inspection service for agriculture).

These issues are looked at in more detail in the following chapters. One major trend that has clearly emerged in the past 20 years or so, however, has been the reorganization of inspection services, from local authorities, from sectoral ministries, from trade unions (as in the case of the former centrally planned countries) into one administration under one central authority. One particularly strong argument in favour of such a development is that location under a central authority facilitates the establishment and application of uniform inspection policies and procedures for the country as a whole. This has for some time been a preoccupation of overriding importance with managers of labour inspection systems, and government and employers' and workers' organizations.

Notes

[1] The operative paragraphs of Convention No. 81 are reproduced in Annex I.
[2] Article 7, para. 3(a)-(d). See Annex I.

THE MISSION OF LABOUR INSPECTION 3

3.1 The trend towards mission statements

Labour inspection's mission in the past often tended to be formulated in very broad, abstract terms. However, in the past two decades labour inspectorates the world over have begun seriously to question their assumed mission and to endeavour to redefine it, often in consultation with workers' and employers' organizations. It may seem self-evident that the process of inspection and its achievable results should be the primary mission of labour inspection. But what inspectors are to inspect, how they should inspect, and the results they should hope to seek from an inspection, are all issues that have been the subject of heated and controversial debate at an international level and within national inspection systems. This has increasingly led managers of inspection systems to aim for "mission statements" as part of their central strategy to give their inspection services a new orientation, to create a sense of corporate identity and to move the system forward. These mission statements are therefore intended to clearly define the purpose of all inspection activities that are undertaken. Such activities may cover all or only some of the core functions of labour inspection. A wide range of approaches can be noted, the variety of which is best illustrated by some random examples:

- the United States Occupational Safety and Health Act (OSHA) was enacted "to assure so far as is possible every man and woman in the Nation safe and healthful working conditions";
- the Government of Canada promotes a "fair, safe, healthy, stable, cooperative and productive work environment for workplaces under its jurisdiction". Some regional entities in that country go even further. As a result, the corporate motto for the Province of Ontario is "an environment that will make Ontario workplaces the safest in the world";

- another similar statement, expanded to include the general public, has been issued by the United Kingdom's Safety and Health Executive (HSE), whose mission is to ensure that "risks to people's safety and health from work activities, including risks to the public, are properly controlled"; and some HSE departments envision their own (sectoral) mission statements;
- Finland takes the mission statement further when the Government includes justice and equality at work as cornerstones of its labour inspection mission; and the Netherlands uses an even wider interpretation in its statement, which includes the obligation to tackle abuse and to provide politically relevant information;
- the Swedish Work Environment Act encapsulates its country's inspection mission: "to prevent ill health and accidents at work and generally to achieve a good working environment". Another government agency has as its mission statement "to improve the performance and effectiveness of organizations by providing an independent and impartial service to prevent and resolve disputes and to build harmonious relationships at work";
- New Zealand's Occupational Safety and Health Service has a mission statement: "Together to Zero", which means that every preventive measure taken is a step nearer towards eliminating workplace-related deaths. This strategy will then result in the decrease and gradual elimination of other kinds of accidents and occupational diseases as well.

The above examples lead to a significant number of conclusions: thus, mission statements tend to be adopted more and more as a key element of strategy. While not indispensable, such statements tend to focus the activities of labour inspection on issues central to its aims. The more succinct a mission statement, the easier it is for the management of inspection services to set objectives and standards against which to implement it, in order to reach the stated goal. Increasingly, therefore, governments see mission statements as central to the effective implementation of all labour inspection activities, or indeed to the reorientation of services towards new goals.

To succeed, a mission statement must be widely accepted by both the inspectorate and the client system it affects, necessitating consultation with all parties concerned. Once accepted, it is necessary to publicize it widely, together with a set of continuously developed objectives, which further define its purpose. These are usually supported by medium-term aims (three to five years), combined with a procedure for setting annual priorities. Today, it is generally seen as insufficient merely to publish a mission statement containing broad aims and objectives, without establishing and publishing annual targets, as well as reports on outcomes as proof of the achievements of labour inspection activities.

3.2   The role and scope of labour inspection

As has been noted, the primary duties of practically every modern system of labour inspection are laid down in Article 3 of the Labour Inspection Convention, 1947 (No. 81). Today, it is generally considered better to prevent than merely to sanction or punish. This change of attitude is reflected in the more recent Labour Inspection (Agriculture) Convention, 1969 (No. 129), which states that inspectorates must be associated with the preventive control of new methods or processes that appear likely to constitute a threat to health or safety. Emphasis on preventive as against corrective intervention is gaining ground. Of course, "traditional" enforcement, namely the various aspects of technical inspection, still continues to contribute substantially to the prevention of accidents and health hazards, particularly if accompanied by advice and comments to employers and workers.

However, enforcement roles of labour inspectors vary greatly from one country to another. They may be general and apply to all labour and social legislation, as for instance in Belgium, Bulgaria, France, Greece, Spain, French-speaking Africa, and most Latin American countries. They may be restricted to certain fields, such as safety and health, and certain aspects of working conditions, such as the work of women and children, as in the Nordic countries, the United Kingdom and elsewhere. Or, conversely, certain matters such as wages may be expressly excluded from the inspectorate's tasks as in the Federal Republic of Germany. Then again, inspectors may have specific responsibilities with regard to certain employers, for example in the case of public works contracts, as in Ghana, Tunisia or the United States (an important feature, since labourers on public works are, by law or practice, frequently exempt from minimum standards of protection).

The enforcement role may also be limited to particular sectors of the economy, often excluding mining and transport. While in this case other inspectorates, such as mining inspectorates, may have been established, certain sectors are sometimes not protected by any external labour inspection, for example offshore extraction industries or, more commonly, public sector activities such as railways, postal services, the police or the armed forces. However, more and more countries (e.g. the United Kingdom, the Nordic countries, most other European Union Member States and Switzerland) have extended the scope of labour inspection to the public sector, and specifically to public administration systems; this is an important development.

Advice, information and publicity provided by labour inspectors in most inspection systems today go far beyond the mere supply of technical counsel on safety and health matters. Clearly a modern inspectorate must command high technical expertise to be accepted as a partner by industry and the trade unions. The latter, particularly, often ask the experts of the labour inspectorate for assistance and advice. Some countries, following the French pattern, rely more on a corps of inspectors with broad enforcement functions. Others, like Germany, have created a dual system, with state labour inspectorates in each of the 16 *Länder* of the Federal Republic of Germany more inclined towards enforcement, and with a more technically specialized inspectorate, run by the Occupational Accident and Disease Insurance Bodies, more inclined towards advice, information and training (although also endowed with powers of sanction).

Many inspectorates experience difficulties in striking a proper balance between enforcement, on the one hand, and advice and information, on the other. Workers' and employers' organizations tend to expect a degree of flexibility and judgement not commonly found in any public service system. Some countries have attempted to solve the inspectors' dilemma: in Brazil, for example, an inspector has to draw employers' attention to the legal con- sequences of their action (or lack of it) before contemplating prosecution. In many countries, it is in practice left to individual inspectors to decide which remedial measures to take. And in times of economic difficulties, there is the temptation, often backed by public policy, to rely too much on advice and information and refrain from "unpopular" enforcement measures. This would not, of course, apply to cases of immediate danger to life and limb, but in some countries it does jeopardize the effective enforcement of compliance with laws and regulations dealing with workers' health and welfare.

Participation in standard setting is a time-honoured role of labour inspec- tion. Inspectors can provide ideas for new legislation and regulations by notifying the competent authority of defects or abuses not specifically covered by existing legal provisions, and by proposing to that same authority improve- ments in laws and regulations. In a large number of countries the labour inspectorate is represented on national tripartite advisory bodies, to which it can bring its knowledge of problems and deficiencies at the workplace to ensure that new laws and regulations are applicable in practice. Labour inspectorates are often also called upon to express their professional opinion or to make proposals for draft legislation on matters of employment or social security. Much as the association of labour inspectorates with standard setting highlights the importance that government authorities attach to their services, these demands can place a considerable burden on the lean resources of inspec- torates. This is particularly true in cases where inspectors are required to carry out statistical surveys on wages or strikes, or to establish cost–benefit analyses in advance of new regulations, or even to make recommendations involving legal consequences (so-called regulatory impact statements), as for instance in

Norway and other countries, a task for which they are often unqualified and lack resources.

Collaboration with workers' and employers' organizations is an important aspect of labour inspection. Most systems have made appropriate arrangements for promoting cooperation between the labour inspectorate and employers and workers or their organizations, in the form of conferences or joint committees at the plant, local, regional or national level. The effectiveness of any action by the labour inspectorate depends largely on the collaboration of employers and workers, preferably already at the stage of policy formulation and standard setting. National tripartite committees therefore exist in countries as varied as Belgium, the Czech Republic, Hungary, Italy, Côte d'Ivoire, the Netherlands, Nigeria, Pakistan, Sweden, Switzerland and the United Kingdom, to name but a few.

Legislation in many countries provides for the establishment, at the level of the enterprise, of safety and health committees, labour protection councils or similar bodies. Their role consists of actively promoting consciousness among the social partner actors, investigating incidents and accidents and means of preventing them, and generally supervising the enforcement of all measures designed to make working conditions more human. These bodies, as a rule, cooperate closely with the labour inspectorate during inspection visits; they may also be empowered by law to request the labour inspectors to be present at their meetings. Such procedures ensure that the interests of workers and employers are safeguarded to the maximum.

In addition to these major roles of most labour inspection systems, other duties are sometimes entrusted to them. Where this is the case, Convention No. 81 specifically provides that such duties should not interfere with the discharge of inspectors' primary duties, or prejudice in any way their authority or impartiality.

In practice, such additional duties abound. Many countries have established labour protection institutes, often under the direct control of, or at least attached to, the labour inspection system. Another duty of labour inspectorates often lies in their contribution to, or participation, in development planning; but this may be a double-edged sword. It may be desirable because it may enable the inspectorate to discourage the location of a potentially hazardous plant near residential areas and enhances the service's delivery capacity vis-à-vis other important government bodies. Similarly, involvement in examining building plans of new enterprises or in licensing hazardous processes can help to ensure that the end result is adequate – but only at the cost of much time and making the inspectorate in part responsible for the outcome. While these additional duties may seem superficially logical and valuable, giving inspectorates more recognition, status and possibly resources within the public administration system, they can also draw slender resources away from major responsibilities, which may already suffer from a lack of political and financial support. In any event, the benefits of positive approval or licensing should always be carefully assessed against the costs, and against the aspect of partial transfer of responsibility that it entails.

In some countries, labour inspectors are required to carry out, or contribute to labour market surveys. They may be called upon to supervise the payment of contributions to social security schemes. They may be asked to collect statistics on conditions of work, or they may be entrusted with a host of administrative duties. They may have responsibilities with regard to unemployment benefits, or they may supervise vocational training centres or programmes. In terms of Convention No. 81, some of these additional duties will be borderline cases, depending very much on the actual workload involved.

Opinion is divided on the role of labour inspectors in industrial relations, particularly their participation in collective bargaining procedures and the settlement of industrial disputes. In countries following the British system (Germany, the Nordic countries and others) negotiation of agreements is left entirely to labour and management. In countries influenced by the French tradition, and in most Latin American countries, collective bargaining procedures often require labour inspectors to attend, or even to chair, relevant meetings. These arrangements are found in Chile, France, Greece, Mexico and French-speaking African countries. While participation in collective bargaining is generally considered an acceptable additional charge, as labour inspectors may contribute to the improvement of industrial relations, their possible role in the settlement of industrial disputes is controversial. In France and countries following the French system, conciliation is one of the major functions of labour inspectors. The Labour Inspection Recommendation, 1947 (No. 81), however, states that the functions of labour inspectors should not include conciliation or arbitration, on the grounds that conciliation and inspection duties are incompatible with the main functions and obligations of inspectors, in particular, the need both to be, and to be seen by the parties to be, impartial in the exercise of their duties. The Labour Inspection (Agriculture) Recommendation, 1969 (No. 133), on the other hand, recognizes the possibility of labour inspectors acting as conciliators, at least on a temporary basis. If the ILO itself seems divided on this issue, so, indeed, is the rest of the world. At one end of the spectrum, one finds countries such as Cyprus, Denmark, Germany, India, Japan and the United Kingdom, where regulations prohibit inspectors from playing any role in dispute settlement, while at the other end, in France, Greece, Spain, Turkey and many other Latin American countries, disputes must be submitted to a labour inspector. In between, every variety of law and practice can be found.

It is noteworthy that in 1997 the European Union agreed on common working principles of labour inspection for Member States to supervise safety and health at work.[1]

3.3   Social promotion, social policing

Article 3, para. 1 (c) of Convention No. 81, in spite of its considerable, far-reaching importance, is a provision often ignored in the practice of labour inspection. It postulates that one of the functions of any system of labour inspection should be to bring to the notice of the competent authorities defects or abuses not specifically covered by existing legislation. A similar Article (6,1 (c)), in the Labour Inspection (Agriculture) Convention, 1969 (No. 129), goes even further, requiring labour inspectorates with agricultural competence to submit specific proposals on the improvement of laws and regulations.

This function, if dynamically managed, is an important factor in social progress. Properly understood, and properly carried out, it will promote new labour protection measures across the range of other inspection functions. Labour inspectors are the primary agents of government in the world of work. They alone can assure a regular state presence in enterprises. Some may feel that this, in fact, is not desirable. Liberalization, deregulation and other political trends tend to downgrade the importance and impact of this primary duty. But it is thanks to their direct knowledge of the working environment, continuously updated in the course of virtually all their activities, that labour inspectors are best situated to alert the competent authorities to the need for new, or the revision of existing, regulations that would be better adapted to meet the needs of workers and employers alike.

Making the best use of this mandate presupposes an ongoing process of social dialogue at enterprise level, which labour inspectors must lead, encouraged by their hierarchy. It also assumes that labour inspectors have an active role in subsequent drafting of labour protection regulations. This involvement can sometimes be quite direct, as when representatives of the inspectorate are members of a national labour advisory board, or similar high-level tripartite consultative body. In quite a number of countries (for instance Denmark, Norway and others), the inspectorate is responsible for assisting the Minister of Labour in drafting subsidiary regulations for which he is mandated under the legislative framework (e.g. the Working Environment Act, the Labour Code, etc). In some cases, inspection bodies are even empowered to themselves adopt legally enforceable standards on prevention of occupational safety and health hazards (as in the case of OSHA in the United States, or that of the *Berufs-genossenschaften*, the Mutual Accident Insurance Associations in Germany).

Whether inspectorates have such far-reaching powers or not, the basic issue is whether they define their mission as being promoters of social equity at the national level, and stimulators of social dialogue at the enterprise level. Are they being encouraged by the system to play such a role in a proactive manner? Do they play it with the indispensable impartiality and openness that it requires? And can they reconcile, and integrate, this function with their core mission: to be, and to be perceived to be acting as, social police? In the final analysis, this is the essence of their mission. If it is compromised and dialogue is sought at the expense of authority and consistency, then this vital function of promoting social progress risks degenerating into little more than talk without any ensuing action. Striking an equitable, clearly defined balance between what to some appear to be conflicting interests, but which in fact are complementary, if intelligently managed, is one of the great challenges facing labour inspection today.

3.4   Prevention

Prevention in the context of labour protection, and the mission of labour inspection in this regard, is referred to in numerous international labour standards (notably Conventions Nos. 81, 129, 155, 174 and others[2]). In addition to the main inspection functions relating to the application of legislation, which already have an evident preventive objective, these instruments contain a number of provisions specifically outlining several important aspects of the preventive role of inspection services, such as the inspection of new establishments, materials or substances and work processes, and the prevention of occupational accidents and diseases.

Specifically, Convention No. 129 (adopted some 20 years after Convention No. 81, which contains several important new principles relevant also outside the sector, thus underlining significant developments in the international conception of, and approach to, prevention) provides that labour inspection services must be associated in the preventive control of new plants, new substances and new methods which appear likely to constitute a hazard. The Convention even contains some, albeit flexible, provisions as to how preventive action of this kind is to be ensured, although relying essentially on national law and practice in member States to give effect to them. Thus, the special international instruments on labour inspection (the above Conventions, and accompanying Recommendations, No. 81 and 133) are generally conducive to promoting principles of prevention, envisaging a proactive role for labour inspection, and specifically addressing issues at the pre-workplace stage (more explicitly so in paras. 1 to 3 of Recommendation No. 81, and para. 11 of Labour Inspection (Agriculture) Recommendation, 1969 (No. 133)).

As already mentioned, to speak of prevention in the context of labour protection implies, first of all, a determined effort to avoid incidents, disputes, accidents, conflicts and occupational diseases by assuring compliance with existing legislation. This approach, however, not only has its limitations but also reveals a basic dilemma with regard to preventive labour inspection activities. What has occurred, and has been the subject of analysis, intervention, control, advice and/or sanctions, is much more readily measured, documented and validated than what has not occurred, because it has been successfully avoided. How does one measure the number and effect of accidents that did not take place? How does one calculate the costs saved because of conflicts resolved before they erupt? How does one show evidence of effectiveness and efficiency as a result of one's actions, and therefore as proof of achievement of one's mission? Statistical evidence, by itself, is often not conclusive, because statistics tend by their nature to reflect quantity, not quality, concentrating on the number of activities carried out rather than on the actual results achieved, and also because labour inspection action is (and can only be) but one contributing factor in a usually highly complex cause-and-effect relationship. It is ironic that the more successful an inspectorate is in preventing disasters, the less evident it may appear that its activities are of vital importance.

Prevention in the world of work, to the extent that it concerns labour inspection, can have a considerable variety of meanings, depending on what particular area one looks at: working conditions; industrial relations; occupational safety and health; or even employment. Common to all definitions is the notion that prevention can avoid or eliminate risk: the risk of unfair treatment; the risk of physical or mental health damage; the risk of costly conflict; and increasingly also the risk of unemployment and exclusion. Underlying these different categories of risk is the realization that, if not prevented, they will lead to losses for the individual, the enterprise, or society as a whole. It is therefore reasonable to say that loss control has developed as a common denominator to every kind of risk prevention.

Any prevention policy, to be effective, requires the participation of all the parties and individuals directly concerned. It must therefore be subject to regular review and scrutiny by organized social partner representatives and obtain their commitment to such policy initiatives. If these organizations are weak, or if they do not consider the development and application of labour protection related prevention policies at national, sectoral and enterprise levels to be a matter of priority, then the concept cannot be successfully promoted by labour inspection. It also, perhaps first and foremost, implies the active participation, sharing of responsibility, and indeed leadership, of management, with the ultimate goal of developing a consistent "prevention culture" at enterprise level.

Government must enable and promote the sharing of responsibility, and provide the impulse and legal framework necessary for relevant initiatives, whether within enterprises, within different economic sectors, or at national level. At the same time, the State must maintain its role of guaranteeing the protection of workers through the enforcement of compliance with existing legislation and standards, thus maintaining the respect for principles which form the basis of labour inspectorates' utility and credibility. However, for a long time, labour inspection policies in many countries were placed within a framework of state control that was too rigid, aiming mainly at conformity with prescriptive and often overly detailed regulations and standards of working conditions without fulfilling this role in an effective manner. Indeed, this continues to be the situation in quite a number of countries.

In contrast, prevention today envisages a much more anticipatory and guiding role for labour inspection, combined with a higher degree of confidence in the actors directly involved in preventive action. Such action on behalf of labour inspection requires a new system of relations between inspectors, on the one hand, and employers and workers (and their representatives), on the other. Inspectors must, in particular, be careful to follow closely and enhance all preventive initiatives developed in enterprises. To this end, rather than merely limiting their intervention to strictly checking the correct application of standards, labour inspectors must be attentive that their actions are complementary and supportive of initiatives taken at enterprise levels, and where necessary stimulate management to manage health, safety and employment policies proactively. This means that they must strengthen their presence at the enterprise level, or else forge relations with "partners/ allies" within enterprises to allow them to develop this crucial anticipatory capacity. New prevention policies therefore cannot provide a substitute for the reduced presence of inspectors in the workplace.

Notes

[1] Commission of the European Union (DGV): *Common principles for labour inspectorates regarding inspection of health and safety at the workplace* and "Questionnaire for evaluating the policies and practices in occupational health and safety inspection" (Luxembourg, 1997).

[2] See Bibliography, section IV, for a complete list.

A SYSTEMS OVERVIEW 4

4.1 General observations

Labour inspection systems have traditionally been categorized as either "generalist" or "specialist" (or some mixture of both). The former describes systems where inspectors have a broad mandate (usually under a comprehensive labour code) to deal with matters related to a host of functions, such as employment (including vocational training programmes), a range of industrial relations issues (notably dispute settlement), many aspects of general conditions of work (possibly including wages issues), and occupational safety, health and welfare (in particular accident investigation, not necessarily for purposes of prevention, but in relation to workers' compensation claims). The term "specialist" would tend to describe systems dealing in the main with only one of these major labour inspection functions – usually occupational safety, health and the working environment. This categorization has fed many international discussions on the comparison of different systems' performance, more often than not concluding that the systems so described were not comparable, either in terms of resources used, or results achieved. Based on these "traditional" definitions, any attempts at comparison would then appear to result in a rather futile debate.

Another approach would be to look at the general pattern of intervention policies characteristic of different labour inspection services. Typically (and crucially), inspectorates will differ according to whether they follow a "sanctioning" system or a "compliance" model. Thus, while sanctioning models are concerned mainly with punishable contraventions or violations of rules and regulations, compliance systems secure conformity with the law (and beyond), without necessarily using formal methods of enforcement, such as prosecution or the imposition of criminal or administrative penalties or fines (although these, of course, remain available as a last resort).

However, the basic enforcement policies driving such different systems are quite frequently revised, often as a matter of political rather than functional expediency. And while a comparison of compliance (typically, Germany, Japan) versus sanctioning models (for instance, the United States) regarding effectiveness of policy implementation and attainment of labour protection goals would be interesting and useful, these differing approaches are also an expression of the diverse administrative cultures in the respective countries and not necessarily peculiar to, or determined by, the actors of the labour inspection system.

A quite different approach would be to use the functional mandate of various inspection systems as a point of departure for the purposes of classification and possible comparison. This concept allows the inclusion of "federal" systems, although in terms of organization and structures they remain a category apart and will be presented in section 4.3.

4.2   Conventional patterns

In the conventional view, there are perhaps four broad types of labour inspection systems. (Those in the same category do not, however, all have identical features, and some inspectorates share the features of two or more systems.)

The generalist pattern

Within this grouping, labour inspectorates have wide responsibilities embracing not only (and in practice sometimes only to a very small extent) occupational safety and health, but also hours of work, holidays and other labour protection issues such as conditions of migrant workers and illegal employment. Many are responsible for overseeing the correct calculation and payment of wages and social security benefits, as well as for industrial relations, also providing conciliation and sometimes even arbitration facilities. In France and other countries following the French pattern, they may also exercise a quasi-judicial function, akin to that of a "social magistrate", for example in conflicts concerning the dismissal of trade union officials. These inspectorates tend to be accountable directly to government ministers and to be centrally managed, though with a regional and local structure. In addition to France, Portugal and Spain, most French- and Spanish-speaking countries broadly follow this pattern. The Labour Standards Bureau of Japan also meets these two criteria of wide responsibilities and direct accountability to ministers, as well as having a centrally managed organization, as do some anglophone African countries, for instance Kenya.

The Anglo-Scandinavian pattern

The main common features of this pattern are that inspectorates have a mandate mainly for the enforcement of compliance with occupational health, safety and welfare, plus certain general conditions of work regulations (though usually excluding wages). They are accountable either wholly to a bipartite or tripartite board or commission, or through such a board or commission indirectly to ministers. The Nordic countries originally established this model, which was adopted by the United Kingdom in 1975 and more recently in countries such as Ireland and New Zealand. In Sweden, the inspectorate is ultimately responsible to a tripartite National Board. Ministers do exercise a (limited) measure of control through the budget, and the Cabinet is empowered to act if necessary. The Netherlands' labour inspectorate is not accountable to or through a tripartite board (although there is a board with an advisory mandate), but since its responsibilities are also limited by and large to occupational safety and health and hours of work, it therefore resembles this pattern. Similarly, in Austria the labour inspectorate is centrally directed and managed (although a separate Agricultural Labour Inspectorate is organized by the individual states of the Republic). Another characteristic of certain of these inspectorates, for example in the United Kingdom, is the delegation of enforcement functions in respect of low-risk premises to local authorities. The *Berufsgenossenschaften* (Mutual Accident Insurance Associations, MAIAs) in Germany are also bipartite bodies running a labour inspectorate responsible only for occupational safety and health and with full enforcement powers (though differing in certain respects from the state inspectorates).

The federal pattern

Common characteristics of this pattern of labour inspection systems generally (though with some notable exceptions, such as the United States) contain a wide range of inspection responsibilities, including as a rule not only occupational safety and health and hours of work, but also other labour protection issues. Inspectorates also delegate functions from central to provincial or regional governments and authorities. Australia, Brazil, Canada, Germany, India, Switzerland and the United States conform to a greater or lesser extent with this broad pattern. German labour inspectors do not, however, engage in industrial relations activities except in a very general, unstructured way by promoting social relations at enterprise level, and certainly not in arbitration or conciliation. Canada divides responsibility, with the provinces undertaking the bulk of the work and the federal authorities retaining inspection responsibility for nationwide activities such as the railways and other enterprises which cross state boundaries. (The situation is similar in Australia and Switzerland.) Although the United States does not conform neatly to any one pattern, it is closest to the federal one. The Occupational Safety and Health Administration (OSHA) is directly responsible for labour inspection in just over half the states, and oversees the activities of independent state occupational safety and health inspectorates (state OSHA programmes that conform to approved federal standards) in the other half. Federal OSHA inspectors are responsible for occupational safety and health only.

In Spain, though it is not strictly speaking a federal State, there is considerable pressure from the 17 "Autonomous Communities" to have a greater say in labour affairs, including labour inspection; but their input at present remains consultative and advisory, and the Spanish labour inspectorate is organized and directed as a unitary organization under the "generalist" model. Italy also seems to share some of the features of the federal pattern in that responsibility for labour inspection is shared between central government and autonomous local health authorities. Finally, in some federal States, labour inspection remains a responsibility of the central government. This is the case, for instance, in Nigeria.

Specialist and associated inspectorates

In addition to the principal labour inspectorate, many countries have a number of smaller, often long-established specialized inspectorates, which have sectoral or technical specialists and deal with particular, limited areas of industry or technology. The most common specialist inspectorates are those dealing with mines.

Many countries have separate inspectorates to deal with agriculture and forestry, or ports and harbours, or the safety of seafarers. Fire safety is frequently the responsibility of authorities other than the labour inspectorate. Railway safety too, including both the safety of railway employees and the general public, may in some countries be the responsibility of a separate inspectorate. Austria is probably unique in having a separate Labour Inspectorate for Transport. Nuclear power stations are often the responsibility of a separate specialized inspectorate, as may be other sources of ionizing radiation, and in some countries, the inspections of pressure vessels, explosives and even construction are separately organized.

In addition to separate state inspectorates responsible for particular activities or hazards, a number of countries have internal inspection departments in line, or sectoral ministries to oversee labour protection – the armed forces, post and telecommunications or other large public services, to cite some examples, often coming under the ministry in question. The drawbacks of such internal inspection departments, notably their lack of independence from the management of the institutions they are to inspect (and which they may on occasion have to criticize), are evident. So, while such departments have an important function, they cannot be regarded as genuine, independent labour inspectorates.

4.3 A functional approach

A functional concept is based on the notion that the generic term "labour protection", to which all labour inspections subscribe (either explicitly or implicitly), encompasses four, and possibly, five major functional areas:

- occupational safety and health (and possibly "welfare");
- general conditions of work (and possibly wage issues);
- industrial relations (including conciliation, but as a rule excluding arbitration);
- employment-related matters (from illegal employment to employment promotion, including vocational training programmes); and
- social security issues (though this is usually limited to controlling remittances and other workers' compensation matters, as in Spain, but sometimes, as in South Africa, unemployment insurance contributions).

Using these functional categories, most labour inspectorates will fall into either single, dual or multiple-function systems. The OSHA in the United States could be considered as a single-function system: its mandate, by and large, only covers safety and health. This also used to be the case for the United Kingdom's Health and Safety Executive (HSE) until recent legislation extended its mandate to cover working hours, but most experts today consider this essentially an occupational safety and health issue.

The systems in Australia, Mauritius or New Zealand could be described as dual function (usually with two separate services, under one ministry), dealing with safety and health, on the one hand, and industrial relations, on the other. Bulgaria, Germany, Japan, the Netherlands and most Nordic countries fall into this category, but in a different way: their respective mandate covers safety and health, on the one hand, and the full range of general working conditions issues, on the other. Typical multi-functional systems include those of France and Spain (with countries in Africa and Latin America more or less following their pattern), as well as Belgium, Switzerland and others.

This functional approach to systematization clearly allows for a more ready comparison of resources allocated to different functions, and of how effective a system is in accomplishing its mandate in different areas of functional competence. It does away with the nonsensical (strictly speaking) generalist– specialist mould: French inspectors tend to think of themselves as "generalist", although they in fact are highly specialized in industrial relations aspects of labour protection. Their German colleagues, traditionally labelled "specialists", would tend to refute such a (narrow) interpretation of their functions and competence. Furthermore, both terms may mean quite different things in different administrative cultures: the term "generalist", for example, may denote a "jack of all trades, master of none".

What appears especially attractive about the functional approach, moreover, is that it allows observers to keep track of important system developments and changes. These tend very much to take place in the extension or alteration of functional responsibilities, which may then lead to other changes in the system. However, it must be said that such a function-related view of labour inspection systems is not yet common currency in international debates on the subject.

4.4   Towards functional integration

If there was one dominant trend in labour inspection systems development in the 1990s, however, it was the integration, accumulation or concentration of functions under one single state labour inspection service. First of all, in practically all transition economies of Central and Eastern Europe, state labour inspectorates, sometimes newly established to take over functional responsibilities of former trade union inspections, saw their functions extended to cover conditions of employment, in particular related to "black labour" and illegal immigrants (e.g. Hungary). The Baltic States and Bulgaria have successfully integrated occupational safety and health inspection (formerly, and in some countries of the Commonwealth of Independent States (CIS), and of Central and Eastern Europe), still under a separate inspectorate, usually under the Ministry of Health) with that of general conditions of work. Other countries intend to follow suit. Further examples concern the integration of safety and health inspection with certain aspects of social security administration (as in some states of Australia and New Zealand).

These functional mergers have as their leitmotif not only the drive for greater efficiency (i.e. rationalization), but rather that of greater effectiveness: mainly to establish, develop and strengthen the system's capacity for prevention. Indeed, it is difficult to imagine how prevention can be efficiently and effectively organized if, for instance, occupational safety and health remain the responsibility of different inspectorates organized in different, unrelated and usually non-cooperating field services, under the administrative responsibility of separate directorates answerable to different government ministries, as is still the case in the majority of the former centrally planned economies of the CIS, Central and Eastern Europe, Transcaucasia and Central Asia.

Conversely, merging employment functions with some other labour inspection responsibilities (as in Hungary, Kenya and South Africa) has tended to strengthen overall inspection performance, both quantitatively and, with proper training and new enforcement policies, also qualitatively, and to reinforcing the systems' preventive capacity.

Finally, the merging of occupational safety and health inspection and workers' compensation insurance functions (for instance, in Australia (New South Wales, Victoria) and New Zealand) has led to the creation of strong, prevention-oriented organizations. These organizations have access to a single enterprise-level database, capable of closely monitoring occupational accidents and diseases in enterprises and sectors, enabling inspectorates to set improved priorities for intervention in areas where it is most needed, and to considerably optimize available (and always scarce) resources.

THE CLIENT SYSTEM 5

5.1 Who are the clients?

In the early days of labour inspection and almost certainly up until the Second World War, the role of inspectors was relatively clear-cut. It was essentially one of "social police", rather like an auxiliary police force established to safeguard the initial achievements of social progress. The inspection service was therefore empowered to enforce whatever labour protection laws had been enacted in a given country, to redress the main inherent imbalance in the organization of work and to redress the dependence of the workers on decisions made by the employers. The latter had the right to organize production in the manner dictated by the best interests of their investors. Previously, they were rarely compelled to take workers' interests into consideration, although some certainly, tried to reconcile what, by and large, were considered to be conflicting positions.

The advent of the ILO's Labour Inspection Convention, 1947 (No. 81), brought about a notable change in perception. It established the principle that to supply advice and information to employers and workers on the most effective means of complying with existing legal provisions was as important a task as that of securing enforcement of these provisions through inspectors' direct interventions. Enforcement clearly began to have a "dual" nature: it now encompassed an advisory as well as an inspectorial function. Supplying technical information and advice, as postulated in Article 3 of Convention No. 81, meant that labour inspectors were called upon to provide a service to employers and workers – at every level of their relationship: enterprise, branch or national.

This considerable change in the perceived role of labour inspectors was commensurate with a fundamental change in the perception of the role of public administration after the Second World War (a process still continuing in many countries today). No doubt as a result of experience with totalitarian regimes and the bureaucracies that executed their designs (with little or no regard for citizens' legitimate interests), emphasis began to be placed on the need for the different elements of the public service to provide exactly that: a service to the public. This orientation towards organizing a needed and useful service is, today, at the heart of labour protection policies in almost all countries with an efficient and effective high-performance labour inspection system.

Certainly, in the final analysis, labour inspectors will continue to remain "social police", to enforce labour laws, and to ensure compliance, by means of sanctions if necessary. But how this is best done is a matter for considerable discussion. In many countries, it is felt that to provide a service, indeed different kinds of services to different actors, may in some cases be a more effective, or at least as effective a way, of ensuring compliance. If inspectors are to provide services in the different areas of their functional competence – conciliation services in the field of industrial relations, information services in safety and health or general conditions of work – then one must accept the notion that there are clients for these services; and, indeed, in modern labour protection systems inspection services strive to build structured relationships with a host of clients inside and outside enterprises, and to be more aware of, and sensitive to, the needs of what is considered to be the client system.

5.2   Workers

Labour inspection was established for the protection of workers. Clearly, they are the primary clients of its services. It is therefore both inevitable and indispensable that labour inspectors and workers should have close relationships. These can be established outside enterprises, through trade union organizations and within enterprises, through workers' representatives in works councils and labour protection committees, through shop stewards or safety representatives.

International labour Conventions dealing with labour inspection define the principle of collaboration with workers and employers. How this is organized varies from country to country and system to system. Generally, at the national level, and more frequently the sectoral or branch level of the economy, institutions have been created with the purpose of enabling and encouraging social dialogue. As a rule, labour administration represents the State; if these bodies deal with labour protection issues, the labour inspectorate is the interlocutor of the employers and the workers. It provides information and advice to them, and in some cases even decides, on policy and other issues. This is the case in countries such as Sweden or the United Kingdom, where national tripartite bodies formulate labour protection policy and supervise the work of the labour inspection services.

As a condition for social dialogue, organizations representing workers must be sufficiently representative. The continuing decline in trade union membership in many industrialized countries has had the effect of eroding trade unions' status as representatives of their constituency. In this context, services provided by labour inspection acquire increasing importance. The task of ensuring compliance with regulations designed to guarantee that workers' representatives can exercise their functions, and that representative bodies can function constructively in such conditions, takes on a new dimension. Labour inspectors in many countries have an important role in overseeing the observance of trade union rights, the protection of legitimate workers' representatives, and the effective operation of statutory bodies designed to engage in social dialogue. This is also an important domain for inspectors' advisory services, to workers and employers alike.

In many countries, labour inspectors are also charged with the task of providing training for workers' representatives on all issues related to labour protection. If the inspectorate does not organize this training itself, inspectors will regularly participate in training activities organized by other parties.

Of course, inspectors also provide direct services to individual workers, in so far as they react to complaints or give advice. Although the decision on what action to take rests with the inspectors, it is in this context that an inspectorate will be judged as to whether or not it provides a service, and whether this service is performed to the satisfaction of its primary clients, the workers. In some countries, trade unions or individual workers, if they are dissatisfied with the way a complaint has been handled, will refer it to their parliamentary representative, which may result in its being made public, or referred to an ombudsperson, showing the inspectorate in a bad light.

5.3   Employers

The effectiveness of labour inspection services is considerably enhanced if it is supported by the concerted action not only of workers but, first and foremost, employers and their representatives. There is a global tendency to associate both workers and employers more closely with the work of the inspectorate. Many countries' safety and health inspection systems, notably in the European Union, but also in Australia, Canada, Japan and New Zealand, focus on the employer as the person unequivocally responsible for labour protection within the enterprise. New policies in these countries aim to stimulate (the Netherlands) or influence, indeed persuade (United Kingdom) employers to do whatever is reasonably practicable to improve and safeguard working conditions and the working environment and, in doing so, to go beyond the legal minimum standards of protection. If these policies are to succeed and have a sustainable effect at the workplace, labour inspection must also be seen to be providing services to employers. In the main, these will concern advice and information, but in more and more countries, inspectors also provide training for employers' representatives or staff, for example, safety engineers or occupational nurses. Increasingly, in the small enterprise sector, employees are offered training programmes that combine elements of business management and basic labour protection issues as a service by the inspectorate. So-called voluntary compliance programmes can also be considered as a new type of service provided by the inspectorate to employers, such as those practised in the United States.

Again, the relevant international instruments provide for collaboration, in particular for advisory and information services. Going a step further, the Labour Inspection Recommendation, 1947 (No. 81), advocates the establishment of bodies enabling representatives of the labour inspectorate to engage in social dialogue with representatives or organizations of employers and workers. Very often, the establishment of bodies, such as joint committees, is provided for by legislation, and supplemented by collective agreements supervised by the inspectorate.

As with trade unions, the organizational structure and scope of employers is an important determinant of how and to what extent the labour inspectorate can engage in social dialogue and provide effective services. Central federations facilitate cooperation. In many industrializing countries, employers that are members of a national federation, though often in the minority, tend to provide substantially better conditions than non-organized employers. They are more available to share information and experience, and are generally more open to the service orientation of labour inspection.

5.4 Other government services

Article 5 (a) of Convention No. 81 provides that the competent authority – as a rule the Ministry of Labour – must make appropriate arrangements to promote effective cooperation between the inspectorate and other government services and public or private institutions "engaged in similar activities". (A corresponding provision is found in Article 12 of the Labour Inspection (Agriculture) Convention, 1969 (No. 129).)

The importance of collaboration between the inspection services and other government authorities and institutions is widely recognized, even though the methods and extent of such collaboration vary from country to country. First and foremost, cooperation must be established among the various services of the system that deal with different kinds of inspection or different sectors of employment. Experience shows, however, that such cooperation is frequently absent. While there is an increasing tendency for international exchanges to take place concerning the problems and experience of national labour inspection services, in some countries there is hardly any contact between one element of a labour inspection system and another. This may sometimes be due to the absence of any central coordinating authority. Thus, in countries where departmental inspection responsibilities correspond to economic sectors, labour inspectors responsible for industry and commerce may have hardly any contact with their colleagues responsible for, say, agriculture, who may be attached to the Ministry of Agriculture. The isolation of special branches of the inspection system is inexcusable when they are all part of the same labour administration system; in such circumstances, there seems to be no obvious reason for a lack of central coordination. Even if the isolation does not lead to rivalry about fields of influence or competence, it is bound to be harmful to the standing of labour inspection as a whole, in particular vis-à-vis its clients. It also prevents cross-fertilization of ideas and practices since experience in one sector can often provoke innovation in another.

Cooperation between separate inspection services should be organized at the highest level, particularly for the joint consideration of problems which, at the national level, are bound to concern each of those services, no matter what their responsibilities may be. At lower levels, contacts between services may be organized on an informal basis, although it is preferable that collaboration between inspection services be institutionalized. For example, in certain countries where the inspection of safety and health in mines[1] is the responsibility of a special technical service, the officials responsible for this inspection are obliged by law to inform the labour inspectors of the results of their visits. The latter may also ask to take part in these inspection visits. In one country, the legislation requires that the Ministry of Labour and Social Security, the Ministry of Health and the national insurance body must collaborate in carrying out their activities.

It would seem appropriate that inspection services have continuous contacts with all other services of the labour administration system at both central and field levels, but once again, the reality in many countries is quite different. In Australia, for example, the Commonwealth Arbitration Inspectorate cooperates closely with the public employment services to ensure that the level of wages and conditions of service offered to job seekers conform with the legal requirements and arbitration awards. Another example of a constructive relationship is information services on basic, prevention-oriented occupational safety and health issues, basic minimum employment standards or wages provided to managers of small and medium-sized enterprises (SMEs) in the context of job-creation programmes that are often organized by the public employment services of the labour administration system. In many Central and Eastern European countries, however, labour inspection is under the council of ministers and not the Ministry of Labour, the relic of a very sensitive arrangement when other ministers were in practice the "owners" of all enterprises.

The activities of the labour inspectorate and of the social security institutions are often complementary, notably in the area of occupational accident and disease prevention (even though their respective activities may have different aims). It is therefore particularly important that close and constructive relations should be maintained between these two bodies, concerning the broader aspect of providing information exchange and services and, where the accident insurance bodies have an inspection responsibility, the supervisory level proper. In several countries, this evident need for cooperation has recently led to a merger of the services in question (Australia, New Zealand), while in other countries this is under discussion (e.g. Switzerland). In France, the regional occupational illness insurance bodies must supply the labour inspectorate with the information at their disposal on occupational hazards, and they in turn may request action by the inspectorate to ensure the application of preventive measures provided for by legislation. Regional coordination committees have been set up to ensure the harmonization of these activities, the coordination of programmes of visits and the exchange of information and documents. It is evident that such cooperation will function best if each institution is not only a service consumer but also a service provider. Again, it is quite legitimate to speak of these other bodies as clients of the labour inspection system and the information services and so on, that it can provide.

5.5   The wider client system

Besides governments, employers and workers, many other institutions and individuals can and do benefit from labour inspection services and form part of the wider client systems. This collaboration is partly covered by the relevant international instruments. Article 9 of Convention No. 81 (and Article 11 of Convention No. 129) prescribes the interaction between the inspection services and duly qualified technical experts and specialists. This mutually beneficial relationship is indispensable for the proper functioning of labour inspection. More often than not, it extends to both public and private institutions, universities, consultants and so on.

Technological developments render the task of labour inspection increasingly complex. Indeed, as shall be seen in Chapter 6, this is one of the major challenges facing today's labour inspectors. Even when they belong to a high-performing service, they cannot keep abreast of all developments. In some countries, quasi-government bodies are responsible for providing advice nationally on matters such as radiological protection and, whether as contractors or customers, collaboration. Working together with public or private research institutes is of growing importance. Furthermore, when approved bodies are entrusted with overseeing compliance of certain hazardous installations, inspection services generally work in close contact with them, providing information and also certifying their competency.

Labour inspectors, in the exercise of their functions, may be called upon to maintain effective and constructive relations with other bodies such as the police, the judiciary, town planning authorities or environmental agencies. Increasingly, in their quest to improve their preventive capacity, labour inspectorates are looking for new partners or clients, as vectors for their prevention message to the – difficult to reach – small enterprises or even the informal sector. These "partners" may include chambers of commerce, young farmers' clubs, colleges and schools. Effective cooperation in this context always presupposes that the inspectorate has something to offer: information and advisory services, cooperation in voluntary compliance programmes and so on. This orientation towards new, unfamiliar client groups was, in a sense, spearheaded by the ILO Labour Administration Convention, 1978 (No. 150), which is based on the concept of a system of which labour inspection is a part. Article 7 states that, with a view to meeting the needs of the largest possible number of workers, each member State shall promote the extension of the functions of the system of labour administration to include activities relating to the conditions of work and working life of appropriate categories of workers who are not, in law, employed persons, such as tenants, sharecroppers and similar categories of agricultural workers; self-employed workers; members of cooperatives; and persons working under communal customs or traditions.

This important trend towards enlarging the scope of labour inspection's clientele is reflected, for instance, in the legislation of an increasing number of countries to extend the responsibilities for labour inspection in matters of occupational safety and health also to the self-employed (for instance in the United Kingdom). Indeed, the continuous growth of inspectorates' responsibilities, which more often than not goes hand in hand with reductions in resources, is another major challenge that inspection managers have to face now and in the future.

Notes

[1] See Bibliography, section I.

CHALLENGES FACING LABOUR INSPECTION

6

6.1   Introduction

In all industrialized countries (and increasingly elsewhere), the managers of state labour inspection systems are confronted with a set of similar, global challenges which have different, often dramatic effects on labour protection in their countries. These challenges can be defined as follows:

- the exponential growth of new technologies in the world of work, new scientific fields, new hazardous substances and new processes;
- the appearance of new risks, not only as a consequence of technological innovations, dangerous substances or production processes, but also as a more general phenomenon, related to the changes in the world of work;
- in part as a consequence, an exponential growth of the regulatory framework, even though it often lags seriously behind technological innovations;
- hand in hand with these developments, the continued fragmentation of the labour market, the increasing precariousness of work, the growth of illegal employment relationships (child labour, illegal immigrants), subcontracting (frequently in complex contract chains, through which labour protection problems are handed down the line), and the pseudo self-employed (so-called "dependent independents");
- for industrialized market economies, the demographic factor, as well as the future increase in older (female) employees and the resulting challenges for labour protection (e.g. ergonomics) and, in consequence, the work of labour inspection;
- the unresolved problem relating to the growing provision of cross-border services (foreign migrant workers, e.g. in the construction industry) and the legal and practical difficulties of enforcing labour protection regulations for workers abroad;

- management changes, including the flexibilization of working time; new atypical forms of work; the mobility of enterprises; the diversification of workplaces; the development of virtual enterprises; the insecurity of employment; increasingly tougher competition; and the need for increasingly rapid adaptation under continuously evolving technical, economic or social changes;
- the continued weakening of the traditional partners of labour inspection, both within enterprises and at sectoral and national levels, and therefore the necessary (and indeed increasingly successful) search for new, strategic partnerships.

Also to be considered is the dramatic growth of the services sector, or "tertiarization", which may go hand in hand with a continued decline in industrial employment, much as the latter superseded agricultural employment in many countries in the twentieth century. This development will imply a different approach by inspectors to the "traditional" risks typically related to industrial work.

Globally speaking, labour inspectorates must find satisfactory answers to the following questions:

1. How best to face the changes in the world of work?
2. How to stimulate, in enterprises, a systematic and sustainable improvement in working conditions?
3. How to reach all enterprises, notably the SME sector?

These different forces have to be seen in the context of, and as a result of the consequences of the globalization of the world economy, a process which, in many countries, has also led to a re-legitimization of labour inspection, thus establishing it as the most important external partner of enterprise-level actors in labour protection. A closer look at the different forces of change will underscore this.

6.2 New technologies

At the turn of the century, for example, the introduction of electricity to manufacturing, or more recently ionizing radiation, was considered "new technology".[1] Labour inspection dealt with electricity, for instance, by making detailed regulations which, by and large, remain more or less unchanged in many countries. Today, inspectorates face astonishingly rapid and complex changes in technology, and specifically in such areas as robotics, data processing, nuclear energy and new products and techniques in the chemical industry, to cite but a few.[2] Reacting adequately to these changes becomes very difficult, and often almost impossible.

The rapid pace of change and innovation in manufacturing and services continues to challenge labour inspection. Inspectors must keep abreast of the latest ideas and be quick to identify new – often unfamiliar – hazards. Recent years have seen the introduction of new techniques such as lasers, robotics, computer-aided design, computer-aided management (CAD-CAM), and the use of programmable electronic systems (PES) for controlling processes and machines, as well as for labour protection mechanisms, and developments in microbiology and genetic engineering, which are now being transferred from research laboratories to industrial applications. These are but a few examples of "new technologies" which change traditional production methods and services, thereby often eliminating familiar sources of danger, but often also introducing fresh and less well-understood hazards to workplaces. As we have learned to control the causes of specific diseases such as lead or cadmium poisoning or pneumoconiosis, so workers have become unwilling to suffer from disabling, even if not life-threatening conditions such as upper limb disorders, repetitive strain injury, lung sensitization and asthma.

There is unlikely to be any reduction in the pace of these technological developments, and increasingly the technologies of one industry will be applied in another, such as the use of lasers in medicine, the increasing importance of microbiology in chemicals and pharmaceuticals, genetic manipulation in many fields, and everywhere the application of PES, bringing with them problems of software reliability.

No sector or activity is completely immune to these changes; modern technology often coexists with traditional activities. This coexistence implies that the labour inspectorate must adapt to a variety of new situations. New techniques bring changes to the internal operations of enterprises, the organization of work and the content of tasks. These changes include: transformation of skills; new conditions of work; changes in the nature of occupational risks (often more difficult to discern because they are less tangible); and increased risks illustrated by recent human-made catastrophes (Chernobyl, Bhopal, Piper-Alpha) and accidents resulting from the use of chemical products (especially in agriculture).[3] They pose a new set of problems for inspectorates. How can they keep up with technological and scientific progress? How can they keep abreast of new hazards and ensuing risks? How can they intervene appropriately? According to which methodology? How can they anticipate developments to be able to undertake preventive action? How can they remain responsive to situations which are so varied and constantly subject to change? These questions acquire increasing urgency as today's products are more powerful, as manufacturing processes have increased in scale, and as new products are marketed even in the most remote areas of the globe.

Furthermore, the introduction of new technologies places workers and the surrounding population at risk of major chemical accidents from plants (Seveso, Mexico, Basel), nuclear accidents (Three Mile Island, Chernobyl) or accidents arising from the transport of chemical products, fires in large industrial or commercial centres, the spread of pesticides among rural populations, the risks arising from waste generated by industry, the contamination of food products, and hidden and insidious risks (such as the use of carcinogenic products). The distinction between the workplace and the general environment is increasingly blurred; solutions to the problems of labour protection must therefore increasingly take account of both contexts in order to be truly efficient and sustainable.

Today, environmental protection usually has a higher profile than working environment issues, and labour inspectors will have to learn to use this to their advantage. Industry will increasingly treat both issues as a single managerial function, and in the majority of countries where these problems are dealt with by separate inspectorates, there will have to be a much more coordinated approach with respect to industry.

Developments in communication have had a substantial impact on the reaction to such new technological hazards. Public opinion is pressuring the State to limit the harmful consequences of industrialization: mining catastrophes and industrial accidents receive in-depth coverage and public opinion demands accountability. This is a positive development, provided that one does not seek to defend the environment at the expense of the conditions of work within an enterprise, and that one does not neglect other equally or more dangerous factors in the workplace, whose consequences may only show up in the long term (after 20 or 30 years), such as asbestos[4] or other chemical products. At any rate, the labour inspectorate in many countries is also under the pressure of public opinion; it is made responsible for protecting safety and health not only of workers, but also of the population as a whole.

Finally, the massive introduction of IT into production processes over the past 20 years has led to deep-rooted changes in the organization of enterprises and the content of work. And although one must take care not to adopt a "mechanical determinism" of technology with regard to employment and work, it is possible to identify a number of major trends in the introduction of new production technologies. These include the fact that:

• work is becoming increasingly abstract: the contact between operators and the product is constantly diminishing, although there is an rising level of exposure to signals and images, which require a greater capacity for abstraction than physical capabilities. As a result, conditions of work and ergonomics are undergoing profound modifications;

- the functions of operators are being extended: maintenance and prevention are essential to prevent any prolonged stoppage of machines which, in view of its cost, would be very damaging to the enterprise. Operators are being given new functions, such as "primary maintenance" and the diagnosis of breakdowns;
- new forms of organization are appearing, which are shortening the hierarchical lines to facilitate liaison between those responsible for design and implementation;
- increased training is required to facilitate adaptation to changing techniques, vocational mobility and the flexibility of organizations.

Modernization does not automatically lead to better conditions of work. Lack of knowledge of the risks arising from the use of new technologies makes the prevention of work-related risks more complex.

Possibly as a result of these many pressures, stress and the management of stress-related conditions have become issues for inspectorates in terms of what constitutes excessive demands and excessive, unacceptable stress. How should inspectorates advise employers to manage the prevention of such an individual-related condition? Partly related to this is the problem of violence at work. In banks, social security offices and hospitals, and for lone workers in cities, the fear of verbal or physical assault is real and one inspectors must respond to with advice and enforcement.

The complexity of the problems to be dealt with cannot be resolved through an inflexible application of legislation (if indeed its scope and content apply). The labour inspectorate can encourage employers, in the organization of production, to take account of risks to the protection of workers arising out of production procedures and processes, as well as forms of work organization which make these same workers more effective.

In this context, the activities of the labour inspectorate have been turned increasingly towards prevention, the anticipation of risks and the organization of dialogue with the partners in the enterprise, so that the factors which give rise to risks and exclusion can be integrated in the use of these technologies. Technological change therefore requires an approach oriented not only towards safety and health, but also towards vocational adaptation.

6.3 New risks in the world of work

Work-related mental health problems are on the rise, as indicated in a recent publication of the World Health Organization (WHO) and the ILO.[5] This study shows that the costs of stress are increasing in most countries analysed, and that depression due to unfavourable working conditions is an increasingly widespread pathology. Stress and new stress-inducing factors, as well as aggression and violence, are among the phenomena affecting mental health at the workplace, and a separate chapter (28, "Labour inspection and 'new hazards' ") is devoted to them.

Psychological and sexual harassment at work, or mobbing, is another serious "new hazard". In many countries, incidents of this nature have been rising exponentially. Besides the devastating effects they frequently have on the victims' mental and physical health, they are often a sign of other dysfunctionalities in the enterprise: poor work organization; bad human and industrial relations; and inadequate labour protection arrangements. As such, they call for the special attention of the labour inspector.

Effectively preventing these risks is likely to be one of the major challenges facing labour inspectorates in the coming years. The implications are serious. New studies show that absenteeism due to these new risks is much higher than that related to traditionally recognized occupational diseases and work accidents. However, in contrast to the latter, they are much more difficult to deal with. In consequence, many labour inspectorates still tend to devote the largest part of their resources to occupational safety. This new body of experience demonstrates the need to adopt a global approach to prevention. Chapter 28 goes into considerably more detail on these issues.

6.4   Growing regulatory volume and complexity

Deregulation in the context of globalization seems to be the order of the day and, indeed, in many countries one sees a trend towards a more simple, less complex, less voluminous, more user-friendly regulatory framework. New regulatory approaches are discussed in section 7.3.

In many other countries, one still notes an extraordinary development and increasing complexity of labour legislation. For example, the French Labour Code has over 2 000 articles, and besides that there are many supranational regulations and other labour protection dispositions that have been transposed into national law but are not part of the Code. Although it does not always (and in fact cannot really) keep up with the evolution of technology (and society itself), labour legislation appears continuously to accumulate new provisions concerning the protection of workers. In most of the member countries of the Commonwealth of Independent States (CIS) and other former centrally planned economies, several thousand labour protection standards still apply, which no single inspectorate can hope to adequately enforce. That said, labour inspection's mission can be rendered more difficult when the inspector is asked to improve conditions of work in the absence of suitable, user-friendly regulations.

It is claimed in many countries that the growing number of risks, as well as of solutions, cannot be "integrated" into the legislation. Thus, in order to remain applicable, legislation and regulations must be kept sufficiently broad in content and expression and be adapted to the existing, constantly changing situation. It is undeniable that employers as well as labour inspectors shoulder more responsibility, if they do not have the benefit of detailed legal texts. This responsibility is even greater in certain countries – Anglo-Saxon for the most part – where the law generally states that the level of technical protection, occupational safety, health and well-being must at all times correspond to the technological and social progress of the enterprises in question. Unless there is a "gross disparity" between the cost and the benefit, any appropriate precautions must be taken.

6.5   Labour market fragmentation

Another set of challenges facing the labour inspectorate stems from the increasing fragmentation of the labour market, primarily the creation of a dual society, and the difficulties in protecting even more numerous categories of the working population. The distinction between workers, who are covered by statutory protection, and the increasing numbers of workers who are not, is becoming more sharply drawn. Workers who are not covered by statutory protection include: workers in small enterprises; rural workers; part-time workers; workers under precarious terms of employment; temporary workers; domestic workers; homeworkers; subcontractors; workers in enterprises which are restructuring or which are in financial difficulty – not to mention clandestine workers (including illegal immigrants who, as workers, nevertheless deserve the protection of the inspection system), or workers in the so-called informal sector. It is likely that throughout the industrialized world the fragmentation of large enterprises and conglomerates, if not into separate companies, at least into very much more independent businesses or families of linked enterprises, will continue. There will be an increasing tendency for companies to contract into a central "core" which undertakes the key functions, but which then buys in expertise and services and responds to fluctuating demand by the (often large-scale) use of temporary workers who generally enjoy much less statutory protection. This will continue to lead to a growth in part-time and other forms of precarious employment. There will be a further growth in the number of individual subcontractors, not only in the field of construction and the professions, but supplying a whole range of other functions including maintenance, transport, the provision of sub-assemblies, packaging, finishing, cleaning, installation and repair. And there will be continued growth in the already very large number of small enterprises, for each of these subcontractors will be a small enterprise in its own right, in principle requiring individual attention at some stage from the labour inspector.

How can such protection be organized, let alone guaranteed? How can one prevent the segmentation of society, where some benefit from the protection of trade unions and the labour inspectorate, while others have no protection whatsoever? How is the creation of a privileged salaried class and a (larger) class of have-nots, with all the ensuing inequalities, to be avoided? Labour inspectorates are ill-prepared for these changes, as they retain many of the characteristics which conditioned their origins, when large industry was developing and the key words were solidarity, uniformity and comprehensiveness.

All of this renders the labour inspector's task more difficult and complex. He or she must have an overview of these issues and consider aspects related to the organization of social relations within the enterprise and their internal functioning (possibly with semi-autonomous "profit-centres" and minimal central services), and thus the physical constraints on labour protection.

6.6   The weakness of traditional partners

Since the beginning of the 1980s, many industrialized countries have experienced a decline in trade union membership, often significant, but varying in extent according to each country. (There are notable exceptions, particularly in the Nordic countries.) There are several reasons for this. Among those advanced most frequently are:

*   the restructuring of production systems, leading to the disappearance of large groups of workers which were the traditional base of trade unionism;
*   the development of the tertiary (services) sector, often composed of small units, in which employment is more precarious and therefore less conducive to trade unionism, as well as the continued strong opposition of employers in small enterprises to trade union activities;
*   the context of the employment crisis and unemployment, which encourages employees not to run any risk of losing their employment, and therefore discourages them from exercising statutory rights;

- cultural factors emphasizing individualism and a defiant attitude towards institutional organizations of a political or trade union nature, which tend to give priority to spontaneous action; and finally
- the "success" of the trade union movement, which has afforded its members a degree of upward mobility enabling them to move from "blue-collar" to "white-collar" jobs, and thereby making union membership superfluous for many.

One of the socio-political consequences of these structural changes is likely to be the continuing decline, to some extent, in trade union influence. This may entail a decline in the assertion of workers' rights, except where large private or state enterprises continue to exist, or in countries where there is a long-established and continuing commitment to co-determination.

Today, emphasis is laid on enterprises and the individual. Social questions focus less on collective interests, and more on individual interests; less on the State and more on the inter-occupational level, and especially on the enterprise; less on regulation, and more on collective agreement. Enterprise-level agreements are proliferating. Even within the enterprise, there is a greater diversity of demands: hours of work and remuneration are increasingly determined on an individual basis. The organization of the work-force within the enterprise is also changing fast, with precarious employment tending to increase. This inevitably complicates the task of the labour inspectorate. Each economic and financial structure tends to have its own set of rights and duties. In some enterprises, the parties are engaged in a sort of negotiated deregulation, agreeing to disregard legal provisions concerning hours of work, for example. Labour inspectors find it more and more difficult to monitor conditions of work and to challenge questionable situations, especially in the many countries where the trade union movement continues to grow weak or is disoriented.

The changes in social relations within the enterprise and the challenge to notions of authority which arise from altered attitudes and behaviour, as well as generally higher levels of training and education among both employers and workers, call on the labour inspector to act as much as adviser as controller. This naturally requires labour inspectors to explain, to convince, to counsel and to provide information. The inspectorate can no longer expect to gain legitimacy merely through repressive measures; it must earn its legitimacy through its competence and efficiency. This, of course, is a positive development, provided that the labour inspectorate attracts and retains staff of appropriate personality and intellectual ability, and retains its powers of enforcement. It also constitutes a challenge, as it is often more difficult to act as an adviser than as a censor or as the social police.

6.7 Globalization

The above challenges have to be seen in the context of globalization which labour inspections worldwide must deal with. These include:

- deliberate shifts of labour and capital to those parts of the world where production can be organized most cost-effectively; substantially different local framework conditions may then be seen as a hindrance to maintaining the level of protection in the original producing country;
- the creation of more and more small and relatively independent organizational units, in spite of more global company mergers, which will be increasingly difficult to inspect with reduced resources;
- the continuous trend of more and more enterprises existing only for a short time, changing their form and ownership and becoming geographically more mobile (nationally as well as internationally);
- the increase in different forms of "shadow economy" (including OECD countries);
- the more frequent appearance of virtual enterprises, i.e. networks where every participant does what he or she can do best; virtual employers will become job providers to small micro enterprises (often "dependent independents"), making it impossible for labour inspection to keep track of enterprises on the Internet;
- a further marginalization of labour protection in the small- and micro-enterprise sector as a result of this trend;
- greater cost and competition pressures to the continuing detriment of social considerations;
- changes in the labour market impacting on "traditional" concepts of labour protection, such as shorter or longer working hours, an increase in atypical or precarious work relationships, working for several "employers" at once, the "downgrading" of jobs and new forms of subcontracting;
- insecurity in employment leading to increased stress and reduced solidarity among employees, as well as reduced participation, as workers cannot (or will not) continue to exercise their rights;
- new forms of work organization and, in consequence, new social relations structures in enterprises, creating new and unfamiliar problems in the area of labour protection and affecting "traditional" ones.

However, a number of other trends are also discernible which may have the effect of strengthening labour protection and, as a result, labour inspection in the context of globalization:

- insecurity may also lead to an increasing need for protection and demands for stronger state intervention and control;
- after deregulation and privatization, there may be a need for "re-regulation", because tasks that have been abandoned by the State cannot be satisfactorily handled by market forces;
- the shrinking of the secondary (manufacturing) sector will continue; new risks in the tertiary (services) sector may therefore receive more attention;
- enterprises will increasingly see good social relations and risk management as an opportunity for cost control and loss reduction, and therefore seek to build productive and cooperative working relationships, including those with labour inspection services;
- finally, the need for international compatibility and equality of standards and levels of protection will grow, as will demands for more equitable enforcement and compliance control, nationally, supranationally and internationally. This is an area of particular concern to the ILO, and which is often addressed through the Labour Inspection Convention, 1947 (No. 81), covering labour inspection in industry, commerce, mining and transport.

For labour inspection systems globally, these and other tendencies that are not clearly recognized will have significant, multiple consequences, many of them not yet fully understood. However, managers of labour inspection systems in many countries are trying to meet these challenges in a dynamic and flexible manner. In so doing, they often have to abandon the traditional, narrow approach, characterized by certain specializations in the technical, medical, social or legal fields, in favour of a truly integrated vision, which merges the different factors and functions in terms of effective prevention.

Notes

[1] ILO: *Safety, health and working conditions in the transfer of technology to developing countries*, An ILO code of practice (Geneva, 1988).

[2] idem: *Radiation protection of workers (ionising radiations)*, An ILO code of practice (Geneva, 1987); and Abu Bakar Che Man and David Gold: *Safety and health in the use of chemicals at work: A training manual* (Geneva, ILO, 1984).

[3] ILO: *Safety and health in the use of agrochemicals: A guide* (Geneva, 1993).

[4] idem: *Safety in the use of asbestos*, An ILO code of practice (Geneva, 1984).

[5] WHO/ILO: *Mental health in the workplace* (Geneva, 2000).

RESPONDING TO THE CHALLENGES 7

7.1 The issues

Just as different countries are affected in different ways and to different degrees by the forces of change described in the previous chapter and to the challenges they constitute to managers of labour inspection systems, so these systems have reacted in different ways, developing different approaches and solutions, many of which are still at an experimental stage. However, certain common patterns emerge, as a reflection of the core common issues. The continuous search for, and development of, new models and solutions is, however, overshadowed by an inherent conflict: whether to use (eternally scarce) resources to further refine a concept or to just go out and "do the job". As a high-ranking inspection manager from a Nordic country put it at a 1998 international conference (organized by the International Association of Labour Inspection on its 25th Anniversary): "Our expectations concerning 'Internal Control' may be too high, but it is worthwhile going through this conceptual model and learning from it. The future will tell how useful it is."

Points of reference include:

- Strengthening the role of the State, not only as a controlling authority, but also to promote social dialogue at enterprise level, to develop or stimulate sustainable preventive action and to raise awareness of related issues. Setting up dialogue structures within enterprises is an important condition for maintaining a good working environment. In many countries, inspectors still have a tendency to neglect this aspect of their mission.
- The creation of information and competency networks between the habitual partners of labour inspection, leading to better collaboration, synergies, and greater unity of purpose.

7.2   The changing role of the State

Labour inspection operates at the point where technology, law and socio-economic reality meet. But recently, in a number of industrialized and developing countries, the notion of a state labour inspectorate has come under attack.

The burden, objectives and effectiveness of public expenditure are being contested, alongside the scope and means of action of the State. A number of responses, often in combination, have been developed by governments:

- under the most radical policies, there has been a refocusing of the State around its fundamental functions, including security, international relations and education;
- certain functions have been decentralized to other authorities that are closer to the citizens; and
- measures have been taken to increase effectiveness through new organizational structures and a more unified system for evaluating the effectiveness of policies.

With better-adapted know-how, the labour inspectorate is more effective. In the field of mental health protection, for example, inspectors in Sweden and Switzerland are specially trained to deal with cases of psychological harassment.

The renewed questioning of the role of the State has had the effect of creating a more demanding environment for its services, at a time when the problems to be dealt with are so complex that they cannot be handled by the State alone. Moreover, the principal issues arising in all countries relate to their social cohesion and, by their very nature, lie within the responsibility of the State.

The paradox affecting countries in East, West, North and South alike is that of a smaller role for the State as public expenditure is becoming too burdensome, while greater demands are made on the State because social problems such as health, education, labour protection, marginalization and unemployment are becoming ever more acute.

Consequently, the idea that inspection could be removed from the State's responsibility, or privatized altogether, has been put forward. Misunderstanding of the concept of "self-inspection regimes" has contributed to the confusion. These regimes, which will be discussed in greater depth later, do not substitute for an independent state inspectorate external to enterprises. Quite the contrary, they place more demands on its resources and professional competence. They do, however, necessitate a fundamental change in the role of state labour inspection and the way it interacts with the duty holders[1] in enterprises.

Labour inspection will continue to remain an essential role of the State, not only because it is a constitutional responsibility of every government (as argued above), but also because privatization (or "commercialization") is not a viable alternative, nor is large-scale delegation to local authorities, social insurance bodies or other contractual institutions. Labour inspection is and will remain a central state function for six reasons:

– in the first place, to do otherwise would involve the renunciation of Convention No. 81 (or constitute its violation). Such a large number of countries are signatories that today its ratification and application are considered a hallmark of progressive social policy and civilized government;
– to delegate the functions would weaken ministerial accountability for an important aspect of public protection, a development that would be particularly difficult to sustain following a major disaster;
– it would expose the private sector inspection bodies concerned to almost open-ended financial liability for acts of omission or misjudgement by their staff, and this they might find prohibitively expensive or indeed impossible to insure against;
– those aggrieved by the alleged inadequacies of a state inspectorate or the actions of its inspectors would be much more likely to sue contract inspection organizations than they are at present willing to sue the state inspectorate;
– not only trade unions, but employers too are likely to have greater confidence in the competence, independence, evenhandedness and accountability of a state labour inspectorate than in a number of, possibly competing, private inspection services, in whatever form they might be organized;
– it is clear that contracting out would involve payment for inspection services by industry, although in countries where these payments are made, the process of preventive inspection is perceived as too random and too much at the discretion of the inspection authority to allow charging to be seen as fair.

The conclusion that there will be a continuing role for a central state labour inspectorate into the foreseeable future does, however, bring with it a number of caveats and implications. It does not mean that things can by and large remain unchanged. The challenge is to re-legitimize state labour inspection by demonstrating that an independent, competent service is best suited to accomplish this function to the reasonable satisfaction of its client system. This in turn implies a changing role for the State, and its workplace intervention machinery and mechanisms.

Besides its traditional enforcement role which, in more and more countries, while still visible, is seen to be moving into the background and used with more discretion, there is a new "enabling" role of the State, in which it sets the framework, formulates broad objectives, gives guidance and support where needed, and then allows the principal actors, employers and employees, to get on with the job. Some countries have given clear expression to this role change in their new inspection policies. In the Netherlands, inspectors should "stimulate" the duty-holders (in the main the employer) to comply with their obligations, indeed to go beyond the minimum legal requirements. In the United Kingdom, the role of inspectors is to "influence", to "persuade" the duty-holders to comply, and to aim for sustainable solutions and cost-beneficial improvements. This means that inspectors have to develop new lines of arguments that are more persuasive than the mere citing of regulations. The ongoing and apparently very successful campaign, "Good Health Is Good Business", run by the United Kingdom's HSE for several years, is a perfect illustration of this role change.

Finally, even in countries where the social insurance system responsible for workers' compensation runs its own inspection services, separate from those of the State (such as France, Germany, Switzerland, some states of Australia, etc.), the fundamental role of the State remains crucial. In the insurance services, the employer tends first and foremost to be a "customer". The State must continue to retain responsibility for enforcement and prevention, and to exercise these tasks in an independent, entirely impartial manner. That is no doubt why Convention No. 81 lays down the principle, in Article 6, that inspectors should be "public officials whose status and conditions of service are such that they are assured of stability of employment and are independent of changes of government and of improper external influences".

It goes without saying that in any "dual" system, inspection and insurance services must coordinate and cooperate in uniting their efforts.

7.3   Coping with new technology

According to a recent study by the European Foundation for the Improvement of Living and Working Conditions[2] involving more than 20,000 workers, 27 per cent of those interviewed consider that their professional activity puts their health at risk. Back pain, stress and general fatigue are the most frequently cited problems; and they are on the rise, as are ergonomic problems, or monotonous and repetitive work. More than half the workers concerned complained of increasing work pressures, faster pace of work and shorter deadlines.

Drawing up appropriate regulations is only possible when the risks of new technology are fully understood. Otherwise, the legislation is likely to prove unsuitable, possibly even inhibiting future beneficial developments in industry and services. But in the meantime, the pace of change is quickening. Already, ever-new generations of computers are being developed and inspectorates cannot stand aside. The diversification of new technology is widening and there is hardly an industry untouched or incapable of productivity improvements – the driving force behind the introduction of new ideas. Automation continues to reduce the size of workforces, and remaining workers have had to be retrained and to adjust to new techniques and systems. As automation removes the operator from danger, the setter or maintenance worker now needs to be protected, a task which can be even more difficult. The integrity of safety-critical software in PES has already been cited. Thus in turn, new labour protection problems are beginning to emerge – some technical, some medical and some psychosocial.

Responding effectively to these changes requires the inspecting authority to invest in its own resources and diversify. In order to keep abreast of developments, the inspectorate needs to ensure that its inspectors are kept fully briefed about new technology and receive any necessary additional training. It is not always sensible to consider making all inspectors expert in every new subject. It will often be more efficient to form highly specialized units for the inspection of new technology. In the United Kingdom, for example, a small group of microbiological inspectors specializes in the inspection of establishments where the more dangerous pathogenic materials are stored and used. Several members of this group are inspectors who were already trained and experienced in general safety and health inspection; others have had to be recruited to this specialized work. In the past, a similar method was adopted for the inspection of certain kinds of work involving high-voltage electricity.

Two lessons emerge here. First, the potential expertise is often already present, within the inspecting organization, allowing experienced inspectors to be turned into new specialists, particularly if their original qualification is in the appropriate discipline. Effective personnel management techniques must be employed to identify, select and commit these persons to the new areas, bearing in mind that additional training may be required. Second, when inspectors do not have a suitable background to specialize in the new sciences, it may be necessary to recruit and train new staff. Given that this is a time-consuming process, it is important to recognize the need at the earliest possible stage so that the inspecting authority can meet its responsibilities.

Another method, which might usefully be employed by the inspectorate in ensuring that its knowledge and policies are up to date, is to participate in research, either directly or through funding. In the Nordic countries and, more recently, in some Central European countries, Working Environment Funds have been set up for this purpose. These days, many high-performing labour inspectorates have research laboratories and they are, as a rule, in close contact with other research organizations. Scientists and inspectors are encouraged to publish papers on subjects in new fields of technology with issues relevant to labour protection. The directors of the leading European safety and health laboratories meet annually to share results and discuss future projects.

In this context, it is clear that inspectors need help from the management of the authority in responding effectively to the demands made by new technology. But the problems are not insuperable. Additional training and specialization for some inspectors may be required. Large groups of inspectors can be involved in surveys and campaigns (once experts have correctly assessed a problem) and can soon become effective in applying standards and enforcing improvements. Regular exchanges of information and the preparation of published guidelines can help, as can the holding of seminars in which industry is invited to participate. The labour inspectorate needs to decide to what extent it needs to be involved in research on the labour protection consequences of new technology – in so far as resources and its mandate permit. Research requires the allocation of scarce resources, and resource decisions will be related to the potential hazards, and the cost of assessment and solutions to problems. The criteria for funding research must be based on the experience and knowledge gained by the inspectorate. The results could be utilized to draft appropriate legislation and, above all, formulate realistic guidance for inspectors, and employers and workers at large. The definition of "acceptable risk" and the choice of appropriate controls may then proceed through consultation and discussion with designers and users in industry. By these means, the inspectorate can both improve its knowledge and keep pace with technological innovation.

7.4   New regulatory approaches

As a reaction to increasingly rapid changes in technology and as a strategy to deal more effectively with the impact of these continuing changes and innovations in the world of work, labour inspection managers in many countries, in the past decade or so, have engaged in an ongoing process of legislative reform. Indeed, most countries' inspection systems review regulations on a continuous basis, but the rate at which new regulations are promulgated depends largely upon the aims of the government of the day. Furthermore, in many countries, there is a strong move towards deregulation. EU countries and would-be members have engaged in major legislative reviews, aimed at harmonizing their legislation with existing EU provisions, as well as transposing a large number of new labour protection directives into their own legislation.

Making an input to legislation may seem a surprising function, since in some countries (such as the United States and sometimes in Europe) the labour inspectorate does not have the influence it should in guiding the development of legislation. Of course, politicians make the ultimate decisions, although lawyers have an important role to play, and the social partners and other groups do have their say. Many countries, however, have well-structured mechanisms that ensure an inspection input in the process. This has contributed to the development of more "inspector-enforceable" legislation with wide-ranging coverage, comprehensive obligations to ensure labour protection, provisions which promote the management of safety and health, realistically take the foreseeability of risk into account and therefore require risk assessment. Good legislation has to balance the need for equity and universally acceptable standards against the need to take account of economically realistic timetables in achieving these ends. The empowering of inspectors, in an increasing number of countries, to request improvements, to stop the work and sometimes to impose fines without having to go to a court of law, has been significant.

In this past decade, many countries have witnessed a major shift in the emphasis of inspection from reactive intervention to proactive, prevention-oriented inspection activities. Inspectors tend to inspect less according to detailed, prescriptive and largely rigid legislation, and more with respect to monitoring compliance with (and enforce as necessary) a new type of goal-oriented, enabling legislation, more flexible in its application and allowing for improvements in working conditions as technological changes occur that impact on the working environment.

In the EU, the bulk of new legislation puts the emphasis on enabling employers to manage labour protection in their enterprises by developing good management and risk assessment. This has led to member countries reviewing and, when necessary, amending existing legislation. For instance, in the United Kingdom, over 100 sets of regulations and 750 pieces of guidance were reviewed by early 1997. Countries that have association agreements with the EU are undertaking similar reviews.

Reviews of old legislation have taken place throughout the world – in Australia, Argentina and New Zealand, for example, and the same approach has been taken in the development of management and risk assessment based legislation, placing more emphasis on cooperation. These countries and many others see employers as primarily responsible for achieving the aims of labour protection. They have therefore adopted a new type of inspection audit to ensure that they do so.

In the Netherlands, for instance, it was felt that the Working Conditions Act 1998 was too prescriptive. It was recently amended to make employers responsible for adopting and implementing a systematic policy with regard to labour protection. As an additional aid to compliance, it is expected that policy rules will come into effect which, while not mandatory for employers, if adopted will indicate what the labour inspectorate considers to be an acceptable standard for meeting the aims of the Act. Employers may apply different rules, provided the same level of protection for employees is ensured. For similar reasons, the Swedish Internal Control of Work Environment Act 1992 has recently been extensively amended to ensure that working conditions are adapted to workers' individual aptitudes. Stricter requirements were defined concerning employee participation in the process of change, and a number of stipulations were added highlighting the psychosocial aspects of the working environment. Other specifications in the Act now require employers to systematically plan, direct and inspect their work activities to control hazards.

Worldwide there is a move to develop standards, codes of practice and guidelines to support the goals of new legislation. Nearly all of them are developed within a tripartite framework. Within the EU, standards are being designed for incorporation into the codes of practice and guidelines of governments, workers' and employers' organizations.

Under the Swedish 1992 Act, the formulation of regulations is delegated to the (tripartite) National Board of Occupational Safety and Health. Without reference to the Government, the Board drafts and issues regulations in consultation with social partner representatives. In the United Kingdom, the Health and Safety Commission is also empowered to prepare, publish and establish codes of practice and issue guidance which may be general, or specific to particular sectors of industry. In Germany, the Mutual Accident Insurance Associations (MAIAs) are empowered to issue sector-oriented "prevention regulations" which are endorsed by the Federal Ministry of Labour, thus giving them force of law, enforced by inspection agents of the MAIAs but also used by state labour inspectors as rules of good practice.

7.5   Changes in management

Inspectorates increasingly have to justify their use of resources publicly. If they wish to make a case for increased resources, they have to prove they have used what they had competently and efficiently, that is, they have to show tangible results for their efforts, mainly to other government agencies, notably the treasury. Labour inspection in developing countries is increasingly being questioned as to its – measurable – contribution to the development effort. In many of these countries, the authors of so-called structural adjustment programmes or civil service reform have put forward the idea of drastic downsizing, even abolishing the state labour inspection services. These and other forces have put great pressure on inspection systems to justify their resource allocations, indeed their very raison d'être and, in many countries, one of the major reactions has been a serious, long-term effort in management reform towards managing the system more efficiently and effectively. Many different approaches have been chosen. Internally, the process of audit and review helps inspection managers to set realistic targets, to adjust staffing at the margins, to make best use of what the inspectorate has and to demonstrate its improvement in efficiency and productivity.

The problem lies in applying realistic output and performance measures. To an inspectorate, objectives such as reducing accidents and ill health, improving occupational health, increasing public confidence, decreasing fear, reducing industrial relations conflicts or combating illegal employment are easy to state but difficult to measure. It is necessary to take into account the many other influences that contribute to incidents, conflicts, accidents and ill health, and to examine how to justify the inputs to overseeing high-risk but low disaster frequency activities which demand significant resources but have a low visible output.

Sometimes it is necessary to develop intermediate or proxy output and performance measures such as the number of inspections or investigations, lectures or publications. However, these say little about the quality of the work and a counted visit may be less efficient than a phone call in achieving the same end. Although inspectors are sometimes critical of the pressure for more visits, it is vital that ways be found of enabling them to spend more time on site and less time in the office. In the past few years, Denmark has, but not without a struggle, increased inspectors' time on site from 10 to 30 per cent. The United Kingdom's HSE requires inspectors to write virtually all accident reports in 90 words; these are then computerized with free text search capacity. It can confidently be predicted that internal audits and proof of their effectiveness will become increasingly important components in the role of managing a labour inspectorate.

No inspectorate will ever have "sufficient" inspectors, hence the need to set measurable, quantifiable goals and to define priorities based on certain evident principles which it is worthwhile to recall:

- targeting interventions in response to prevalent risks, and not merely as a function of enterprise size;
- concentrating efforts on the least-motivated enterprises (i.e. those unwilling to cooperate, with above-average numbers of complaints, high accident rates, absence of social dialogue on labour protection, etc.);
- taking into account the competence available in the enterprise;

- giving preference to action that is likely to achieve the best results; and
- promoting "internal control" (or systematic self-regulation) in enterprises, combined with external labour protection systems control.

Many other management tools exist and have been put to good use by labour inspectorates the world over. They will be described and analysed in more detail in Part III.

7.6　New strategic partnerships

In response to the increasing weakness of traditional partners in some countries or, in others, their reluctance to continue the existing partnerships (such as some national employers' organizations), labour inspection has had to look for new partners at international, national and sectoral levels.

There is now considerable international collaboration on labour protection. At the international level, governments come together to review relevant issues, discuss policy and agree on joint action. The ILO, the EU, Australia, Canada, Mexico, New Zealand and the United States meet frequently. The EU's Senior Labour Inspectors Committee (SLIC) meets at least twice every year in the country holding the EU Presidency, to discuss issues of importance to top-level inspection managers. It has recently opened attendance to counterparts from potential new candidate countries contemplating membership of the EU. Within federal States such as Argentina, Australia, Germany and the United States, there is increasingly close collaboration between national and state legislators and enforcers.

The branch of social security responsible for occupational accident and disease insurance, or workers' compensation, has been an important new partner in labour inspection in several countries. Indeed, in some countries, such as France, the cooperation between the French labour inspectorate and the Regional Health Insurance Funds is time-honoured and effective. Similar conditions exist in countries such as Austria and Luxembourg. In others, such as Germany, there is a problematic dual inspection system, mainly as a result of overlap and lack of coordination. Both in certain states of Australia (New South Wales and Victoria) and in New Zealand the occupational safety and health inspectorate and the workers' compensation authority (social insurance body) were merged into a single organization. The labour inspectors (some 250 in New South Wales) remain civil servants, but their salaries and emoluments are now paid from the employers' contributions to social insurance, as are all the necessary means to operate the inspectorate. At the same time, labour inspection now has full access to the comprehensive occupational sickness and accident data banks of the social security system. This is considered essential for the implementation of an effective, comprehensive prevention strategy.

In Switzerland (the canton of Geneva among others), labour inspectors are paid pro rata for time spent in enterprises on prevention activities in relation to occupational safety. The time paid includes preparation and evaluation (reporting). The workers' compensation insurance (SUVA) reimburses inspectorates for preventive labour protection activities in favour of enterprises at the rate of approximately US$80 per hour. A surcharge of 6.5 per cent is levied on the accident insurance premium payable by the employer. This generates an additional 100 million Swiss francs, of which the state (cantonal) inspectorates receive some 7 per cent to finance prevention and control activities in the field of occupational safety (but not occupational health).

Particularly when it comes to dealing effectively with SMEs, labour inspection must look beyond the traditional social partner organizations. In Germany, district artisan associations have proved to be very effective in introducing labour protection awareness and simple, relevant concepts to SMEs with support and guidance from the inspectorates, and also through external multidisciplinary services or by establishing a common service to be used by all associated establishments.

More importantly, labour inspection must endeavour to link up with the growing number of state- or donor-funded programmes for job creation and employment growth programmes through SME development. In many countries, these programmes are organized by, or with involvement, of the public employment services. It seems logical that the concerns of one public body, labour protection administration, should be merged with or fed into that of another labour market administration, under the same roof, so to speak; and logical that labour protection concepts could and should be introduced into these employment-promotion programmes. It also seems natural (though by no means a matter of course) that different departments, which in the majority of countries belong to one and the same labour administration system under the same politically responsible minister, should cooperate on such a vital issue (or be made to do so). Examples of several countries show that this is already being done successfully – for instance, in combating illegal employment – in which case labour inspection and public employment services often form joint intervention groups. Similar collaboration for the benefit of SMEs is being experimented with at national and international levels (including with the ILO).

Notes

[1] The duty holder may be the owner of the premises, or the supplier of the equipment, or the designer or client of the project, rather than the employer of the workers exposed to the risk.

[2] European Foundation for the Improvement of Living and Working Conditions: *Flexibility and working conditions – A qualitative and comparative study in seven EU Member States* (Luxembourg, Office for Official Publications of the European Communities, 2000).

PART II

INSPECTION SYSTEMS: POLICY

"The existence of an efficient labour inspectorate provides the surest guarantee that national and international labour standards are complied with not only in law, but in fact."

ILO Committee of Experts on the Application of Conventions
and Recommendations, 1964

SOURCES OF POLICY REFERENCE 8

8.1   Introduction

The sources of labour inspection policy are closely related to, and often (though not exclusively) based on, relevant international labour standards,[1] and it seems useful to deal briefly with these at the outset. These standards constitute a source of authority, a source of guidance, a source of protection and ultimately a source of strength for labour inspection. Other sources of policy reference will also be dealt with in this section.

8.2   International labour Conventions

The Labour Administration Convention, 1978 (No. 150), as already mentioned, entrusts ILO member States with the obligation to establish a system of labour administration encompassing all aspects of national labour policy and, in its accompanying Recommendation (No. 158), urges members to set up a labour inspection system integrated into the national labour administration structures. Two specific Conventions and a Protocol deal exclusively with general issues of labour inspection: the Labour Inspection Convention, 1947 (No. 81); the Labour Inspection (Agriculture) Convention, 1969 (No. 129); and the Protocol of 1995 to Convention No. 81 dealing with labour inspection in "non-commercial services" covering all remaining activities in public administration and services. By the beginning of 1999, Convention No. 81 had been ratified by over 120 member States, making it the most widely ratified of what are known as "ILO technical standards". These international standards, like Convention No. 150, are based on the concept of a systems approach. The Labour Inspection (Seafarers) Convention, 1996 (No. 178), and its accompanying Recommendation (No. 185), deal with issues specific to labour inspection of seafarers' conditions of work.

International labour Conventions constitute an important *source of authority* (see section 1.3) for national labour inspectorates. In this context, it may be helpful to recall briefly what Convention No. 81 (Article 3, para. 1) describes as the main functions of any system of labour inspection:

(a) to secure the enforcement of the legal provisions relating to conditions of work and the protection of workers while engaged in their work, such as provisions relating to hours, wages, safety, health and welfare, the employment of children and young persons and other connected matters, in so far as such provisions are enforceable by labour inspectors;

(b) to supply technical information and advice to employers and workers concerning the most effective means of complying with the legal provisions;

(c) to bring to the notice of the competent authority defects or abuses not specifically covered by existing legal provisions.

The Article continues (para. 2):

Any further duties which may be entrusted to labour inspectors shall not be such as to interfere with the effective discharge of their primary duties or to prejudice in any way the authority and impartiality which are necessary to inspectors in their relations with employers and workers.

Many other clauses or norms in these Conventions are designed to strengthen the authority of labour inspection vis-à-vis its client system. Other Conventions likewise provide similar support with direct reference to effective labour inspection, for instance the Plantations Convention, 1958 (No. 110), the Occupational Safety and Health Convention, 1981 (No. 155), the Safety and Health in Mines Convention, 1995 (No. 176), and the Worst Forms of Child Labour Convention, 1999 (No. 182). Labour inspection in countries where these norms have been ratified is generally at a significantly higher level of effectiveness and efficiency than in countries where this is not the case.

Even when these standards have not been adopted, however, the Conventions are a *source of guidance*, providing a pattern on which to successfully base national policies, legislation, organization, structures and ultimately action at field levels. Numerous countries have shaped their specific labour inspection legislation along the lines of these standards, sometimes incorporating whole passages verbatim into their national texts. Member States are obliged, by virtue of the Constitution of the International Labour Organization and at the request of the Governing Body, to report at intervals on the position of their laws and practice dealt with in the Convention, and to show the extent to which effect has been given or is to be given to the norm's provisions by legislation, administrative action, collective agreement or other forms of agreement. This constitutional requirement is considered to have a promotional effect towards bringing about the realization of the material dispositions covered by a particular instrument.

Furthermore, in a number of (mostly Latin American) countries, the influence of international labour Conventions is formalized by a clause in the Labour Code stating that cases not covered by any specific legislative provision, as a general principle, shall be determined by reference to the Conventions, regardless of whether they have been ratified or not. In some countries (Italy), ILO standards have been invoked by courts of law interpreting constitutional guarantees of social rights.

Standards, once ratified, provide a *source of protection* for the status of labour inspection, notably against the pressures of deregulation, decentralization, reduction of social rights or of the resources and authority to set up, promote and defend them. No State can be forced, through any form of structural adjustment programmes or other international financial pressures, to renege on its legal obligations under *ratified* international standards.

These standards constitute a *source of strength* in that they provide an indispensable policy reference framework for the status and functioning of labour inspection, labour inspectors, inspectorates and the clients they serve.

8.3   International labour Recommendations

International labour Recommendations are considered to be international instruments and are therefore important sources of policy reference. They are not, however, open to ratification by member States. On the one hand, this makes their application more flexible while, on the other, they do not bestow the same weight and authority on an inspection system. Instead, they provide guidance for policy decisions and, as a rule, they contain important policy principles going beyond the standards of the relevant Convention, which they often complement (although a number of subject areas are dealt with uniquely by Recommendations and, conversely, some Conventions stand alone).

International labour Recommendations are a source of policy reference and authoritative guidance. Labour inspection issues are primarily covered by the Labour Inspection (Health Services) Recommendation, 1919 (No. 5), the Labour Inspection Recommendation, 1923 (No. 20), the Labour Inspection Recommendation, 1947 (No. 81), the Labour Inspection (Mining and Transport) Recommendation, 1947 (No. 82), and the Labour Inspection (Agriculture) Recommendation, 1969 (No. 133). A special Labour Inspection (Seafarers) Recommendation, 1996 (No. 185), deals with inspection of seafarers' issues. The earlier Recommendations (Nos. 5 and 20) have, for the most part, been superseded by updated standards, although the latter contains some interesting concepts on the preventive role of labour inspection that are still relevant. Indeed, on the occasion of the very first session of the International Labour Conference in 1919, the founding year of the Organization, it was deemed appropriate and necessary to adopt a standard on labour inspection. Eighty years later, the Worst Forms of Child Labour Recommendation, 1999 (No. 190), provides clear guidelines on the prevention of this type of labour.

Recommendation No. 81, perhaps the most important of these, contains sets of provisions covering: preventive duties of labour inspectorates; collaboration with employers and workers in regard to safety and health; labour disputes; and detailed points on the structure and content of published annual reports on the work of inspection services (also with a view to their international comparability). Recommendation No. 82 specifically urges member States to apply Convention No. 81 to mining and transport enterprises.

8.4   Other supranational norms

There are no other (non-ILO) international or supranational standards dealing exclusively or specifically with labour inspection. However, some of the large trading blocs have found it necessary to develop supranational standards covering aspects of labour protection. The European Union (EU) has adopted a large number of norms, or "directives", under Articles 100a and 118a of its Single European Act. Although these two provisions pursue the different objectives of the elimination of trade barriers and harmonization, directives issued under them have addressed a wide range of labour protection subjects with a profound effect on labour inspection, its policies, procedures and methods of intervention in the EU[2] and elsewhere. Most aspiring Member States (such as the transition countries of Central and Eastern Europe) have undertaken to transpose the relevant directives into their national legislation in anticipation of membership negotiations. Indeed, countries such as Norway, Switzerland and other trading partners not intending to join the EU at present have judged it at least partly expedient to shape their labour protection and subsequent inspection policies in accordance with these directives, in particular those of the Framework Directive on Occupational Safety and Health (89/391/EEC). This norm has brought about a significant change in many countries' inspection systems, policies and methods, particularly regarding enforcement policies. It postulates in very clear terms the unequivocal responsibility of employers to provide a safe and healthy working environment; and it is thus on the role of employers that new enforcement policies tend to focus. This Framework

Directive is certainly a major source of policy reference both within and outside the EU. The implications of this will be discussed later.

8.5   Other sources

Other sources of policy reference, though not legally binding (even for a limited number of States), have nevertheless had a strong effect on labour inspection policies in a growing number of countries in recent years. The International Organization for Standardization (ISO) has developed a set of standards known as the ISO 9000 series. These standards focus essentially on quality control, from which two concepts have emerged: total quality management (TQM) and quality assurance (QA). Another series of standards (ISO 14000) dealing with environmental management is increasingly being adapted to the working environment. In line with these standards, several countries (notably in the Anglo-Saxon world: some states in Australia, Ireland, New Zealand and the United Kingdom) have adopted national, legally binding Occupational Safety and Health Management Standards, and these in turn have substantially changed the direction in which some of the most effective labour inspection systems have developed their new policies.

Norway and Sweden have taken this concept a step further and introduced systems known as "Internal Control" developed from the ISO 9000 series. This new systems approach has fundamentally changed the way labour inspectors go about their work in these countries. This issue will be discussed in more detail in Part III. It is important to note that there are numerous sources of reference for policy outside the national level with various degrees of legal value, which are nevertheless useful and suitable for labour inspection managers to analyse in their continuing quest for greater efficiency and effectiveness. The technical norms developed by other standard-setting institutions such as the European Standards Commission (CEN) and the International Electrotechnical Commission (IEC), and by national standards institutions such as the British Standards Institute, the Canadian Standards Association, the German Institute for Norms (DIN), the Japanese Industrial Standards Committee, or the American Standards Association (ASA) in the United States, must be added to these. These bodies have major roles in determining best practices and encouraging higher standards that impact on occupational safety and health.

A final source of policy reference that merits mention includes the host of guidelines and codes of practice that exist on specific labour protection issues, both internationally and, increasingly, at a national level. The ILO has published numerous codes and guidelines incorporating the experience of best practices in member States and addressing particular sector-relevant issues.[3] For example, there are ILO codes of practice and guidelines on: safety and health in the use of chemicals at work; maximum weights in load lifting and carrying; safety and health in construction; safety and health in forestry; and recording and notification of accidents and diseases. A large number of similar national codes of practice and guidelines are now in use, or are being developed, to complement many countries' statutory framework. These constitute a useful source of reference for managers of inspection systems in countries moving in this direction.

Notes

[1] The operative paragraphs of the major international labour standards on labour inspection are reproduced in Annex I. See also ILO: *International labour standards concerned with labour inspection: Main provisions* (Geneva, 1990).

[2] The EU currently has 15 Member States.

[3] See the Bibliography, section I, for a list of ILO codes of practice and guidelines.

THE CONTRIBUTION TO POLICY FORMULATION

9

9.1   Some general considerations

Labour inspection's mandate to contribute towards policy formulation and development or to take charge of this function directly can be derived from Article 3 of the Labour Inspection Convention, 1947 (No. 81), calling on inspection systems to bring to the notice of the competent authorities deficits in the existing regulatory framework. This is the foundation of the labour inspectors' role as promoters of social progress. These inspection initiatives, if well researched and justified, often lead to new regulatory ideas. Of course, policy formulation is not limited to contributing to development, or reviewing laws and regulations, but new policies often have to be given legal expression in order to become effective and operational.

A common definition of "policy" is that it is a specific, deliberate course of action adopted by a government or public body (such as labour inspection) in response to a challenge or problem in its mandate. "Policy" (in the English language) also carries with it the connotation of prudent conduct or sagacity. It is part of, and an important instrument for, decision-making processes. However, any policy must be anchored in, and derive its authority from, formal legal powers, obligations and intentions.

An important concern of labour inspection managers is to contribute to the formulation of policy relevant to labour inspection. These policies and any derivatives or sub-policies are in effect situated in a hierarchical policy "pyramid". At the top, one finds the different components of national socio-economic (development) policy. National labour policy is a function of a larger policy or set of policies. Labour protection policy is merely one important element of national labour and social policy. At this level of policy hierarchy or system, managers of inspection systems are able to intervene directly and influence policy concepts and decisions. The notion of a "pyramid" indicates the degree – increasing as one moves down the hierarchy – to which inspection managers can control the shape and content of the respective policies.

The next level leads to a comprehensive labour inspection policy. And finally, an inspectorate's enforcement policy lies at the heart of any inspection policy. This is the centrepiece of any labour inspection system's strategies and operations. Its "quality" has a decisive impact on the success or failure of an inspection service. That is why managers of high-performing inspectorates devote so much time and resources to formulating and constantly refining their enforcement policy concepts and the different operational elements they require. For example, in 1996/97, the United Kingdom's leading inspectorate, the Health and Safety Executive (HSE), allocated 410 work-years to policy formulation (though not exclusively at headquarters, or to enforcement policy alone). Section 12.2 outlines the HSE's concepts.

9.2   The design process

Policy formulation has two major aspects: the design process and content. Policy design is best anchored in a framework of tripartite consultations. Many countries have established tripartite bodies specifically mandated for social dialogue in this context. In other countries, tripartite bodies set, guide, monitor and control the policy formulation and implementation process. This is notably the case of Sweden's National Board of Occupational Safety and Health, a policy-making body that manages policy implementation at the level of the district labour inspectorates; and of the United Kingdom's Health and Safety Commission, which has a similar function vis-à-vis the labour inspectorate, the HSE.

Social dialogue in labour protection at different levels of any community has become increasingly important for labour inspection managers. Examples can be found from the work patterns of the EU, for example the Advisory Committee on Safety, Hygiene and Health Protection at Work, and obviously in the machinery and institutions for the adoption of ILO Conventions. Tripartite advisory committees or councils exist in many countries, with responsibilities in the area of labour protection. Within a national labour protection policy, the tasks of these bodies should be elaborated. The need for regional and/or sectoral councils should be addressed, as well as how to make them operational. Social dialogue at enterprise level usually takes place in the form of bipartite collaboration, although in many countries labour inspection is involved to a larger or lesser degree. This is more common in the French and Spanish-speaking world than in Anglo-Saxon countries following that pattern. Nevertheless, labour inspectors are widely seen as useful animators of, or contributors to, social dialogue at the enterprise level and as monitors of social relations (see section 10.1).

The basic duties, characteristics, responsibilities and rights of members and services of tripartite and bipartite collaboration bodies and their organization should be laid down in a national labour protection policy. Guidance can be found inter alia in the Occupational Safety and Health Convention, 1981 (No. 155), and its accompanying Recommendation (No. 164), and also in the EU Framework Directive on Occupational Safety and Health (89/391/EEC).

In so far as labour protection policy design (the umbrella for subsequent labour inspection and enforcement policies) concerns the preparation of legal provisions, an appropriate way to start the process would be to compare existing legislation with the provisions of relevant ILO Conventions, and with other sources of reference as described in Chapter 8. Where labour inspection managers are directly concerned and can exercise direct influence, there is an indisputable need to formulate a comprehensive, coherent, and consistent national labour protection policy.

The object of national policy on labour protection is to create a general framework for the improvement of working conditions and the working environment. Such a policy should be applied, if possible, in all areas of economic activities and in the public and private sector. In this scenario all stakeholders may also have to be consulted.

The required framework should contain principles for the prevention and ultimate elimination of occupational risks, protection of workers' social rights and other industrial relations issues relevant in a national context. It should provide for the safeguarding and continuous improvement of general conditions of work, elements of employment protection, and modalities for information, consultation and balanced participation of workers and their representatives. In addition, the policy should indicate the functions and responsibilities, according to national conditions and practices, of public authorities, employers, workers and others who may have complementary functions in the area of labour protection.

Concerns for the development of labour protection activities should be specified to include legislation, inspection functions, organization of labour protection, collaboration with other agencies, activities at enterprise level, and the main issues of working conditions (working time, accidents, risk factors, occupational diseases and absenteeism).

9.3   Policy content

National policy as set down in legislation and supported by codes of practice and advice should set standards and give guidance on how to achieve the main objectives and components of modern labour protection. A comprehensive national labour protection policy should deal with the following primary concerns of any labour inspection system:
* the objectives of labour protection, in the context of expected socio-economic developments;

- tripartite collaboration at national, regional, sectoral and enterprise levels;
- consultation on and drafting of legal provisions (also in the light of international labour standards[1]);
- general unequivocal employer obligations for labour protection;
- the inspection of general working conditions;
- occupational hygiene and health inspection and promotion;
- provisions concerning the obligation to contract (external) services.
- the development of training and education in labour protection;
- information, data collection and dissemination on labour protection issues;
- the commissioning and management of research on labour protection issues (and by whom);
- the development of international cooperation in the area of labour protection; and
- the responsibility for identifying special problem areas and needs for the development of labour protection concepts, and action programmes to deal with them.

In the field of occupational safety and health, a national labour protection policy should operate through:

- general obligations on employers, for example, to ensure and commit themselves to the health, safety and welfare of their employees; to carry out risk assessments; to implement remedial action; to evaluate risks which cannot be avoided; to combat risks at source; to adapt work to the individual and to technical progress; to replace the dangerous by the non-dangerous or the less dangerous; to give collective protective measures priority over individual protective measures; and to give appropriate training and instructions to the workers;
- general obligations on workers, for example, to make correct use of machinery and other means of production; to use personal protective equipment; to refrain from misuse of safety devices; to inform the employer of any work situation representing a serious and immediate danger to life or health; and to cooperate with the employer in labour protection matters;
- measures to ensure that those who design, manufacture, import, provide or transfer machinery, equipment or substances for occupational use observe appropriate labour protection measures, including prior testing and the provision of information concerning the correct use of plant and equipment, and the possible hazards and appropriate precautions for any chemical, physical or biological substances supplied;
- appropriate systems of inspection including law and regulation enforcement, and the imposition of sanctions;

- measures to provide guidance and advice to employers and workers on all aspects of occupational health and safety (or ensure that it is available), and to assist SMEs in achieving acceptable levels of prevention;
- arrangements for the establishment of national, regional and/or sectoral tripartite advisory bodies on labour protection, and support to ensure their effectiveness;
- arrangements for cooperation between management and workers and/or their representatives at the enterprise level;
- provisions concerning appropriate health and safety training for workers following recruitment, after a transfer or a change of job, or in the event of the introduction of new work equipment, new technology and any other situation where staff may need additional knowledge and skills in risk assessment and avoidance;
- measures concerning workers' health surveillance;
- measures for coordination between various authorities and bodies dealing with labour protection, and cooperation with relevant academic and professional bodies; and
- intentions regarding transparency, publicity and relations with the media.

9.4   Labour inspection policy

Once a comprehensive labour protection policy anchored in comprehensive legislation is in place, design (or review) of a labour inspection policy is the next step. The policy should describe how the inspectorate is organized and managed, how it receives medical, technical and specialist support, how the inspection process is planned, programmed and monitored, how priorities are set, how special campaigns are organized and how resources are to be divided between proactive inspection, the reactive investigation of incidents and complaints, and ongoing advice and promotional activities.

This type of labour inspection policy is based on the number and size of workplaces subject to inspection, available resources, a specific number of planned inspections, the nature of the inspection, the role of enforcement, and the amount and areas of legal or technical advice given. The policy might also discuss different inspection approaches. It could, for instance, concentrate on the "hardware" or the effectiveness of the enterprise's management of safety and health, modifying its approach with SMEs or different sectors of economic activity, and discuss how best to assist SMEs and enhance their labour protection efforts.

Arrangements for cooperation and coordination with other inspection authorities should be defined (such as those responsible for hazardous technical plants and installations, mines and agriculture, electrical inspection, radiation inspection, hygiene and health inspection[2] (as appropriate in the national context)), as well as issues related to the inspection of the general environment or to relations with other bodies with primary responsibility in this area.

Different types of inspection concepts, such as advance notice inspections, preventive inspections, targeted inspections and campaigns, as well as routine or surprise inspections, might be developed. Advance notice inspections may be focused on machines, equipment and materials prior to their acquisition or on plant, production lines, processes and facilities during the planning process. Preventive inspection is a process where inspectors judge an employer's ability to effectively manage labour protection issues in his or her enterprise in accordance with the legal requirements. Targeted inspections are usually limited inspections. They focus either on those responsible for a given risk, or on less well-controlled activities, for example noise,[3] or groups of problems, such as accidents in certain types of factories, or sectoral problems in docks[4] and harbours, construction and agriculture. Campaigns or special action programmes usually include a combination of targeted enforcement instruments, backed up by information leaflets, folders, publications, websites and videos, and possibly the use of local radio and television stations. Time must be allocated to the investigation of complaints, accidents and incidents, but this must also be controlled. Other devices, such as financial incentives (or disincentives) and certification may be included. It may be appropriate in large enterprises to use teams of inspectors and specialists to make a comprehensive appraisal and advance notice of team inspection is usually given.

An inspection policy will specify how inspectors are to contact and involve workers or workers' representatives in the inspection process and receipt of information. The enforcement policy will give guidance on the procedures to follow when deficiencies are found, and the circumstances in which it is appropriate to give verbal advice, confirmed by letter or formal notice, and (depending on national practice) when to order the cessation of work or a process, when to impose an administrative fine and when to institute or recommend legal proceedings.

Notes

[1] The operative paragraphs of the major international labour standards on labour inspection are reproduced in Annex I. See also ILO: *International labour standards concerned with labour inspection: Main provisions* (Geneva, 1990).

[2] See the Bibliography, section I, for a list of ILO codes of practice and guidelines.

[3] ILO: *Protection of workers against noise and vibration in the working environment,* An ILO code of practice (Geneva, 1984).

[4] ILO: *Safety and health in dock work,* An ILO code of practice (Geneva, second edition, 1992).

NEW POLICY ORIENTATIONS 10

10.1 Monitoring social relations

Monitoring social relations is a time-honoured responsibility in a number of inspection systems following the French and Spanish pattern. Other inspectorates are changing their policies in the light of the increasing impact of changing employment and social relations at enterprise level on traditional patterns of safety and health and general conditions of work. This in turn, has a negative effect on inspection systems' capacity to accomplish their mission in the traditional manner. New forms of work organization – short-term or temporary contracts, subcontracting, the increase in "dependent independents", or the pseudo self-employed – force inspectorates, traditionally concentrated on safety and health protection and prevention, to expand their vision in order to understand and keep abreast of changing forces in the working environment.

Some countries still deny their labour inspection any competence in the monitoring of social relations in enterprises. This is the case in Denmark, Germany and the United Kingdom, and, with few exceptions, Hungary and Poland. However, some countries allow labour inspection intervention, either under the aegis of a third party, as in Sweden and in some states of Australia (e.g. New South Wales), where supervision is undertaken jointly with the social partners, or as a specific competence forming an integral part of normal labour inspection activities. Monitoring social (or industrial) relations represents a significant proportion of labour inspection's overall activities in numerous countries.

In the majority of countries, where inspectorates have a mandate for industrial relations issues, inspection is seen as an agent of industrial peace, entrusted inter alia with the task of familiarizing employers and workers with labour legislation, as well as preventing disputes. In addition, where different preventive measures have not produced the expected results, inspectors may intervene by means of conciliation or mediation to resolve a conflict. This is often considered to be an essential service by both the labour inspectorate and the social partners.

The position of labour inspection as a system that monitors and moderates relations between the different partners in the world of work presupposes a policy empowering it with broad authority to ensure compliance in the protection of personnel and representatives of employers' and workers' organizations. Protection by the State is deemed indispensable in many countries (although procedures may vary considerably), and labour inspection is usually responsible for dealing with this vital issue. It often forms the basis for the existence and effectiveness of actors from the workers' side to conduct social dialogue at the workplace and elsewhere.

While some countries have a separate conciliation and arbitration service, others have introduced a conciliation procedure through the labour inspectorate for individual labour disputes. In the case of collective disputes, labour inspectors must examine, propose and explain methods of preventing conflict and facilitating its settlement. Training officials in this field is considered extremely important to promote both attitudes and actions conducive to monitoring and constructing balanced interaction between the parties in the enterprise. Japan has introduced measures to promote communication between workers and employers in order to maintain and develop constructive social relations. Its labour inspectorate is also concerned with social relations in the working environment. Labour inspection officials' responsibility in other countries is limited to the protection of workers' representatives, protection of trade union rights and participation in the various consultative bodies.

In Australia and Finland policy covers a broader sphere. Finland has a wide-ranging system of collective agreements, ensuring the absence of labour disputes during the validity period of collective agreements. Bargaining takes place at different levels with the greatest impact at the union or federation stage. Labour inspection has to monitor and supervise the implementation of collective agreements. Beyond that, intervention focuses on workers who are not covered by a collective agreement or a trade union. Labour inspection also ensures the protection of workers' representatives.

In Australia, at national level, the Federal Department of Industrial Relations (DIR) is responsible for providing information, assisting and consulting with employers' and workers' organizations on the content and priorities of "Certified Agreements" (CAs) negotiated between an employer and a representative workers' organization, and other agreements. The Office of the Employment Advocate (OEA) ensures the supervision of freedom of association and investigation in sectors where these agreements are negotiated. The main purpose of the 1996 Workplace Relations Act was to provide a framework of cooperation for good industrial relations at the workplace, by promoting competitiveness while respecting the workforce, and by providing information on the rights and obligations of employers and workers and their organizations, in order to enable them to implement these agreements effectively. Inspectors monitor compliance with the relevant laws enacted in each state or territory. The Department of Industrial Relations, to which they are subordinate, strives to work with employers, workers and their representatives in an equitable, innovative and productive manner. The fact that the standards have been agreed with employers and workers makes compliance more acceptable.

10.2 Sectoral policies

Countries such as the United Kingdom have found it extremely useful to develop sectoral priorities, programmes, guidance and advice through tripartite sectoral advisory committees. Comprising employers' and workers' representatives, and where appropriate specialist support services exist, these committees not only encourage compliance through their recommendations and publications, but also ensure that inspectors visiting sector enterprises work to common standards and treat all employers consistently. Compliance in these conditions is also more acceptable.

10.3 Employment inspection

Protection of the labour market, and more precisely the protection of legal employment against a host of different forms of illegal work, has recently attracted urgent discussion. Traditionally, labour inspectorates are ill-equipped to deal with phenomena such as illegal employment of immigrants or migrants, "grey" labour, moonlighting or the illegal employment of children and young people below the minimum age of employment (15 according to the Minimum Age Convention, 1973 (No. 138), or 18 years for heavy work or work likely to jeopardize the health, safety or morals of young persons). Few inspectorates have an "employment inspection" policy; few have special institutional or procedural arrangements for dealing with the most difficult aspects of illegal employment.

A number of inspectorates recently merged their labour inspectorates with inspection bodies or activities under the responsibility of public employment services (Hungary, Kenya and South Africa), in a bid to make their intervention in this field more effective. Though not without teething problems, this has had the welcome result of considerably strengthening, and in some cases (Hungary), almost doubling the number of staff under the responsibility of the labour inspectorate.

The Netherlands enacted the Aliens Employment Act 1995, whose underlying policy implications merit a closer look.

10.4 Small and medium-sized enterprises

Increasingly, small and medium-sized enterprises (SMEs) have moved into the central focus of labour inspection's attention, and inspection managers in several countries have felt it necessary to develop policy concepts to address the very special needs of this sector. Here the policy challenge is how to promote small enterprise development combining economic efficiency and job creation with adequate social standards, working conditions and labour protection.

The views of legislators, employers and workers on the application of general labour standards sometimes vary considerably, reflecting competing demands of reduced regulation, economic stimulus and safeguarding equitable standards of employment. The ILO opposes any kind of deregulation that abrogates the most essential protective legislation or opens the way to unsatisfactory or exploitative conditions. It does, however, accept both the elimination of unnecessary provisions and a more flexible application of regulations, if balanced by other acceptable measures.

An Australian report found that an average small business spends 16 hours a week on administration and compliance activities. This does not capture lost opportunities and disincentive effects created by the "compliance burden". "Burden" is defined as the time and expense outlaid over and above normal commercial practice.

Article 137 of the European Treaty specifically requires that any directive made under it must "avoid imposing administrative, financial and legal constraints which would hold back the creation and development of SMEs". The EU Framework Directive on Occupational Safety and Health (89/391/ EEC) states that the improvement of occupational safety and health must not be subject solely to economic considerations.

A recent review of strategies, policies and measures to reduce administrative burdens for SMEs has been undertaken in the EU. It was discovered that Member States were using a variety of the approaches and strategies described in detail in Part IV, Chapter 23, "Labour inspection and small and medium-sized enterprises".

Policies and regulations should enable enterprises to be competitive without undermining the achievement of social objectives. Article 2 of the same Framework Directive establishes that minimum rules are applied to all private and official job fields, independent of the size of the enterprise. The continuing growth of SMEs as a source of employment highlights the challenge of finding ways to support such enterprises while combining business efficiency and competitiveness with adequate protection.

ENFORCEMENT POLICIES $\quad$ 11

11.1 Rationale and needs

An inspectorate's enforcement policy relates to other (higher) levels of policy, but at the same time it is an umbrella for different components of enforcement, containing its own set of policy principles and addressing issues relevant in the national context.

The background to this overriding concern with enforcement policy in high-performing inspection systems is that these systems tend to reflect procedures and practices developed in the context of a general national public administration as it has evolved historically in different countries. Social and cultural characteristics are reflected in these policies, procedures and practices. In consequence, these approaches have to be regularly adapted to the very specific needs of labour inspection enforcement procedures and practice.

Heterogeneous, sometimes contradictory approaches may exist in one and the same country. When separate inspectorates are responsible for different sectors of industry (agriculture, mining, transport and commercial services), or for overseeing diverse elements of social and labour legislation, significantly different enforcement policies and practices may exist between various labour protection inspection bodies. Sometimes, particularly (but not exclusively) in federal States, one finds a variety of approaches between individual states, provinces or regions. One of the current major preoccupations in labour inspection in the EU is that common regulations and directives are being enforced to significantly different degrees of effectiveness in different countries. The ILO is increasingly concerned that widely ratified standards such as the Labour Inspection Convention, 1947 (No. 81), are not always, or not sufficiently applied in many member States, owing to a lack of adequate and effective enforcement policies.

The formulation of comprehensive labour inspection enforcement policies, the proper choice from a range of enforcement strategies, the development of effective enforcement procedures and uniformity of enforcement practices at national and, increasingly, international levels are therefore high on the agenda of the directors of labour inspectorates in many ILO member States. These strategies, procedures and practices must address, inter alia, the setting of priorities through determination of risk, the desired balance between advisory and mandatory elements of enforcement, the development of a flexible, graded system of sanctions and its effective application, the evaluation of existing prosecution procedures, the degree of discretion available to inspectors, the need and means for training to make these procedures and practices operational, and follow-up procedures to monitor enforcement, whether in different sectors of industry (construction, agriculture, off-shore petroleum) or in different-sized establishments, or in companies with across national or international outlets.

Above all, the enforcement policy has to flow from a set of basic principles that is commensurate with labour inspection's basic role of social police officer and promoter of social justice.

11.2 Basic principles

In the development of an inspection enforcement policy it is therefore necessary to be guided by a set of principles which should, inter alia:

- provide for uniformity of criteria for and standards of enforcement;
- provide for consistent implementation of legislation;
- provide equal protection for workers in similar situations;
- eliminate unfair advantage to employers (obtained by non-compliance);
- provide for a common and consistent approach to common problems;
- provide for logic and consistency in the selection of priorities;
- provide for consistency in the provision of resources;
- provide for the consistency of procedures;
- provide clear guidance to inspectors on the use of their discretion;
- be clear, transparent, coherent and manageable;
- provide for collaboration with the social partners; and
- encourage cooperation with other agencies and actors.

As discussed in section 9.1, inspection policy leading directly to enforcement policy requires a number of crucial elements.

- **Focused priority setting:** How can one determine the enterprises to inspect, for instance by establishing data banks on enterprises and applying ratings to established criteria to provide a numerical rating for each enterprise? The rating score would then determine which enterprises are to receive priority for inspection visits.

- **Prevention aspects:** Will inspections be reactive or proactive? (In practice, however, many countries may not have a real choice between reactive and proactive inspection, due to the lack of (human) resources. Severe lack of staff constrains inspectors to "run after events" (accidents) rather than to organize their work so as to anticipate and prevent them.) What use can be made of accident reports, sickness reports, incident reports, or individual complaints to prevent similar problems in future? What can be done, using media campaigns, targeting particular sectors, industries and enterprises, to prevent accidents and contraventions of the law?
- **Methods:** Will visits be random (all the building sites in an area) or selectively planned? Will the inspection be a safety systems audit or a full worksite inspection? Which people *must* be contacted? Which people *might* be contacted?
- **Specialist support services:** What specialist support services are available? How will these be accessed? Will staff members or external consultants provide support?
- **Reporting:** What will be the reporting content and format? What will be the time frame for reporting? How will reporting be coordinated at district, province and headquarters levels?
- **Making enterprises take responsible action:** The new risks outlined in section 6.2 and more specifically in Part IV, Chapter 28, make it necessary to train and retrain inspectors, and to stimulate competency building within enterprises to deal with these new risks adequately. Is training providing improved skills and know-how (see section 12.4)?
- **Sanctions policy:** Will prosecution be used as a first or a last resort? Is it possible to envisage an enforcement "pyramid" which relies on persuasion/advice in the first instance, moving on to warning letters, then formal contravention notices, followed by sanctions or prosecution, and finally to licence revocation?

There is, of course, no single answer to these questions. What is important is that they are reflected in a policy which provides the basis for deliberate decisions, and not left to individual inspectors to make arbitrary ones.

Focus and transparency are keywords. Focusing on priorities means making sure that inspection is aimed primarily at activities that give rise to the most serious risks or where the hazards are least well controlled. Thus, action is focused on the duty holders,[1] who are responsible for the risk and who are in the best position to control it, whether employers, manufacturers, suppliers or others. Enforcing authorities should have systems for prioritizing visits according to the risks posed by a duty holder's operation, and taking hazards, and the nature and extent of risk into account. Management competence is important, as a poorly managed, relatively low-hazard site can entail greater risk to its workforce (or the public) than a higher-hazard site where effective risk-control measures are in place. There are however, high-hazard sites (nuclear installations, offshore installations, highly hazardous chemical plants or processes) which receive regular visits so that enforcing authorities can be sure that even remote risks continue to be effectively managed.

Transparency means helping duty holders understand what is expected of them and what they should expect from the enforcing authorities. It also means making clear to those in positions of responsibility not only what they have to do, but also, where this is relevant, what they do not. It means distinguishing between statutory requirements and advice or guidance about what is desirable but not compulsory. Duty holders need to know what to expect when an inspector calls and what rights of appeal and complaint are open to them. Complaints procedures, in the case of administrative decisions, and appeals in the case of statutory notices must be envisaged. (Often this will be provided for under a country's general administrative procedure laws.)

11.3 Sanctions

Enforcing authorities must seek to secure compliance with the law. Most of their dealings with those on whom the law places responsibility (employers, employees, the self-employed, and possibly others) are informal. Inspectors offer information, advice and support, both face to face and in writing. They may also use formal enforcement mechanisms, as set out in law, such as improvement notices where a contravention needs to be remedied, prohibition notices where there is a risk of serious personal injury, withdrawal of approvals, variations of licences or conditions, or of exemptions, or ultimately prosecution or similar forms of sanctions.

The enforcement of labour protection law should be based on general principles of public (executive) administration, such as proportionality in applying the law and securing compliance; consistency of approach; focusing of enforcement action; and transparency about how the inspectorate operates and what those under its purview may expect. The United Kingdom's Health and Safety Executive has set out the following basic rules of law in its Enforcement Policy Statement:

> Proportionality means relating enforcement action to the risks. Those whom the law protects and those on whom it places duties (duty holders) expect that action taken by

enforcing authorities to achieve compliance should be proportional to any labour protection risks and to the seriousness of any contravention. Some labour protection duties are specific and mandatory – others require action so far as possible. In general, the concept of proportionality is built into the regulatory system through the principle of "Reasonable Practicability". Deciding what is reasonably practicable involves the exercise of judgement by duty holders and discretion by enforcers.[2]

Consistency of approach does not infer total uniformity. It means taking a similar approach in similar circumstances to achieve similar ends. Duty holders managing comparable risks expect consistency from enforcing authorities in the advice given, in the use of enforcement notices, *procès-verbaux* and approvals, and in decisions on whether to sanction or to prosecute. In practice, consistency is not a simple matter. Inspectors are often faced with many variables: the level of hazard, the attitude and competence of management, or the history of incidents may vary between companies in cases which may otherwise appear similar. The decision on enforcement action is a matter of judgement and the enforcing officer must exercise discretion, including effective arrangements for liaison with other enforcing authorities, as appropriate.

Prosecution or sanctioning is another issue to be addressed by enforcement policy. Enforcing authorities must use discretion in deciding whether to initiate prosecution. Other approaches to enforcement can often promote labour protection more effectively but, where circumstances warrant it, prosecution without prior warning and recourse to alternative sanctions may also be appropriate and indeed essential.

When formal enforcement action is necessary, the person responsible for creating a risk should be held accountable. The duty holder may be the owner of the premises, the supplier of the equipment, or the designer or client of the project, rather than the employer of the workers exposed to the risk. Where several duty holders share a responsibility, enforcing authorities should take action against those regarded to be primarily in breach.

Most inspectorate managers will consider prosecution when appropriate, as a way of drawing general attention to the need for compliance with the law and the maintenance of standards required by law. Prosecution is especially appropriate in cases where there is a standard expectation that punitive action be taken or where, through the conviction of offenders, others may be deterred from similar failures to comply with the law; or when there is judged to have been potential for considerable harm arising from a breach; or when the gravity of the offence, together with the general record and approach of the offender, warrants it, for example, apparent reckless disregard for standards, repeated breaches or persistent poor standards.

Some systems such as the OSHA in the United States apply a relatively rigid approach to sanctioning violations. Others may have adopted a "hands-off" policy and rarely use formal sanctions, if at all. Some systems empower inspectors to levy administrative fines against which, as in the case of enforcement notices or orders, there is a right of appeal.

11.4 Balancing advisory and enforcement approaches

This time-honoured issue has, often with an inconclusive outcome, animated many a debate at national and international levels. It is, however, accepted that if the objective of inspection is to ensure compliance with the law, then clearly it has both an enforcement and an advisory component. It is not an "either or" question. That said, there are systems (such as the OSHA in the United States) which do not permit inspectors to give advice on the occasion of an unannounced inspection visit, although many provide advice and information on appointment or through other programmes. Other systems (such as the Netherlands) may discourage inspectors from giving advice to employers of larger enterprises. Instead, they oblige the latter, by law, to buy the expertise necessary for adequate market compliance. Conversely, Dutch inspectors are encouraged to use a more advisory approach vis-à-vis SMEs. Other countries' inspection systems tend to rely extensively on advice and information, adopting a non-confrontational approach, at least on the occasion of a first contact or inspection visit.

It is important that the chosen approach is a consequence of a deliberate policy decision (often indeed a result of years of discussion and experiment), and that it is applied with consistency. If inspectors are given a (smaller or larger) degree of discretion in this matter, then consistent management of this discretion will be a major issue of attention for the inspectorate management.

Article 3 of Convention No. 81 clearly gives equal weight to the enforcement and advisory components of inspection. In the practice of many countries, it is still left entirely to the individual inspector to decide what remedial action to take. This is not without drawbacks, as there is the temptation to rely too much on advice and information and refrain from "unpopular" enforcement measures. Different inspectors will treat similar cases quite differently, and employers burdened by a particular inspector's decision will, in these cases, complain of unfair arbitrary treatment and competitive disadvantages.

Some countries have developed a policy of "negotiated compliance", which consists of inspectors applying quite forceful pressure, but at the same time giving advice. This has, in Denmark, resulted in a relatively high level of subsequent prosecutions, but it is noteworthy that the policy is fully supported by Danish employers. The Netherlands has practised a similar system, a staged approach of purposeful negotiation of programmed compliance, backed up by the use of *procès-verbaux* or enforcement notices. In Sweden, there is some pressure on inspectors to negotiate at the initial stage of intervention rather than move on too quickly to formal enforcement.

There are strong advantages in seeking to persuade before turning to formal sanctions, which may explain the relatively infrequent use of criminal pro-secution in most countries. In particular, it is felt that, if successful, persuasion can ensure that matters are permanently changed once inspectors leave the premises, and does not depend on the continued threat of their presence (which in reality is not very great). It is, however, important to ensure that if "negotiated compliance" is adopted as a policy, negotiations do not drag on endlessly through slow incremental improvements, monitored at repeated, costly visits by inspectors.

While the enforcement notice procedure or *mise en demeure* has the effect of concentrating the efforts of enterprise management on the rectification of deficiencies rather than preparing a defence against criminal prosecution, the option of punishment must exist – and be seen to be used. This is especially the case of non-compliance with enforcement or prohibition notices, where there are serious or flagrant contraventions, in cases of the obstruction of labour inspectors on official duty (unfortunately on the rise in many countries, often including violent incidents against inspection officers) and where it is necessary to motivate those who are unresponsive to persuasion.

The choice between advisory and supervisory, or more coercive measures will, in practice, depend on the motivation, the commitment and also the competencies available in different enterprises. If an enterprise has competent specialists at its disposal but lacks motivation and commitment to solve the problems, then the preferred choice of inspector's intervention tools will be improvement or prohibition notices, possibly combined with sanctions, rather than advice or information (though the latter can, of course, be combined with the former).

Most major inspectorates operate somewhere between the extremes, giving advice as long as it is accepted and turning to sanctioning when it is not. A few – particularly in the Netherlands and, to some extent in Denmark – have taken the concept of self-regulation to its logical extreme. Having identified the deficiencies in an enterprise, they negotiate a programme of rectification, generally including improvements in managerial procedures to prevent a recurrence of the problem and confirming this in an enforcement notice. In the Netherlands, the State has taken the view that the role of inspectors is not to advise, as this is not what they are paid to do, and that if enterprises require advice, they should obtain it from advisers or consultants and pay for it.

This perhaps somewhat extreme but entirely logical application of the market principle in enforcement is supported by the EU Framework Directive (391/89/EEC) requirement that employers should have access to occupational safety and health advice from competent people. Inspectors can therefore activate and check compliance with this requirement. However, in some countries, the State wishes to limit its commitment of resources and therefore the cost of the labour inspectorate, in a climate where there is considerable political sympathy for SMEs, and therefore pressure on inspectorates to be "helpful", understand their problems, and adopt a "hands-off" approach at least up to a point. This puts pressure on inspectors to spend time advising. If one recalls that one of the most costly aspects of an inspectorate is getting the inspector to the front door of an enterprise, once she or he is there it seems somewhat wasteful not to make use of the expertise, at least to put the enterprise on the right track and to advise it on the correct criteria to apply, although perhaps not to act as a free consultant.

Therefore, inspectors and inspectorates are subject to two kinds of pressure. The first is to improve the quality and availability of authoritative advice, and the second is to make inspectors more disciplined in limiting their assistance to individual companies, thereby spreading the benefit of their expertise more efficiently.

Taking the second point first, the problem is that inspectors often become too interested in an issue, get too involved with a company, enjoy giving advice and helping to solve a problem, like to be appreciated (even though they are sometimes disappointed at the results), and in short are too perfectionist. From the inspectorate manager's point of view, it is much more important that once inspectors have identified problems, given some general advice on legal compliance and put the company in touch with sources of detailed assistance, they should move on to inspect other enterprises which have probably not been visited for many years. Inspectors traditionally resist this pressure as "the numbers game". However, this is not how it should be seen. Instead, the inspector should recognize that he or she is a very valuable resource, which the State must use to make the maximum impact on the maximum number of problems in the maximum number of enterprises in the course of a day or a week. If there are competent sources of consultant advice and well-prepared guidance documents, leaflets and information booklets, it will be easier for inspectors to accept this approach. This is linked to the first point, the need to stimulate and, if necessary, create sources of authoritative advice, in compact, readable form, to satisfy the increasing demand. Advice can be prepared by insurance organizations, trade associations, bipartite or tripartite bodies or by the state labour inspectorate itself.

Given this dual strategy for ensuring both economy of inspection effort and the availability of comprehensive authoritative advice, the Netherlands pattern of enforcement-oriented inspection becomes more attractive to resource-pressed inspectorates. They will still have an advisory role, albeit a more selective, more considered one, as "third parties" rather than impacting directly on the recipient.

11.5 Procedural issues

A number of other issues can and should be dealt with by means of a comprehensive enforcement policy. Some may apply to specific sectors (construction, agriculture, the informal sector), while others would address specific methods or intervention procedures. Some may be considered marginal to an inspection management's central preoccupation, whereas others will reveal their value only after considerable discussion and experiment. For example, most inspectorates have a standard procedure to deal with the question of whether (regular) inspection visits should be announced by appointment with the management of an enterprise, or unannounced, capitalizing on the surprise element. There is something to be said for (and against) each approach. It has been observed that, in any well-organized enterprise, the only person to be surprised is the gatekeeper (news of the inspector's arrival travels fast enough).

However, if the main objective is to influence, stimulate or encourage employers to not only comply with, but also to go beyond minimum standards, then it is indispensable that an inspector should meet and discuss matters with the employer or very senior management representatives on the occasion of his or her visit. An appointment is the most likely and most cost-effective way of ensuring this objective. Unannounced visits will still be possible, but more and more enforcement policies now make the visit-by-appointment, at least on the occasion of a first inspection, part of their standard procedure.

It may be desirable for the inspectorate's management to lay down a set of similar policy decisions related to other inspection procedures and methods of intervention. These will certainly vary from one system or another. What is important is that they reflect a considered choice, appropriate to particular circumstances. Some systems allow inspectors a considerable measure of independence, resulting in a heterogeneous approach to enforcement. This type of policy often cites Article 6 of Convention No. 81 alleging that the provision "inspection staff shall be ... independent of changes of government and of improper external influences" implies that inspection should also largely be independent of instructions from their superiors. This is by all accounts a misinterpretation of the Convention which, in a preceding provision (Article 4) clearly states that: "So far as is compatible with the administrative practice of a Member, labour inspection shall be placed under the supervision and control of a control authority."

For most other systems, therefore, coherence and consistency are policy objectives of overriding importance. Even in these systems, inspectors still enjoy discretion, but the effective and consistent management of this discretion becomes a crucial issue for enforcement policy to address. It goes beyond achieving a balance between the different intervention tools, and between advice and sanctions. It embraces the whole way inspectors go about their work. It requires a very complex, but also a very flexible mechanism. In addition to guidance, it demands individual training of inspectors, not only in the techniques, but also in the "software" of labour inspection, of persuasion and of influencing people and of social skills development, such as managing conflict. It requires the creation of confidence in inspectors operating within guidelines both sufficiently wide to allow a proper response to individual circumstances, and also sufficiently defined to ensure consistency. Provided inspectors operate within these guidelines, they should be confident in the support of their management for conscientious decisions, regardless of how much opposition or protest they provoke. No inspectorate can ever be confident that all is well in its management of discretion, but it poses a particular problem for those whose staff has been trained to follow rigid "methodologies".

However, an inspectorate can only fulfil these demanding roles effectively if the qualifications, competence, training and expectations of labour inspectors are satisfied. These are subjects in their own right and ones which continue to preoccupy inspectorates in respect to their internal management role, and for which coherent internal management policies have to be developed.

Notes

[1] The duty holder may be the owner of the premises, or the supplier of the equipment, or the designer or client of the project, rather than the employer of the workers exposed to the risk.

[2] HSE: *Enforcement Policy Statement* (Sudbury, Suffolk, 1995).

INTERNAL POLICY ISSUES

12

12.1 Systems management policies

As mentioned in Part I, the ILO concept of labour inspection, as expressed in the set of relevant international standards, is based on a "systems" approach.

This involves managing the inspection service in terms of work systems rather than concentrating on individual problems. Its focus is on organizational structure, responsibilities, practices, procedures, processes and resources for implementing and developing labour protection policies. This management system spans the entire organization by relating the inspectorate to its environment, setting goals, developing comprehensive strategic and operational plans, designing structure, setting performance standards, and establishing monitoring and control processes, including the review and development of the legislative framework. Setting objectives and targets, establishing a management programme with procedures for achieving targets, measuring techniques to ensure these targets are reached and making arrangements for feedback into the process of defining and reviewing objectives are of particular importance.

Under a systems-based approach, management as a process can be modelled to permit predictions of the probable outcomes if no changes occur in the elements of the current system. The aim of systems management is to highlight these elements, and show how each one relates to the goal or process the system is designed to achieve. For example, labour inspection management systems may have particular goals to prevent and control occupational injuries and illness, and the process by which these are, or are not, attained can be modelled.

In general, systems management is considered to be successful if it achieves the stated objectives in an efficient and effective manner. Systems theory specifies five conditions, which must be established if an effective and efficient control system is to be established:

- the system must have a defined purpose, a set of objectives, or expected standards of performance with which to compare its actual achievements or outputs;
- the actual output of the system must be measurable in the same terms as the objectives in order to assess the extent to which the objectives are being achieved;
- a model of the process being controlled is necessary to identify reasons why objectives are not being met;
- the output of different elements of the system should be capable of being related to the resource input of these elements so that priorities can be assessed and resources redirected if necessary; and
- the system must be capable of responding to and rectifying any significant non-compliance.

This concept for managing complex organizations evolved from quality management approaches, which became highly influential (and successful) during the 1980s. Of these, as already mentioned, the concepts of total quality management (TQM), and to a lesser extent of quality assurance (QA), have come to dominate the field. Traditionally, TQM aspires to provide management with a framework in which to build quality into every conceivable aspect of organizational work. It is a management policy that institutionalizes planned and continuous performance improvement.

Many inspectorates do not have a comprehensive or consistent management policy framework and often do not feel ready to adopt one. Reservations concern the applicability of these concepts in a public service context; more specifically, the notion of management of labour inspection is contested in countries where individual inspectors insist on a quasi-statutory independence, allegedly backed up by ILO standards. It has already been pointed out that this is an apparent misinterpretation of the Labour Inspection Convention, 1947 (No. 81). Of course, the ILO concept of a labour inspector is that of a competent public servant capable of sound professional judgement and enjoying a predetermined measure of discretion in the exercise of his or her responsibilities. This does not prevent inspectors from being part of a service or system properly managed by a central authority, whose responsibility is clearly to put scarce resources to optimal use to meet the objectives of its overall labour protection, inspection and enforcement policies. Giving instructions down the line is an indispensable element of such a management process.

There are currently many "ready-made" management policies available for public sector organizations that have particular relevance for labour protection. What is important is that one coherent policy approach is chosen, containing details of the objectives to be met, the activities to be carried out and how they are to be carried out, and that the process is evaluated to provide feedback on the suitability and attainability of the original set of objectives. The policy should be capable of relating outputs in terms of activities or achievements to resource inputs. This policy should also be consistent with organization development strategies that emphasize management commitment, organization culture and identity, effective and efficient implementation and monitoring, evaluation and control. As the creators of this approach (in the mid-1980s) emphasized: in a well-managed system, everybody wins. It is also argued that the (inadequate) design of management policy (or its total absence), rather than human error, is the source of most problems in organizations, and that the quest for efficiency must start with a restructuring of the system of management itself, a process invariably preceded by a reflection on the best management policy.

In this context, it may be relevant to recall that a growing number of countries (Ireland, New Zealand, Norway and the United Kingdom) have adopted statutory requirements for enterprises to set up labour protection or occupational safety and health management systems. In many other countries, enterprises are encouraged to set up these systems voluntarily, with guidance from the inspectorate. However, inspection systems managers are also, in a sense, employers. As such, they must look critically at their own management systems. There is a clear synthesis between good management systems and labour protection management systems. Therefore, it would appear logical and appropriate that managers of inspection services should – to the extent practicable – apply the same policy concepts to their own organizations that they expect their clients to apply. This would make them more sensitive to the fact that what they are asking from other employers is often no easy task.

12.2 Organization development policies

Much has been published on suitable organizational development policies for public administration bodies. Labour inspectorates without these policies are often characterized by poor performance, stagnation, and a lack of purpose or low motivation among officials. They regularly tend to be caught "off guard" when major reform initiatives sweep through the civil service in a given country. A proactive approach to creating and continuously developing a more functional, efficient and effective organization would not only help in dealing with the demands imposed by structural adjustment, civil service reforms, downsizing and outsourcing; it would also strengthen the organization, correct its weaknesses, improve performance and maintain a level of quality services to the clients. Being able to prove that one has used one's existing resources to best effect considerably strengthens an application to government for additional resources.

It is not the intention of this book to promote a particular model of organizational development policies. Labour inspection managers should be aware of the various policy concepts and explore their potential useful application. This would preferably be done at the initiative of the inspectorate management. More often than not, this kind of pressure comes from external sources. It can also lead to important changes and positive results. The case of the HSE in the United Kingdom can be cited here as an example.

In 1995, a central government initiative in that country prompted a review of the senior management organization of government departments. This resulted in a recommendation that the HSE should have a leaner senior management structure and proposed bringing all the inspectorates into a single "operations group" under the line management of a single deputy director-general. At the same time, the HSE developed a set of aspirations (broad policy objectives) outlining the organization it aimed to be. These aspirations were to:

• encourage permeability of people within the organization;
• improve the effectiveness of teamwork;
• ensure the quality of the activities;
• be less bureaucratic;
• be open and increase the flow of information;
• learn from each other, sharing good ideas and good practice more effectively;
• encourage personal development;
• recognize and value the contribution of all staff.

The Government also wanted to cut red tape and review the existing labour protection legislation. The review of regulations increased the attention given to the accountability of HSE to its various duty holders, and in particular its responsiveness to the needs of employers. The consistency of enforcement and the appropriate use of enforcement tools came under close examination and gave rise to a new HSE enforcement policy.

Furthermore, a cross-inspectorate project team was set up to see how these new principles and objectives could be taken forward in the organization. This resulted in the formation of an operations management forum, consisting of senior managers to support the deputy director-general with the following key roles:

• to secure consistency of approach (where it matters);
• to seek continuous improvement in operational activity;
• to act strategically by developing high-level goals for common issues, and the principles and standards to guide the ensuing strategies;

- to share ideas and information across the operational group and more widely across the HSE.

A series of further projects was also set up to tackle a number of particular issues across the operations group, such as resource allocation, quality and accident investigation. The findings were used to define the organizational policy for resource allocation, the core processes of inspection, investigation, formal enforcement, and audit and safety case assessments. Methodologically, the framework used in the HSE publication (for employers), *Successful health and safety management*,[1] was found to be useful in testing the adequacy of its own internal organization development policy and arrangements. In a manner of speaking, the HSE is learning to take its own medicine and its overall development policy is to become a permanent learning organization.

Where does this leave the inspectorate's management? It has to ensure that its policies are put into effect. If they are to be effectively implemented, they should preferably be discussed and explained to staff, as well as being set out in terms of practical guidance.

The following subsections may serve as a convenient checklist for managers implementing the most important policies.

12.3 Recruitment

Every country has its own recruitment system, but it is generally easier to recruit than dismiss the inadequate inspector, who may have been with the organization for up to 40 years. The selection process should therefore be concerned not only with the knowledge of candidates, whether technical, legal or specialist, but also with assessing their qualities as individuals, their motivation, their self-reliance and their ability to combine firmness with diplomacy.

Clear descriptions should exist, not only of the job, but also of the sort of personality required. It is equally desirable that senior managers are involved in the process, because of the financial and managerial implications of poor recruitment.

12.4 Training policies

In the context of an organization development policy, training will probably be the single most important tool at the disposal of labour inspection managers to improve the performance of their inspectors and support staff and, in consequence, that of their organization. Training is the instrument of choice to bring about change in an organization. It is the main management strategy used to transfer knowledge, develop skills, change attitudes, and impart a set of organizational and societal values. In order to be effective, however, training must be based on a clear and comprehensive training policy.

Training is part of the process of change. It brings about planned modifications in people to enable improved work performance. It provides people with new knowledge, new skills, new techniques and often substantially different attitudes that alter their behaviour. However, at this stage, we are not concerned with the training services an inspectorate may provide to its clients. We are interested in the adequate training of labour inspectors, which does not simply imply systematic induction training on entry to the service but, equally important, acceptance of the concept of continuous and further training, usually of an in-service nature. Training may be pre-service induction or further training, including training for higher responsibilities, and is an important element of labour inspection both at collective and individual levels. At the collective level, training is an integral part of organizational development; at the individual level it is closely linked to career development.

Training has both a task orientation and a motivation orientation. Task orientation reduces the gap between the job requirements and the qualifications of the jobholder, and prepares officials for increased responsibilities in the future. The goal of motivation orientation is to provide clear, distinctive and challenging incentives or rewards resulting from training, job enrichment and promotion opportunities. Successful motivating activities are best expressed through an inspection training policy.

Because training is expensive, in terms of both money and time, it is important to make it as effective as possible. Will the planned training enable officials of the labour inspection system to better fulfil their existing tasks and to undertake new and more challenging tasks? Is the training planned relevant to the role, scope, functions and administrative culture of the inspection system for which it is organized? The process of appraisal requires careful examination of training proposals before implementation at the policy-formulation stage, to assess whether they are likely to be beneficial and cost-effective.

A comprehensive training policy must also address the question of how the training function is to be organized and what its place in the organization will be. In many, low-performing inspection systems, inspectors' training receives little or no attention. It is frequently not undertaken in a systematic manner. Sometimes, there is little understanding of the central role of training as a management function. There is no clear job profile of trainers and their career prospects are often bleak. Either they are deadwood to start with, or they are subsequently sidetracked. Their motivation is often low, as are the resources available to them, and in consequence their impact. Being poorly organized and with the wrong kind of training is probably worse than having no training at all.

Conversely, high-performing inspectorates usually make considerable investments in training, particularly initial training. Many countries have special training institutes for their inspectors (France, Germany, Poland and the United States, for example), where a wide range of training programmes is organized. Others have training departments within the headquarters of the inspectorate (Denmark and the United Kingdom, among others) that develop training curricula and methodologies, and organize or fund training pro- grammes. All of them operate under a comprehensive and regularly reviewed training policy. One major inspectorate carries out update-training for new legislation, using travelling trainers who visit each major office. In contrast, refresher training on technological developments is given by a wide variety of two-day courses to which nominated inspectors are invited. Attendance at these courses is usually discussed and agreed between the inspector and his or her superior at the annual staff appraisal and is part of the inspector's "training allowance" for that year.

The EU's Senior Labour Inspectors Committee (SLIC), in a report by one of its working groups, gives a good example of a broad training policy statement:

> [Member States will need to ensure that] inspectors are provided with sufficient and suitable training to enable them to attain the levels of competence necessary to fulfil their duties. Newly recruited inspectors should undergo a period of intensive training and work experience to provide them with the knowledge and skills necessary to enable them to [take action carrying out inspection of health and safety at the workplace]. All inspectors will from time to time benefit from periods of refresher training to bring them up to date with advances in technology and developments in law and good practice.[2]

Issues such as making enterprises responsible, or the "new workplace hazards" discussed in Chapter 28, mean that labour inspectorates need to stimulate competency building with enterprises, if they are to deal adequately with these hazards. Mere motivation is not enough, but must be accompanied by adapted know-how.

12.5 Initial training

As already indicated, there is a wide range of different models for training inspectors, and the content and format can be expected to change in the light of experience and changing circumstances. Training will cover important areas such as understanding the law, techniques of prevention, the demands made by occupational safety and health, and employment protection. Training will also include an explanation of inspection and sanctioning policies, and unavoidable administrative procedures, such as the management of office work and reporting arrangements. It is equally important to ensure that inspectors understand the attitudes and psychology of employers and workers, as well as the processes of management.

Time should therefore be allowed for training in influencing skills, the management of conflict and the use of the media. For these purposes, it is often wise to involve external specialists and not to rely solely on the senior staff of the inspectorate, important as their input may be.

12.6 Post-probationary and in-service training

Most effective inspectorates have post-probationary programmes and in-service training to prepare staff for new duties or work in new sectors of the economy, or to alert them to the latest technological developments. In order to ensure the best use of such programmes and consistency in keeping staff up to date and in staff development, some inspectorates allow a certain number of training days per inspector a year or over a particular period. The programme includes managerial training for those about to assume responsibilities.

12.7 Information management policies

This section is not about information services provided by labour inspectorates to their wider client system. It is about the management of knowledge and information within the inspectorate, and what policy issues should be discussed in this context.

Information management has to contribute to making the inspectorate more efficient and effective – irrespective of the mandate of the inspection system. Proper decisions on the choice of information management policy demand an objective appraisal of the role of the inspectorate and inspectors in the context of the social and political environment in which they work. For example, an inspectorate may be generally reactive, dealing mainly with complaints about conditions of employment. Another may have a wide remit with regard to labour inspection, taking in welfare, social security, safety and health matters, conciliation, illegal employment and so on. Inspectorates may be close-knit communities working from a small number of offices, or built up from several government departments with very little internal liaison. Most probably, the real inspectorate will be an organization with a range of different formal and informal features.

The appraisal itself, though a necessary starting point, will not offer any solutions. It creates a framework against which policy managers can discuss those functions of the organization amenable to information management and the degree to which they can be exploited. The appraisal can also be used to balance costs against benefits, determine the information flow and data requirements, and help keep an open mind on alternative solutions. In short, the appraisal will give direction as management draws up the objectives for an information system. Decisions on the introduction or development of information technology will play a major role in this context, and the following paragraphs can also be applied to that decision-making process.

The detail with which the objectives are produced is determined by their purpose, which is to help identify user needs. They must therefore be comprehensive without developing any one aspect to excessive lengths. Essentially, one has to identify where a shortage of information or difficulty in accessing information is hampering the work of the inspectorate. Data may exist, but not in a readily comprehensive and available form to the right point in the inspectorate at the right time.

At first glance, these problems may be difficult to see, as the organization could have adopted makeshift solutions to cover the worst difficulties, or not have appreciated that there are missing elements. Pressure of day-to-day tasks can preclude this necessary self-examination, but it is most important if information management is to be correctly applied. The objectives will be used as the standard against which missing data are identified and indicate where gaps need to be filled.

Information collected by the inspectorate cannot have much value unless it is accessible. Often, the assets locked up in a system can only be fully resourced by users, as they apply it to support the purpose of the organization. Users within the inspectorate therefore have a critical role to play. With their knowledge of labour inspection from a government and industrial point of view, they have the capability to assess the relevant information provided by management. These are the people who can discuss problems and opportunities, reject impracticalities and assess the implications of proposals.

There is another reason for regarding staff in the inspectorate as primary data users. Much of the data going into the system will derive from inspectors: much of it will be specific to conditions in premises and require professional assessment. Unless the provider can see some gain from the information, then cooperation and quality may suffer.

Some method has to be adopted to control fact finding. To approach users without a policy framework against which to identify needs will result in a tangle of detail difficult to unravel. It is far better to start a policy with some structure within which needs can be discussed and rationalized. Clearly needs have to be compatible with the aims and objectives of the information system, and constant questioning of the use to which data are to be put can weed out redundant elements. Top management should resist the temptation to make enquiries solely for management purposes, but should aim to work on the basis of data already collected for inspection, technical or policy purposes.

The issue remains: how can one match the data one has, or can have made available, with the organization's information needs? There are four questions to be addressed in this context, the answers to which will help the designers of the system assess the solutions that are open to them, primarily:

– How does information flow through the inspectorate from its source to the users?
– What analysis and collation are required?
– What are the permanent data storage requirements?
– What service should present information to the users?

The information flow must include all sources of information and all users, but can otherwise be left in fairly broad terms. Its purpose will be to check that the alternatives considered satisfy each channel of the information flow.

This depends on the different purposes for which information is collected, on the users, on the functions exercised by the inspectorate, and so on. If the inspection service has a major role in policy development, analysis must be comprehensive and in depth, focusing on both policy and operational requirements. For purely statistical purposes, analysis and collation will generally be less comprehensive and less resource intensive.

Permanent data storage refers to the paperwork associated with the enterprises dealt with by the inspectorate. Some will be prescribed by legal requirements. Planning applications, notification of accidents and notice of occupation of factories will need to be kept for a period of time on paper. Furthermore, the inspectorate has to continue to function during a system failure.

Which service provides information will depend entirely on the way in which the inspectorate functions. At its simplest, an inspector may be given an annual list of sites to visit with no initial briefing. Here the service provided can consist of an annual printout, with no particular demands on methods of access or response times.

More realistically, inspectors will be working to a general annual plan, but with frequent diversions requiring them to react to requests for advice, incidents and complaints. They will need the best possible information about the enterprises and their previous involvement with the inspectorate. This environment places demands on the speed and the methods by which that information should be managed. The need for some types of information may be foreseeable at perhaps a week's notice; other types will be far more interactive, requiring both faster response and an ability to browse through information sources.

Essentially, information management policy is an exercise in formulating and analysing alternative solutions, identifying the associated constraints, risks and cost–benefits, and deciding the way forward.

The way information is collected, the geographic location of the offices of the inspectorate, the types of analyses and data required by the users, the volume of data and the number of daily transactions either to or from the database, will allow an estimate of the hardware, software and communication network costs. Some cost–benefit analyses can be made in terms of the likely savings in inspector and support staff time; the benefits improved information systems bring to the effectiveness of the inspectorate may require time to materialize and may well be left as a hidden bonus.

Much of the information relating to data flow, requirements of the different users, volumes of information and so on can then be carried over, expanded and confirmed. This will suffice for the basic functional design and construction of a computer system. Other requirements, equally important to successful information management, can then be introduced. In general terms, these are the principles that managers wish to be applied between the information-processing facilities and the user (the inspector), and to the long-term management of the system.

Finally, the agreed solution will have to be developed, in every aspect, into a clear user-friendly statement. There are a number of ways a well-designed information management policy may benefit the inspection service and, consequently, its client system.

- All legislators and policy makers need raw information. They need accurate facts to support proposals and to assess the cost-effectiveness of new regulations. The existence of good data, however, can show where problems are occurring, and point the way to solutions. This is at the lowest level of active cooperation between the inspectorate and the information system.
- Using an information system to good effect in communication, planning and monitoring of inspectors' activities will challenge preconceptions. It will bring into question the way in which staff are deployed and the line management posts that are necessary for those staff.
- Another active role for an information system is that of building links between the technical knowledge and solutions in one database, and the problems faced by industry. The question is simple: "I have the knowledge: where can I find a problem to solve?" The demand will be for a system that collects information and is capable of directing the inspectorates' resources to good effect by identifying where given problems exist.

- A well-briefed, well-trained inspector is likely to earn respect. If she or he is seen as part of an organization capable of acting through its information systems in an even-handed manner, then there is more likely to be a change in attitudes. The inspector is working as a more effective agent in achieving the objectives of the organization.
- The organization may react well to this increased effectiveness. It provides an option to change enforcement policies, in other words, it permits the balance between advice and control, and coordinated inspection, data collection and dissemination functions to be altered. All of these will in turn have some effect on the tasks that are demanded of the information system.
- The final step will be to help inspectors interpret situations using the information system. It is difficult to visualize the application of a truly "expert" system, which can take in certain factors about a site or organization, predict the likely problems and offer solutions. More foreseeable is a type of knowledge-based system that not only helps the user interrogate the database but gives suggestions for the type of questions that ought to be asked when dealing with conditions found in an enterprise, and points the way to go about finding the answers.

The active potential mentioned here cannot be realized in one step. The inertia in any organization would not permit it, nor has any single individual sufficient foresight to gauge the cause and effect of any particular move. Organization and information systems have to change hand-in-hand. All that can be asked is a constant questioning of the status quo and sufficient flexibility in system designs to keep the options open.

Perhaps, above all, the whole system has to be positively managed in order to ensure compatibility of hardware, the exploitation of new techniques, the protection of security, where necessary, and the maximum benefits in terms of efficiency and service.

Notes

[1] HSE: *Successful health and safety management* (London, 1997).

[2] European Commission, Senior Labour Inspectors Committee (SLIC): *Common principles for labour inspectorates regarding inspection of health and safety at the workplace* (Brussels, 1997).

PUTTING POLICIES INTO EFFECT   13

13.1 Planning and programming of inspections

Preferably after discussion with middle managers in the field, policies must be translated into an annual programme nationally, regionally and locally. These programmes should specify the amount of time to be devoted to proactive inspection and special initiatives, thereby ensuring that such activities are not eroded by excessive demands of reactive work, such as the investigation of accidents and complaints. Some time may also be allocated for lectures on publicity activities. Inspectors need guidance on the extent of their enforcement role and to what extent they should give advice. This may not be the same in the case of SMEs and large enterprises. These work programmes enable progress to be monitored during the year and the performance of each unit to be assessed at the end of the year.

13.2 Style of inspection

Inspectors need to be given clear guidance on the style of inspection expected from them, be it the comprehensive assessment of hardware or chemical processes, selective sampling of particular departments or areas of activity, evaluating the quality and competence of risk assessments undertaken by employers themselves, or examining the occupational safety and health management systems. There is no single right model, but the inspectorate's management needs to make clear what approach it expects in different circumstances or at different times. The badly or incompetently managed enterprise may initially require a very thorough hardware inspection, although many experienced inspectors can adequately gauge standards by selective sampling. The use of identified deficiencies to demonstrate the inadequacy of the risk assessment process or the managerial control of safety and health can also be effective. Inspectors should also be clear about what is expected of them in terms of interviews with senior management and contact with unions and workers.

13.3 Discretion

Section 11.3 of this book described the range of sanctions available to inspectors. However, clear guidance needs to be available on the circumstances in which each option is appropriate. Obviously, it is necessary to give inspectors and their managers a significant measure of discretion to enable them to adapt their actions to the particular circumstances in question. However, the limits of discretion need to be clearly delineated so that inspectors and middle managers are confident of support in whatever actions they embark upon.

13.4 Procedures for influencing manufacturers, suppliers and importers

When an inspector discovers an inadequately protected piece of plant or inadequately packed or labelled substance, the manufacturer, supplier or importer seldom has an office locally. In order to have inadequacies rectified by the people who are in the best position to do so, the manufacturer or supplier, it is essential to have a system to collate evidence of similar deficiencies found elsewhere and to coordinate an approach to the manufacturer, supplier or importer to ensure that matters are put right.

13.5 Ensuring equity and consistency of treatment

While on the one hand, employers value the use of a certain amount of discretion in the inspector's role, as distinct from simple mechanical enforcement, they are on the other hand greatly perturbed if it appears that their competitors are being treated more leniently, in another part of the country. If this occurs, it will attract criticism of the inspectorate. Obviously, an effective organization should have procedures that ensure broad consistency in the interpretation and enforcement of standards across the country. These procedures may involve specialist units at headquarters or they may be delegated to individual regions for different sectors of the economy.

13.6 Responsibility for cooperation with other authorities and bodies

Although emphasis has been placed on the importance of cooperation with other authorities and bodies concerned with labour conditions, it is insufficient to leave this as a matter of good will or at the discretion of the local manager. If the inspectorate attaches importance to cooperation with particular bodies, then the way this should be done, the frequency and the nature of this cooperation, should be clearly stated in guidelines to middle managers.

13.7 Handling the media

While the labour inspectorate may have a general policy for handling the media, problems may arise with local press, radio and television. This can occur in a climate where there is a conflict of interest between the public's expectation for openness and information and the need to maintain confidentiality on situations or individuals, still under investigation, or indeed plants or processes subject to commercial exploitation. Local inspectors or managers may suddenly be faced with these conflicting demands and need guidance on how to respond in a manner that does not risk embarrassing the entire organization.

13.8 Monitoring quality

The inspectorate's management cannot assume that all programme activities developed in accordance with perscribed guidelines will be correctly carried out. Positive monitoring and evaluation programmes are vital. They should cover output in terms of time spent or number of visits or inspections achieved, and should seek to assess the quality of the work.

At an individual level much can be gleaned by the senior manager accompanying an inspector on a follow-up inspection. They can assess not only how he or she deals with the current visit, but also the impact and effectiveness of the original inspection. Similarly, senior managers should assess the performance of regional and local units, not only by examining records and statistics, but also by meeting and periodically inspecting local staff. These monitoring activities are in effect a two-way process because senior managers will become aware of misperceptions or misunderstandings enabling them to modify guidance or instructions. Most importantly, the proper systematic evaluation and presentation of results, both in terms of quantity and quality, enhance the inspectorate's credibility in the eyes of ministers and help ensure continued financial and political support.

INSPECTION POLICIES AND PREVENTION ECONOMICS   14

14.1 The issues

The aims of this chapter are to:

*   give labour inspectors and those responsible for inspectorates an overview of how different countries have tried to calculate the costs of workplace accidents and ill health to the national economy, to employers and to individuals;
*   summarize the factors which have been taken into account in making the calculations;
*   give an idea of the scale of the resultant figures;
*   describe the opportunities the data give to labour inspectorates to use in the course of their inspection and enforcement activities; and
*   illustrate the issue through selected case studies.

The cost of workplace accidents and ill health at national level[1]

Of the approximately 115 million workers in the EU, over 10 million are victims of occupational accidents or diseases every year. Of these, more than 8,000 die each year as a result of occupational accidents alone. The number of fatal occupational diseases is estimated to be many times higher, possibly by a factor of ten or more.

In the EU alone, the money paid out each year as a direct result of work accidents and illnesses is estimated to be more than 26 billion ECU. In the United States, the cost of non-prevention in the manufacturing industry has been given by the Department of Labor as around US$190 billion annually. Similar cost estimates for the German economy give total annual losses due to non-prevention of work accidents and diseases at around DM52 billion.

Adopting a total loss approach, the overall cost to the British economy of workplace injuries and work-related ill health in 1995/96 was estimated at between £2.9 billion and £4.2 billion. If the costs of avoidable non-injury accidental events are included, the figures rise from between £4.2 billion to £8.6 billion, the equivalent of 0.6 to 1.2 per cent of the total British gross domestic product (GDP). The cost to employers of workplace injuries and work-related ill health was estimated to be around £2.5 billion (£0.9 billion for injuries and £1.6 billion for illness). This is equivalent to between 4 and 8 per cent of all United Kingdom industrial and commercial companies' gross trading profits, or between £143 and £297 per person employed. Over the same period, it was estimated that individual workers who suffer work injuries and work-related illnesses lost around £558 million in reduced income and additional expenditure, quite apart from loss in the form of pain, grief and suffering.

In Germany, asbestos-induced occupational diseases, which account for more than 80 per cent of all fatal work-related illnesses, are calculated to be in excess of DM1 million in direct costs for each single case.

In Norway, a relatively small country with a very high level of labour protection, 2,500 cases of occupational diseases and 25,000 occupational injuries are reported each year, allowing for the fact that the inspectorate estimates that only one out of every four occupational injuries is actually reported. Recent studies estimate the social costs of non-prevention at NOK40 billion per year, or approximately US$550 million.

According to the Finnish Ministry of Labour, the costs of work-related diseases and occupational accidents were calculated as FIM18.3 billion in 1992 (approximately US$3 billion), nearly 4 per cent of GNP.

In arriving at these estimates, countries have applied different calculations and factors, but they all encompass various aspects of medical costs, costs of productive capacity and other economic costs, human costs, damage to property and equipment, administrative costs, emergency service costs and insurance administrative costs.

Costs at enterprise level

Costs to the employer include costs resulting from the worker's absence, the cost of replacing workers, damage to materials and equipment, and compensation and insurance. Generally speaking, employers' liability for sickness and compensation and their liability to third parties for damage are covered by insurance. However, other costs include damage to products and materials, to plant and buildings, to tools and equipment (not to mention the cost of recruiting and training replacement workers or temporary labour), possible additional payment at overtime rates and administrative costs, as well as legal costs and fines that cannot be covered by insurance. Uninsured costs have been estimated to come to twice or even eight or more times the insured costs of accidents.

In addition, there is an unquantifiable loss of goodwill and the reputation of the firm with its workforce, customers and the local community, which can have a longer-term effect upon the economic well-being of the company and the morale and productivity of the workforce.

Costs to the individual

In contrast to the cost to the economy and to the enterprise, the costs to the individual worker continue. They include lost earnings, loss of future income, reduced earning capacity, additional living costs, loss of quality of life, and pain, grief and suffering. The section "The human factor", below, looks at the mental health picture.

The broader economic perspective

In the Nordic countries there has been varying interest in assessing the influence of the work environment on the economy, at the level of both the company and society as a whole. Debate continues there as to whether economics will be misused – by limiting interventions to safety and health problems to the cheapest solutions – rather than used to solve the problems workers experience. However, economics can act as a catalyst promoting a healthier working life. The principal arguments for this perspective are that:

• the use of economic breaks are not an extra cost problem, because investment in safety and health ultimately results in considerable savings;
• the prevention of accidents and diseases can save billions on the state budget, although safety and health is seldom mentioned as a priority area in national budgeting;
• in the face of rapid technological change, fierce competition and new political demands, there is an increasing need for competent and flexible employees. Problems in the work environment are often reflected in low motivation, high sickness rates and high turnover of personnel, resulting in a negative company image which can have a deleterious effect on the marketing of its products; and
• the expectations of a healthy working life are higher today; more people are motivated to do something about their health when informed of the consequences of unhealthy workplaces.

The Finnish labour inspectorate explicitly recognizes that while some investments are paid back in a short period and are economically profitable to a company, there are other investments that are positive for society but not necessarily from a company perspective. When a company is obliged to make investments for legal and ethical reasons, the appeal to company self-interest and self-motivation for economic reasons must be reinforced – and supplemented – by the traditional inspection and enforcement work of the labour inspectorate.

14.2 The role of labour inspection in prevention economics

Contributions to national prosperity

Although the EU Member States and many other industrialized countries have carried out studies of the costs to the national economy and to individual companies of workplace accidents and ill health, it is not enough to simply publish these results. They will seldom have an impact at enterprise level unless their significance is translated into terms and scale of costs relevant to the enterprise's size, sector and economic prosperity. Making these cost estimates relevant to individual management is a vital function of the labour inspectorate. It is not enough to pass laws, promote self-regulation or introduce a system of "internal control", just as it is not enough to publish cost studies without the inspection and enforcement activities of the labour inspectorate.

Labour inspection has a key role to play in developing and promoting the concepts of costs and benefits in terms of occupational safety and health, and designing specific policies and operational procedures to promote cooperation with other key players, such as trade associations and insurance organizations. The aim is to inculcate the possibility of cost and loss reduction into management thinking, to the extent that it results in practical preventive action.

It is increasingly common practice for governments to require a cost–benefit analysis or regulatory impact study, before introducing new safety and health regulations. Although it is by no means an easy task to estimate the prospective benefits in terms of reduced suffering and reduced costs, the labour inspectorate, through its experience on the ground, its knowledge and its studies, is pivotal in contributing to the estimated costs of non-prevention. It is, in part, the studies and data provided by labour inspectorates that have made the information available on worldwide losses from workplace accidents and ill health, as described above.

Changing inspection policies

Traditionally, labour inspectorates have operated through a combination of "surprise" routine inspections, investigations of reported accidents and ill health and special visits either at the employer's request or to undertake some particular inspection initiative. Increasingly, inspectorates have focused on getting management to manage occupational safety and health in the same way as it manages other organizational activities. An awareness of the costs of accidents and ill health and the ability to speak convincingly about their reduction will assist the individual inspector to motivate management more effectively.

To accomplish this, the first prerequisite is to convince inspectors of the validity of this approach, which is at least as effective in appealing to managements' self-interest as is the threat of legal sanctions. The second prerequisite is to have documentation ready to convince management that "Safety Pays" and that "Good Health is Good Business".

Influencing management

The introduction of an inspection policy requiring the inspector, when appropriate, to present the economic as well as the legal and ethical case for improved safety and health is a significant challenge to the individual inspector. He or she is operating on new ground, and economic arguments are rarely either quite so convincing or incapable of being challenged as they first appear. Employers will be aware of their immediate costs, availability of suitable staff, the demands of customer services and the day-to-day problems of production or service. The inspector will have to take these considerations into account when presenting the economic argument for improvement.

The object of inspection is to achieve permanent positive change in terms of improved working conditions or improved procedures. This in turn involves motivating those in charge to initiate change of their own accord. By promoting improvement, inspectors can utilize their knowledge and experience to advise and support management in dealing with occupational safety and health problems and in developing solutions. While continuing to argue the economic case, inspectors must bear in mind that, where seriously unacceptable conditions are found, the law will require action.

Being realistic about the costs and benefits of prevention

While presenting the economic benefits of improved preventive measures, the fact is that inspections usually result, initially at least, in some additional costs. Management generally notices the cost but not the advantages and ultimate savings of preventive measures. While some inspectorates have developed means for measuring and recording costs and benefits, it is well to acknowledge that not all measures are equally cost-beneficial.

Occupational safety is not always profitable. An inspector must choose the best approach to present to a particular enterprise. Emphasis on the economic aspect may not be appropriate or necessary at every inspection, especially if the economic advantage of an occupational safety measure is so small that it would not motivate management to make changes. In these cases the inspector has to appeal either to the need for good health or the provisions of the law.

The Finnish Department for Occupational Safety and Health suggests that better housekeeping (a "tidy" workplace, keeping gangways clear, arranging a logical layout for production and processes, increasing the flow of information and general improvements to the workplace atmosphere) tend to be profitable. Improvements to the safety of machinery, and dealing with chemical problems, dust and fumes, and noise abatement, while often essential, are not automatically cost-effective. Similarly, obeying orders from inspectors or company officials tends to be less profitable than listening to the views of workers, enabling and encouraging them to participate and to take responsibility for their own safety and health. However, a Swedish study suggested that reducing exposure to chemical fumes and dust was relatively "profitable".

On the other hand, an occupational health service that meets only minimal statutory requirements or concentrates on medical treatment is more likely to profit from active occupational health care aimed at prevention and rehabilitation. Ergonomics involving the improvement of individual workstations without considering the work processes as a whole will be less beneficial than the application of ergonomics to planning and purchasing. A comprehensive Nordic study showed that an inspection process that identified occupational safety and health problems and related them to legal provisions resulted in the lowest costs for management, but required very careful analysis, and the final decision had to be left to management. The enterprise in question was its own best judge in terms of finding the most economic solution and in this case the system of inspection was effective because the standard to be met to satisfy the law was made unequivocally clear.

However, an informal style of inspection can be least advantageous to an enterprise if it leaves management unsure of what is actually required. As a result, management might either do nothing or might delay action. According to a Swedish study, the development of an ergonomic solution to problems, and the application of ergonomics, proved to be relatively easy technically and economically viable.

A United Kingdom leaflet aimed at SMEs suggested that taking the inspector's advice may often save a company money. For instance, intending to install a fire-resistant spray booth for flammable substances, the owner of a small firm had flameproof lights and switches in mind. The inspector advised the owner that he would be satisfied if ordinary fluorescent lights and switches were sited outside the booth with the lights shining through sealed wired glass panels – a much cheaper method. In another instance, the owner of a provender mill proposed putting the mill itself in a substantial "blockhouse" type of building. The inspector suggested a less substantial building with a lightweight roof that would vent the pressure of any explosion to a safe place, saving the company £60,000.

The human factor

Mental well-being has an important, if not decisive, significance in the productivity and economic results of most enterprises and organizations. Signs of a workplace's state of well-being are the employees' positive experience of the working community, high work motivation, low absenteeism, tolerance of conflicts and uncertainty, reasonable staff turnover and the organization's ability to promote fruitful cooperation. Good working conditions, good management and good interaction have a positive effect on employees' well-being and motivation, and subsequently on the quality and productivity of the enterprise operations.

An absence of mental well-being can be observed in various disturbances of the operations and production, and in a negative impact on work efficiency and the profitability of the company. The direct consequence can be high absenteeism, high staff turnover, willingness to take premature retirement, an increase in the number of visits to the company's health centre, repeated difficult conflicts and the splitting of the workforce into factions, as well as a general feeling of uncertainty and insecurity. The impact of mental health problems in the workplace has serious consequences not only for the individual but also for the productivity of the enterprise.

Deficiencies in the physical working conditions tend to make it difficult to do the job and cause unnecessary strain. Resources are also consumed by stress, burnout, conflicts within the working community, discrimination, bullying and the threat of violence at the workplace (see Chapter 28). The promotion of mental well-being is more a question of easily understood and easy-to-implement changes in lines of action and the promotion of good interaction rather than through large economic input. Emphasizing the economic significance of both positive and negative consequences may further provoke the action required to achieve improvements in the workplace.

Productivity and profitability are affected by many different factors. A Swedish study suggests that the style of management and management's relationship with workers, the type of work and the individual's motivation, the workplace atmosphere, the extent to which the tasks take ergonomics into consideration, training and orientation were the main factors contributing to well-being in the workplace, and that factors such as housekeeping, lighting, temperature and noise were secondary considerations in terms of staff turnover and absenteeism.

Such basic requirements include good physical working conditions, smooth relations between workers and between workers and management, equitable work planning, job security and adequate wages. Any continuing growth of productivity requires positive work motivation, appreciation of the individual's contribution and a feeling of affinity with the organization. If inspectors are able to give some consideration to these factors, they can simultaneously affect the company's productivity positively.

Root cause analysis

Emphasis in the foregoing sections has been on reducing avoidable losses and minimizing unnecessary expenditure. The United Kingdom's HSE has developed a model for safety and health management, and a methodology for costing accidents. Recent research has built a link between the two and a method is being developed to test a way to cost accidents, together with a tool for analysing the "root cause" of a given incident, in order to enable organizations to target safety and health expenditure more effectively. If the costs of accidents could be clearly identified and linked back to specific management failures, companies would be able to target their improvement effort in a cost-effective way by concentrating on well-defined areas of management activity.

Two trials have been undertaken, one for capturing data on accident costs as simply as possible and the other to develop a "root causes analysis tool" from first principles. The financial costs include both material and labour costs, while the opportunity costs include those arising from workers having to stand idle or being unable to produce their regular output because they have been redirected to deal with the consequences of an accident. In addition, there are the usual administrative and legal costs.

The development of the root cause analysis tool involves assessing incidents and accidents against a six-stage model following quality principles and best company practices, namely policy, organizing, planning, measuring, reviewing and auditing, discussed below ("A state hospital").

A comprehensive literature review revealed widespread agreement on a basic analysis accident causation model for barriers, computing:

- awareness of a hazard;
- barriers failing; and
- people or objects being in the way.

This model was later made into a more systematic process through the development of MORT (management oversight and risk tree) analysis, providing a disciplined method for determining the causes and contributing factors of major incidents. The process seeks to identify the root cause of an accident: inadequate definition of policy; inadequate organization in terms of control, cooperation, communication or competence, inadequate planning, implementation or measurement; or a failure to review the whole process.

Two subsequent case studies showed clear weaknesses in the organization's own communication system and the competence of its workers, as well as its planning ability, although it scored high on implementation. In another study of a state hospital, described below, policy and organization were found to be above average, although planning and implementation were both below the acceptable standard, with a total absence of any review process. The analysis enabled the organization to improve its weak elements and lower its accident costs.

The economic input to risk assessment and enterprise action programmes

In the EU and increasingly elsewhere, enterprises are being required to base their action programme on risk assessments. Thus, the seriousness of the risk may be judged not only in terms of the outcome in damage or ill health, but also in terms of the economic consequences of an incident. For instance, a calculation of the risk of interruption to the power supply might indicate the need for urgent action, even if the risk of physical injury as a consequence was relatively low. Economic considerations stemming from a safety and health risk analysis can effectively contribute to an action programme that would minimize loss, as well as the risk of injury. Similarly, it is possible to estimate the economic effects of eliminating or reducing health risk – the cost–benefit effects of a strain injury, for example.

For example, in the United Kingdom, the widespread introduction of lifting aids, transfer equipment and height-adjustable beds, together with the adoption of a "no lifting" policy in hospitals, has led to a significant reduction in injuries to nurses and significant savings in individual establishments. Knowledge of various cost effects provides the inspector with important additional information, when seeking to motivate enterprises to carry out risk assessment and to manage those risks proactively.

14.3 Selected case studies

A car business

The Finnish TYTA model is a computer programme by means of which it is possible to explain and evaluate costs due to sickness, accidents, labour turn-over and disability, and input costs of occupational safety on an annual basis. This model is particularly applicable to large enterprises where the amount of sick leave and the number of accidents are high. Using the model, the inspector is able to draw the employer's attention to the costs caused by risks in the working environment and thus motivate the employer to focus more on improving conditions in the workplace.

An enterprise dealing in cars, with a high level of accidents and sickness absence, applied the model over a period of three years and succeeded in identifying the causative factors. They decided to concentrate on enhancing the working environment, enhancing job satisfaction and taking similar measures to prevent incapacity. As a result, absences due to sickness and accidents were reduced by two-thirds and fell below the average of other enterprises in the project.

A wholesale business

A model was used by the Finnish labour inspectorate to explain the costs and advantages of improvements in the working environment and to occupational safety and health. If the cost of a preventive measure can be determined, it is possible to draw up a cost–benefit calculation for the investment and determine the period of repayment.

In a wholesale business, the workplace inspection showed a high accident occurrence rate. The model was used to demonstrate the economic impact of these accidents and the effects of preventive investment. A particular problem concerned personnel and forklift trucks criss-crossing in the same yard space, and also a risk of people slipping when walking. The enterprise decided to build a footbridge and to estimate the costs and benefits. Costs were incurred in the planning, materials and bridge-building work; advantages were accrued through a reduction in absenteeism, the speeding up of work, energy savings, the lengthening of the service intervals for forklift trucks and more efficient use of storage space. On this basis of a cost–benefit analysis, the period of repayment of the investment was 25 months.

Construction site A

At a poorly organized construction site, the potential profitability of improved housekeeping was calculated by means of a cost–benefit analysis, which showed that the losses caused by the lack of organization were three times as large as the investment costs. Necessary improvements were made to the site layout and its organization, with a consequent improvement in site housekeeping.

A water authority

Applying the standard categories for the cost of work accidents, (employee lost time, investigation time, operational inefficiencies, clean-up costs, treatment/ claims/administrative costs) to both reportable (three-day) injuries and lost-time accidents, enabled the water authority to focus on the main causes of accidents (falls from a height, manual handling, slipping and being struck by a moving object).

The enterprise also extrapolated the cost of non-injury accidents or incidents. Having tracked these costs and introduced a new safety and health management system, over a six-year period, management calculated a saving of some £2.5 million by accident prevention alone.

In the case of ill health, the company concentrated on work-related upper limb disorders, hand/arm vibration syndrome, occupational stress and noise-induced hearing loss. Collecting the same cost data on work-related illness enabled the enterprise to adopt a preventive programme. In the case of work-related upper limb disorders, personal one-to-one interviews were carried out with every user of display screen equipment. Control measures in all work-station aspects were adopted on the spot, as well as referrals to occupational health services, additional training and software development. The total cost over a ten-year period was approximately £30,000; claims for work-related upper limb disorders are increasing both in number and in the size of settlement. The company reckons it will have saved some 175 referrals, at a compensation cost of just over £5,000 each, providing a saving of over £900,000 over ten years. The estimated ten-year cost for the compliance programme was £34,000, which is easily outstripped by the ten-year saving in compensation costs.

In the case of hand/arm vibration from the use of tools that vibrate and equipment used to break open and reinstate road surfaces, the enterprise concentrated on the provision of leaflets, health surveillance and anti-vibration upgrading of equipment. The total cost of the compliance programme, including an allowance for maintenance, was £50,000. Since 10 per cent of the 200 employees already showed symptoms, management assessed that they had prevented some 20 cases over the next ten years at an average cost of £11,500, thus saving some £230,000 over ten years.

Construction site B

This case study concerns the construction of a supermarket, with a contract value of about £8 million, which took place over a period of 18 weeks. There were some 29 subcontractors. All accidents above the threshold value of £5, and considered by the main contractor to be preventable, were recorded for the whole site. An accident was defined as "any unplanned event resulting in injury or ill health of workers, or damage or loss to property, plant, materials or the environment or the loss of a business opportunity".

A total of 3,620 accidents meeting this definition were recorded over the 18 weeks, resulting in direct financial losses of over £87,000, with opportunity costs, mainly wages paid during periods of no production, amounting to a further £158,000, making a grand total of £245,000. Assuming that accidents occurred at this rate throughout the entire contract, the total losses were estimated to be in the order of £700,000, or approximately 8.5 per cent of the £8 million tender price.

In total, 56 minor injuries and 3,570 accidents damaging property were recorded. No major injuries or over-three-day injury accidents occurred during the study period, despite national accident construction data suggesting at least one serious over-three-day injury during the study period. The ratio of insured to uninsured costs was estimated at 1:11. The nature of this study – a project of limited life – precluded a "before and after" comparison, but the results in terms of cost and loss should convince managers of construction companies that there is ample scope for cost-saving in their industry.

A state hospital

Applying the root cause analysis approach described above, a 13-week study of a hospital identified total accident costs of £26,000 (almost £2,000 per week or £104,000 per year). Each incident had to be an unplanned event that management could have controlled; to have resulted in harm to a person or have had the potential for harm; and to have caused costs above a minimum threshold of £5 or 15 minutes of an individual's time, directly incurred as a result of the incident.

During subsequent investigation, information was gathered on individual incidents and whether any hazard controls were present. Events and causal factors were charted to clarify the sequence of events and identify the root cause ("the most basic cause that can reasonably be identified and that management has the ability to control").

The root or basic cause was in turn described in the HSE's publication,

Successful health and safety management.[2] This document suggests that the components of a safety and health management system involve:

- **policy** – setting a clear direction for an organization to follow;
- **organizing** – setting effective management structures and arrangements to deliver the policy, including control, by assigning appropriate roles and responsibilities, ensuring adequate competencies, establishing effective communication mechanisms and achieving the cooperation of all staff;
- **planning and implementing** – ensuring that risks to safety and health from work activities are controlled by using formal written risk assessments which are implemented in work practice;
- **measuring performance** – agreeing standards to measure against; and
- **auditing and reviewing performance**.

In assessing costs, the study did not take account of long-term health effects resulting from, for example, needle-stick injuries, equipment damage (reporting of which was poor due to staff reluctance), management costs (regarded as already counted for) or litigation potential. The analysis identified the strongest aspects of the hospital system as its policy, communication, cooperation and performance. Areas for further development included control, planning and implementation. Management found this outcome highly informative and, as a result, prepared a prioritized, detailed action plan. The data were also persuasive in reinforcing positive attitudes to safety and health within the organization.

Notes

[1] The data in this section were provided by departments of labour or directorates of labour inspection in the countries concerned.

[2] HSE: *Successful health and safety management* (London, 1997).

PART III

INSPECTION SYSTEMS: ORGANIZATION AND MANAGEMENT

LABOUR INSPECTION AND TRIPARTISM

15

15.1 General observations

Social dialogue equates with tripartite cooperation at different levels. Tripartite cooperation is essentially a means of reaching compromises between economic and social imperatives that are acceptable to all the parties concerned. While tripartite cooperation cannot function in the absence of a market economy, it does aim to restrict, to a certain extent, the free play of market forces.

The various forms of tripartite cooperation (including informal arrangements) are an especially appropriate and, in the event of a serious crisis, indispensable means of ensuring that better account is taken of social considerations at the national level. Social dialogue has an important contribution to make towards providing an international social framework for the globalization of the economy. Tripartite cooperation can also help reconcile the concern of enterprises to increase their competitiveness, while respecting the requirements of social justice and solidarity.

In many Central and Eastern European countries and in some developing countries, the main difficulty hampering the effective functioning of informal and formal tripartite arrangements has been the slow emergence of truly independent employers' and workers' organizations, with clearly distinct functions for independent and state organizations.

In countries where tripartite cooperation has functioned well, it has been based on a conscious effort by employers' and workers' organizations to seek common ground, even in the face of ideological opposition, whether between competing groups on the same side or between workers and employers. The State must be open to the usefulness of the social partners' input into dialogue, and the workers' and employers' organizations must have the capacity to be effective participants.

In fact, the effectiveness of inspection services will be greatly increased if they receive the support of employers and workers, their organizations and their representatives. This tripartite concept is not new, and indeed it provides the basis on which the ILO functions. Not only does it reflect the composition of the Organization itself, but it is also embodied in the procedure through which international instruments are formulated and presented. It is exemplified by the Tripartite Consultation (International Labour Standards) Convention, 1976 (No. 144).

As in any form of cooperation, tripartism requires a degree of trust amongst participants, which in turn is conditioned by a willingness to exchange honest information on the issues involved. For example, workers and employers must know the facts on which government bases its policies, and each of the social partners must be prepared to clarify its own position in regard to productivity, working practices, occupational safety, hygiene and health, the framework of social relations at enterprise level, and so on. The aim should be to establish one's own position, explore common interests and, as far as possible, eliminate divergencies.

15.2 Collaboration within the enterprise

A growing number of countries have introduced legislation that requires joint committees to be established in industrial, commercial and even non-commercial enterprises above a certain size, although this has not occurred to the same extent in agricultural enterprises. These committees complement some of the functions of the labour inspectorate, exercise in-plant supervision over conditions of work and, in particular, occupational safety and health, and generally help prevent occupational and ever-increasing social and economic risks. A parallel development has been the introduction of safety delegates elected by the workers in enterprises, usually when there are more than ten workers in the enterprise (but sometimes more than five) or, occasionally (for instance in the United Kingdom), but not exclusively, when they are appointed by trade unions. The latter approach is not problem free, as trade union rivalries may be introduced to the shop floor in the context of labour protection, often to the detriment of the latter. In recognition of the value of both joint safety and health committees and safety delegates, the tendency on the part of governments is to give them increasingly extensive powers, for example to allow them time off (by law) to accompany labour inspectors on their visits – an important point, since they can indicate hazards which might otherwise escape the inspector's notice and generally add considerable value to the inspector's presence in the workplace.

The collaboration of the inspection services with workers' representatives is not confined to questions of occupational safety and health. In a number of countries, legislation states that trade union delegates and other staff representatives within the enterprise should have special responsibilities for conditions of employment and work. These delegates and representatives are specifically responsible for submitting complaints and observations relating to the application of the legal provisions and regulations to the labour inspectorate.

15.3 Collaboration at sectoral, regional and national levels

Many governments have established statutory tripartite bodies responsible for labour protection at national, regional and sectoral levels. These bodies deal with a wide variety of topics, which may include labour protection legislation, wages policy, safety and health, occupational hazards, industrial relations issues and even vocational training. In most cases, qualification for membership is set out by regulation, and is usually confined to workers' or employers' representatives or members of professional organizations, with a vested interest in the matters under discussion. The government department responsible for labour administration invariably provides administrative support, and its effectiveness is directly related to the quality of this support.

Sectoral bodies can be particularly effective in interpreting legislation for the processes or activities of the industry or sector in question, by agreeing and publishing detailed guidance. This reassures employers that the same requirements are being imposed on competitors, as well as assisting inspectors in their enforcement of agreed standards.

The logic of tripartism requires no emphasis and its advantages are plain. Cooperation yields better results than confrontation, at least in terms of social peace, and the more the labour inspectorate can do to foster cooperation between employers, workers and the government, the greater its contribution to the economic and social well-being of the country is likely to be. Collaboration can also be bipartite. Both employers and workers often consult the labour inspectorate informally about their problems. These contacts should be encouraged, subject to the proviso that the inspectors' impartiality is preserved and they do not become biased advisers to either party. It is also incumbent on labour inspectors to maintain contact with representative bodies of employers and workers. Inspectors will find it useful to call on them regularly, not only to discuss particular issues, but also to discuss matters of general interest in the sphere of working relations and conditions. The costs of such action will have to be weighed against the potential benefits.

15.4 Membership of advisory and decision-making bodies

Members of the labour inspectorate frequently share in the work of advisory bodies (in addition to providing the secretariat). They may be appointed, by name, as representatives of the minister to whom the particular body is responsible, in which case their appointment is based on the public character of their duties, their rank in the national civil service, or their personal ability to represent the department. On other occasions, the labour inspection service may be requested, together with other technical units, to send representatives to meetings to provide information that the service has obtained in the course of its day-to-day work. This information may be essential in guiding discussions or in deciding on a course of action. Sometimes it is necessary to make use of the labour inspectorate's knowledge of labour relations in a given area or a particular industry, or to examine the difficulties which might arise in the practical application of a legal text in the course of preparation. In these cases, the representative of the labour inspectorate merely attends as an observer or expert, takes no real part in making decisions, and is limited to the provision of advice. The position is quite different when the inspectors' attendance is part of their routine duties, and when it is the labour inspection service itself that is represented because of its technical responsibility (as is the case, for instance, in France and other countries following the French system). This usually involves participation in a collective decision.

Occasionally, the inspectorate is asked to give its approval before a final decision on a particular issue is made. This kind of participation is routine in the case of boards set up to examine and approve new plant and equipment, and in the case of safety and health committees at the local, regional and national levels. In these circumstances, the labour inspector may draw attention to the inadequacy of proposed protective measures, suggest others, or point out the practical difficulties involved in applying a particular regulation. The inspector's job is to represent the technical and practical views of the authority responsible for enforcing the decision or texts after they have been formulated. The role of an inspection service, in a sectoral planning committee, is directed towards drawing attention to the labour problems that should be considered before a particular measure is decided on, and to problems that could result from the introduction of such a measure.

STRUCTURAL ASPECTS OF ORGANIZATION   16

16.1 Labour inspection as a government department

The location of inspection systems within a central authority, such as a ministerial department, facilitates the establishment and application of a uniform labour inspection and enforcement policy for the entire country. This is why both Labour Inspection Convention, 1947 (No. 81), in Article 4, para. 1, and Labour Inspection (Agriculture) Convention, 1969 (No. 129), in Article 7, para. 1, stress the desirability of placing labour inspection under the supervision and control of a central authority "so far as is compatible with the administrative practice" of a member State.[1] This clause, as straightforward as it might appear, has repeatedly given rise to controversial interpretations. One issue of concern is whether the administrative practice referred to simply relates to the organization of the inspection service, or to any (similarly structured) part of the executive system, in other words, a country's public administration and its field or decentralized services. In the first case, the given organizational structure of an inspection system may indeed not be historically compatible with the notion of a single government department or central authority responsible for labour inspection (the case of federally constituted countries will be looked at later). However, in most countries other public services are under a central authority (e.g. tax inspection).

Behind this lie several important considerations, one of which is the aspect of ministerial responsibility. In countries where labour inspection is organized as a central government department, usually with decentralized field services under its direct supervision and control, it will, as a rule, be part of the Ministry of Labour or its equivalent (Social Affairs, Employment, etc.). Clear political (ministerial) accountability and indispensable political support for all labour inspection issues are then easily established. This political backing is essential for the day-to-day running of an inspection system and for labour inspection policy and structural reform, as well as for generating – though by no means guaranteeing – the necessary support for additional resources.

This form of organization may take labour inspection management out of the political limelight, but it tends to assure a measure of stability and continuity indispensable for the implementation of existing and new policies. The ILO's experience in different member States has shown that it may take three to five years before a major new policy initiative actually reaches the enterprises' shop-floor, signifying that it has been understood and effectively implemented. In 1981, the Netherlands demonstrated understanding of this principle by adopting a new labour protection policy in the form of the Working Environment Act. Entry into force of the Act, however, was staged. First the provisions on occupational safety, with which the client system was already quite familiar, came into effect. After three years, the parts dealing with occupational health came into force, to which the social partners needed more time to adjust. Finally, after seven years, the arrangements concerning "well-being", a completely new, far-reaching policy concept involving, inter alia, issues such as job satisfaction, and with whose application and oversight the inspectorate had to become familiar, acquired force of law.

Today, the global trend is to completely separate the policy (design, monitoring, evaluation) function of labour inspection, as described in Part III, sections 9.2 and 9.4, from the "service delivery" function, or labour inspection proper. In recent years, reforms in Australia, New Zealand and elsewhere have gone in this direction. How this service delivery component is best organized remains a matter of continuing debate. For example, in Belgium the labour inspection function is organized into three different government departments (technical inspection, medical inspection and inspection of social laws) under the same government Ministry (Labour). Coordination in this case tends to pose a considerable problem. In most English-speaking African and some Asian countries, two services (labour inspection, responsible for general conditions of work and industrial relations, and factory inspection, responsible for occupational safety and health) exist side by side as government departments of the respective Ministry of Labour. Coordination or cooperation is generally poorly developed; coherence of labour protection and consistency in the application of respective policies tend to suffer.

In the transition countries of Central and Eastern Europe, two separate government departments, one responsible for occupational safety (under the Ministry of Labour) and the other dealing with occupational hygiene (under the Ministry of Health), exist side by side. Institutional coordination and cooperation tend to be almost non-existent. Instead, there is competition and considerable waste due to friction and duplication. Effective and efficient inspection tends to suffer in these conditions. In contrast, countries such as Finland, the Netherlands or Norway, where the functional responsibilities of labour inspection are organized as one inspection system in a government department under the Ministry of Labour, tend to provide strong, well-organized, well-coordinated, coherent, effective and efficient labour inspection services to their client system. They may still have organizational problems at a more advanced level, but they tend to be in a better position to deal with these problems. It comes as no surprise that a number of high-performing labour inspectorates are choosing this type of model.

16.2 Tripartite systems management

In a growing number of countries, labour inspection is organized under a tripartite body, board or commission, which in turn supervises the inspectorate proper, sets the policy, monitors its implementation, evaluates the results, attributes resources and assumes overall responsibility for the proper running of the inspection service. This tripartite body may itself be politically accountable to a government minister (in a relatively loose way), or directly to parliament, as is the case in some countries.

The United Kingdom provides a typical example of a country with a tripartite management structure. The Health and Safety Commission (HSC) develops draft legislation and supervises the inspection service, the Health and Safety Executive (HSE). In Sweden, the tripartite National Board of Occupational Safety and Health supervises labour inspection in the country's seven districts.

Other countries have tripartite bodies that deal with labour protection. In Hungary and the Netherlands these bodies have an advisory function and, although they are highly respected, they do not act as the head of the executive. In systems where social security runs an inspection service (Germany and Switzerland), the supervision of the social security bodies and their preventive activities may be confined to bipartite bodies or boards, but this is very much the exception.

Tripartite management structures are only possible in systems where the social partners are strong, well organized and independent, have a keen interest in labour protection issues, and are accepted by the government as a partner in labour inspection matters. In such circumstances, considerable devolution of government ministry powers can occur. The example of the HSC in the United Kingdom may illustrate this. The aims of the HSC and the HSE, whose existence and functions derive from the Health and Safety at Work Act 1974, are to protect the health, safety and welfare of employees, and to safeguard others, principally the public, who may be exposed to risk.

Primary responsibility is placed upon those directly engaged: mainly employers, but also the self-employed and suppliers. The Commission and Executive are there to inform, stimulate and guide those with duties of care (duty holders[2]), and others concerned with labour protection, towards actions leading to higher standards, and in particular to:

- define standards, inter alia, by:
  - proposing reform of existing legislation, through regulations and approved codes of practice under the Act;
  - issuing guidance; and
  - cooperating with other standard-setting bodies;
- participate, through negotiation, in relevant standard setting in the EU and in other international bodies, taking account of the principles of the Trade Union and Labour Relations Act 1974;
- promote compliance with the 1974 Act, and other legislation as relevant, in particular by:
  - inspection, advice and enforcement in enterprises where the HSE is the enforcing authority; and
  - proposing and keeping under review arrangements for the allocation of enforcement responsibility between the HSE and other enforcement bodies with a view to satisfactory and consistent standards;
- carry out, publish and promote research; and investigate accidents and industrial health problems, disseminating findings as appropriate;
- provide specific services related to the Commission's main functions, such as an Employment Medical Advisory Service;
- contribute to the process of open and democratic decision making, transparency, accountability and consistency of approach on health, safety and welfare issues by:
  - providing advice and information as required to ministers;
  - making as much information as practicable available to the public;
  - cooperating with regulatory bodies in related fields;
  - representing United Kingdom interests in the EU and other intergovernmental fora; and
  - encouraging well-informed public discussion of the nature, scale and tolerability of risk.

The business of the HSC and the HSE is to ensure that: health risks and safety at work are properly controlled, in ways that are proportionate to the risk; technological progress is allowed for; and due regard is paid to the costs as well as the benefits. The two bodies act in close consultation with those whom their work affects and in all they do seek to promote better management of safety and health, using a systematic approach to identify hazards, and assess and control risks.

In Sweden, the National Board of Occupational Safety and Health has very similar functions. It receives its budget from the Ministry of Labour, but that is practically the only form of control the government exercises.

While the advantages of systems management organization on a tripartite basis are evident, in that the people most directly concerned have a real say in formulating and running policy issues which directly affect them, this is not entirely problem free. Political support at ministerial level may not very strong if the department does not come directly under the Minister. In the United Kingdom, the responsibility for the HSC/HSE has repeatedly shifted from one government ministry to another. If one of the social partners decides to withdraw from tripartite cooperation at national level for political reasons (as was the case for a time in Sweden), the whole concept is endangered. In Finland, the labour inspectorate used to be organized under a (tripartite) National Board of Labour Protection until it was abolished and transformed into a central government department, initially under the Ministry of Labour and currently assigned to the Ministry of Social Affairs and Health. However, tripartite management continues to be an important concept for the organization of labour inspection, and other countries are joining the ranks of these, by and large, high-performing systems. To cite another example, Australia set up a National Occupational Health and Safety Commission (NOHSC) in 1995, which has the following broad mandate to:

- achieve major planned outcomes (MPOs) annually;
- report to the Minister (for workplace relations) annually;
- collaborate with the Department of Labour Standing Committee (DOLAC), responsible for a comparative performance measurement in the federate units;
- to make recommendations to the Labour Minister's Council (federal and state territories) on any future regulations and standards;
- to consult with advisory bodies and other interested parties; and
- to supervise the operation of the NOHSC office, which has a set of executive responsibilities.

16.3 The need for integrated systems

It has already been noted that, in many countries, for a variety of historic, political or functional reasons, discrete labour inspection services have been established over time. These services often have different functional responsibilities, sometimes they overlap partially, and sometimes they have parallel responsibilities. In countries with "dual" systems, the need for coordination and cooperation is widely recognized. In practice, however, collaboration is mostly non-existent, and at best haphazard, often relying on the good will or personal relations of individuals in the different services. Even where cooperation is institutionalized by ministerial decrees or "agency agreements" between the managements of the services, there is no guarantee whatsoever that it will in practice function effectively. Yet dual or parallel inspection systems, often organized within one and the same government Ministry (usually Labour), are costly. Administrative duplication, separate data banks and lack of coordination in the use of human and material resources (which are always scarce) lead to waste and inefficiency. Added to that, the client system is often at a loss to understand the differences in the nature of the separate systems' intervention. Sometimes, inspectors from the different services give conflicting advice on labour protection issues. Often, they will appear to be insensitive to issues that do not fall within their own, often narrow, legal mandate.

Yet to the employers and workers concerned, these issues are usually so closely related as to form an intangible whole. This is how modern, high-performing systems tend to approach labour protection: in a holistic manner, adopting a global vision, trying to understand, to anticipate, and to come to grips with the different interrelated issues of labour protection, be they of a technical, medical, social, legal or economic nature. A holistic approach is increasingly seen as quintessential for the successful development and implementation of prevention policies in the world of work. Integrated labour inspection systems combining the major functional responsibilities of labour protection such as labour relations, occupational safety and health, general conditions of work and the fight against illegal forms of employment, are being set up in an increasing number of countries. In ILO member States, several typical constellations have emerged since the beginning of the 1990s.

Several countries, notably among the former British colonies, have inherited an unfortunate dichotomy of inspection services: a labour inspectorate, usually responsible for industrial relations, general working conditions and wages; and a factory inspectorate for occupational safety and health. When there were institutional links between these systems (until the end of the colonial period), the factory inspectorate was usually a part of the labour department. In the 1980s, the division between these services tended to increase, and factory inspectorates in many countries have become separate government departments.

Labour administration in most English-speaking African countries (and elsewhere) receives no more than 1 per cent of the national budget (in some cases, the figure is 0.1 per cent, while in many others it hovers around 0.25 per cent). Labour inspection, in turn, receives only a fraction of these resources. In consequence, its status is often unacceptably low. Labour inspectorates, as a rule, are grossly understaffed, underequipped, undertrained and underpaid. They are further characterized by a low transport and travel budget, insufficient training and inadequate means of communication. These factors lead to a lack of motivation and, often, a serious lack of orientation.

Integrated labour inspection is not a new concept in the African countries. It has simply not yet been effectively applied in much of the continent. In most countries its introduction would, therefore, involve a significant policy change.

In African countries, even in the formal sector, visits by inspectors to enterprises are few and far between. In many countries, inspectors (of either service) visit less than 10 per cent of formal, private urban sector establishments per year, in other words, they visit once every ten years. Rural establishments (of the formal sector) stand to be inspected much less frequently. Thus, when an inspector (labour or factory) does visit a workplace, it is unacceptable that he or she should turn a deaf ear to complaints, or a blind eye to violations, simply because they do not concern his or her field of legal or technical competence. To the workers concerned, the inspector represents the only agent of labour administration they are ever likely to meet. For labour inspectors to be insensitive to violations of occupational safety and health regulations, or factory inspectors to disregard complaints about the non-payment of wages, for example, as is presently the case in most countries of the region, is quite unacceptable. Not only does it defeat the purpose of all labour inspection, to protect workers and promote better working conditions and a better working environment, but it undermines and destroys the authority of both inspection services and the labour administration system as a whole.

Moreover, it constitutes a serious waste of resources. Labour protection managers know that the most costly part of organizing labour inspection is actually getting an inspector to the shop floor. If and when this happens, then that inspector should be mandated and competent to address – and be receptive to – all labour protection issues brought to his or her attention. Furthermore, factory inspectors are often highly trained specialists, and to send them haphazardly, as is still often the case, to enterprises on the assumption that they will always find something, is a most inefficient and costly way of organizing an occupational safety and health inspection service. For them to spend time in SMEs attending to details of low-complexity safety and health problems (which nevertheless have to be looked at by the employer) is a waste of time and resources. On the other hand, the exclusion of occupational safety and health from general labour inspection activities is unjustifiable, as it is too serious an issue to be neglected in this fashion.

A more functional systems organization would designate the (usually more numerous) labour inspectors as "points of first contact" with the labour force at the workplace, responsible for all aspects of labour protection, including "screening" basic, or non-complex, occupational safety and health issues (and basic industrial relations issues). More complex matters could then be referred to the occupational safety and health specialists stationed in provincial offices or areas of industrial concentration. To illustrate this point: in Kenya, the Labour Department conducted over 26,000 inspection visits in 1993 (with 182 inspection officers); the Department of Occupational Safety and health Services conducted some 3,000 inspections with 85 inspectors that same year. One may reflect on what an immense difference in occupational safety and health protection it would make in that country if labour inspectors were mandated (and, of course, adequately trained) to address basic safety and health issues during their visits as well. This is what the integrated systems approach (or "one-stop-shop") is all about, making optimal use of available, but always scarce, resources in the inspection system.

A second constellation concerns the Central and Eastern European countries (CEECs) emerging from the former Soviet-style labour inspection system. In many CEECs the dichotomy between a labour inspectorate responsible for labour protection and safety, and local hygiene units responsible for occupational health, continues into the twenty-first century. While the labour inspectorates are, with certain exceptions, accountable to the Ministry of Labour, the hygiene units form part of the network of regional and local hygiene stations responsible for public health, child health and immunization, and are accountable to the Ministry of Health.

This arrangement throughout the Soviet system was grounded on the perceived need to deal with people's health "holistically", taking account of the interaction between occupational and community exposure. Unfortunately, although substantial medical and scientific resources were devoted to periodic examinations, measurements of contaminants in the workplace and the classification of workplaces into hazard groups, little or nothing was done to modify the processes themselves, to improve control of the working environment, or to reduce exposure, let alone to stop unhealthy or dangerous processes.

One of the most pressing structural reforms is the integration of health and hygiene inspection with safety (and general conditions of work) inspection in all but a few countries, such as the three Baltic States and Bulgaria, where they have already taken the step. While in most CEECs the state sanitation and epidemiology inspectorates are staffed with doctors, hygienists and scientists who carry out laboratory analyses, they are not inspectors, and they do not generally achieve improvements in working environment conditions. As a rule, inspectors do not make good doctors, and doctors do not make good inspectors. They are different professions requiring different knowledge and skills.

Some major deficiencies result from this divided responsibility and the confusion it creates. Most importantly, it is not logical for inspection authorities to preach to employers on the importance of treating health, safety, labour protection, quality and efficiency as a single integrated management activity, when in advocating this approach they are themselves illogically divided.

The overriding argument in favour of change is that the systems in the CEECs over the past 40 years have failed to protect workers' health, and it would be irresponsible for any government not to consider the need for a different approach. Perhaps the guiding principle is that everyone should do what he or she does best. Doctors should examine people, hygienists should measure substances, scientists should analyse results, and inspectors should inspect and enforce. In most industrialized market economy systems, inspectors call upon and use the knowledge of doctors, hygienists and scientists, and that support is essential, indeed vital, to their credibility (provisions to this effect, again, are contained in Convention No. 81, Article 9). It is for the inspectors to judge, give preventive advice, enforce the recommendations and, if they are resisted, justify their actions with evidence provided by doctors, hygienists and scientists, before a court or labour tribunal if necessary.

Integrated inspection does not of course mean that every country will follow the same pattern. The systems in almost all industrialized market economy countries differ in some way, as already noted. Some will choose to recruit doctors, hygienists and scientists into the state labour inspectorate. Others will place a statutory or contractual obligation to provide the services of doctors and hygienists, as well as analytical support to the labour inspectorate on demand from the staff of hygiene stations and public health authorities. Another approach is for the labour inspectorate to require the employer to commission (and pay for) the services of approved doctors and hygienists to undertake appropriate examinations, tests and measurements to enable the employer and the inspector to judge whether, and if so what, action is necessary.

What will not work is the conclusion of agreements to cooperate, which can be (and tend to be) ignored at grass-roots level. Then there are the inherent difficulties that the costs of coordination and cooperation pose between different government departments, which are either under one ministry, or worse, under separate ministries, as the considerable additional resources consumed by attempts at effective cooperation would, by necessity, have to be siphoned off the meagre resources available for inspectorates' field operations. The state labour inspectorate in CEECs should have a clear, comprehensive, statutory responsibility for securing the enforcement of legal provisions relating to working conditions and the protection of workers in accordance with the provisions of Article 3 of Convention No. 81. It should strive to become a fully integrated system, which does not mean that it may not commission the advice of specialists from other departments.

Two other situations have recently led to more integrated systems. First, because of the growing unemployment rate in many countries, the issue of controlling and reducing significantly illegal forms of employment has received growing political attention. This has led to labour ministries intensifying the pursuit for more effective and efficient approaches to this particularly exploitative form of abuse. Persons employed illegally are especially vulnerable, whether children or young people, illegal immigrants, women in precarious work situations, or nationals engaging in "black labour" or moonlighting, to name only the most prevalent forms of exploitation.

In many countries, fighting illegal employment is primarily, or at least also, the task of the public employment services, but this has often proved ineffective. The result, in a growing number of countries as diverse as Hungary and Kenya, is that inspection or control functions of the employment services have been merged with, or transferred to, the state labour inspection services, substantially strengthening the latter, particularly in the control of illegal employment.

The second area where recent changes towards systems integration have occurred is the relationship between labour inspection's occupational safety and health activities and related activities, notably in the domain of prevention, undertaken by the social security organizations responsible for occupational accident and disease insurance, or workers' compensation.

As noted in Part I, a number of countries have, mainly for historic reasons, established labour inspection services that deal with occupational safety and health (and often other functions) and parallel compensation systems running separate inspection services, sometimes as parastatals (France, Germany, Luxembourg), and sometimes organized under private law (Austria, Switzerland). These systems are financed from employers' contributions and usually have a prevention mandate, as it is generally less costly to prevent accidents and diseases than to compensate for the consequences.

In New Zealand and in the Australian states of New South Wales and Victoria, the occupational safety and health inspectorate and the workers' compensation authority (social insurance body) have recently merged into a single organization. The labour inspectors remain civil servants, but their salaries and emoluments are now paid from the employers' contributions to social insurance, as are the inspectorate's operating costs. Labour inspection now has full access to the comprehensive occupational accident and sickness data banks of the social security system, a fact considered to be essential for the implementation of an effective, comprehensive prevention strategy in the context of an integrated inspection system.

16.4 The case of federal states

Article 4, para. 2 of Convention No. 81 makes provisions to accommodate the notion of a "central authority" responsible for labour inspection in federally constituted ILO member States. The central authority can be at the level of federal government, or of each federated unit. States with a federate structure have developed a considerable variety of solutions to this issue, and the underlying problems of coherence and consistency in implementing a national (federal) enforcement policy countrywide. In practice, three obvious "models" have emerged: a central authority at federal level; separate "central" authorities at the level of each federated unit; and a combination of these two. In a number of countries, the situation is made even more complicated by the existence of parallel or dual inspection services, which may be organized differently from the general (state) labour inspection systems. A number of States may have sectoral (e.g. agriculture) or functional (e.g. industrial relations) responsibilities, or may only inspect federal enterprises or the application of certain (federal) laws.

Brazil, Nigeria, the Russian Federation and Venezuela are among the countries with a central authority at federal level. Germany is a typical country without a central authority at federal level, but with one in each state of the federation.

Among the countries in the third group, with both federal and state central authorities, there are two subgroups. The first consists of countries with a central authority at federal level, and central authorities in some of the federated units as, for instance, in the United States. In that country, the federal agency, the Occupational Safety and Health Administration (OSHA), is directly responsible for safety and health inspection in 27 of the 50 states and six of the eight territories. In the other states and territories, OSHA has approved state programmes which comply with a framework developed by the federal authority under which the states then set up and run their own state inspection service (e.g. California OSHA, New York OSHA). However, the United States is also a typical case of a dual system, since it operates a separate, federal labour inspection system, the Employment Standards Administration (ESA) – in fact, the older and the larger of the two inspection services – which essentially enforces and administers laws governing wages and working conditions as one central authority for the whole country.

India also appears to be in this first subgroup, with an occupational safety and health inspectorate operated by the central government for the whole country, and labour inspectorates operated by the state governments under their own respective ministries responsible for labour and social affairs in each territory.

The second subgroup is made up of countries with a federal labour inspectorate for enterprises under federal jurisdiction and for federal employees, and certain "strategic" sectors, and/or specific (federal) laws under exclusive federal execution; and central authorities at federate unit level for enterprises and employees that do not come under federal jurisdiction. This is the case in Argentina, Australia, Canada (for occupational safety and health inspection) and Mexico and Switzerland (for all functional responsibilities). The case of Switzerland is complicated by the fact that a third inspection service, with its own agents, is operated by the social insurance system, SUVA (a similar dual system exists in Germany, organized along industrial sector lines, and whose agents have inspector-like status, powers and duties). SUVA is competent in the field of prevention of occupational diseases in enterprises. Its inspectors supervise compliance with legal provisions relating to occupational safety in enterprises with particular hazards (chemical industry, construction, etc.). The state (cantonal) inspectorates are responsible for occupational safety in all other enterprises, as well as for all general provisions concerning workers' health protection (e.g. length of working time and rest periods).

Finally, there are some countries which, according to their constitution, are not federally constituted states but where labour inspection organization does have certain "federal" features. In Spain, for instance, there is a central labour inspection authority under the national Ministry of Labour. However, the 17 autonomous communities in the country have labour inspection responsibilities accorded to their regional labour ministries. In practice, coordination and cooperation between these different bodies can be difficult to achieve on an institutional basis, and the application of a uniform, equitable national enforcement policy, as described in Part II, Chapter 11, seen as a crucial element for success by managers of high-performing inspection systems, can be problematic.

Notes

[1] The operative paragraphs of Conventions Nos. 81 and 129 are reproduced in Annex I.

[2] The duty holder may be the owner of the premises, or the supplier of the equipment, or the designer or client of the project, rather than the employer of the workers exposed to the risk.

THE ORGANIZATIONAL FRAMEWORK 17

17.1 Cooperation within component services

There is usually no special problem with vertical relations within the same branch of an inspection service. Nevertheless, the central authority must keep in mind that it has to coordinate and promote action. The tendency for central departments to settle down into a comfortable routine must be resisted. On the contrary, the inspectorate's top management must utilize its broad view of matters referred to it to continue to pass down guidance and instructions. Officers required to take executive action must not be allowed to feel forgotten or neglected, and senior officials must always be ready to deal with their requests for advice, explanations, documents, and support against improper external interference or, in cases of conflict, to address the concerns of employers, trade unions and other public bodies. In order to remain fully in touch with developments on the ground, senior management should actively seek and welcome feedback, be it proposals for new initiatives or criticism of existing procedures.

While there may be a tendency for a central authority to cut itself off from its operational external units in the field, the reverse occasionally occurs. In other words, the central authority may interfere unduly and unnecessarily, and this is again incompatible with efficient labour inspection systems management. Field units must be left a certain, if defined, freedom of action and it should be mainly through their periodical reports that senior officials oversee their activities. An inspector in charge of a local or regional office must be given full responsibility for its organization and activities with an eye to local requirements and conditions, and within the framework of the national enforcement policy and annual operating plan described in Part II.

Within branches, there may be horizontal contact in the course of day-to-day work, for example, when an inspector responsible for a regional office feels that it might be useful to discuss a common problem with a fellow official from a neighbouring area. These contacts should be encouraged, and it is common practice in many countries for senior officials to meet regularly for joint discussions and an exchange of views on working procedures, difficulties encountered and action to be taken. This is a management instrument that proactive, high-performing inspection systems use routinely. In contrast, in low-performing systems, the heads of the regional/provincial offices often do not meet with their headquarters managers in a formal fashion, nor do they receive visits from headquarters. In consequence, an important management instrument and a forum to air issues, sort out problems and generally advance the organization is ignored.

Top managers should, at the beginning of the year, programme a series of visits to various field units. They will invariably learn something significant of which they were unaware. But if these visits are not scheduled, they will seem less important than immediate day-to-day concerns and will not be made.

Cooperation between separate inspection services should be organized and institutionalized at the highest level, particularly for the joint consideration of problems, which are bound to concern each of those services, irrespective of their responsibilities. At lower levels, contacts between services may be organized on an informal basis, although collaboration between inspection services is again best ensured when institutionalized. For example, in certain countries where the inspection of safety in mines is the responsibility of a special technical service, the officials responsible for inspections are obliged by law to inform the labour inspectors of the results of their visits. In other countries, the legislation requires that the Ministry of Labour and Social Security collaborate in the exercise of its activities with other ministries, for example, the Ministry of Health or the national social insurance system.

An unusual but productive means of promoting cooperation is for the inspectorate to organize a two-day technical symposium on a subject such as noise or programmable electronic systems, and to invite papers from different parts of the organization. The resulting discussions between policy makers and scientists, inspectors responsible for factories, agriculture, nuclear installation or mines, and between engineers, doctors and researchers, not only promote better mutual understanding and appreciation but can also create new policy initiatives.

17.2 Cooperation with other bodies

Article 5 (a) of Labour Inspection Convention, 1947 (No. 81), and Article 12 (1) of Labour Inspection (Agriculture) Convention, 1969 (No. 129), state that arrangements must be made to promote cooperation between inspection services and other government services and public or private institutions engaged in similar activities.[1]

Cooperation must first be established among the various branches of the service that deal with different kinds of inspection or different sectors of employment. Experience indicates that this cooperation is frequently absent. While there is an increasing tendency for international exchanges to take place concerning the problems and experience of national services, there is often hardly any contact between one branch of a labour inspection system and another in some countries, despite the fact that almost all governments recognize the importance of collaboration between inspection services and other authorities.

This lack of contact may be due to the absence of any central coordinating authority. Therefore, when departmental responsibilities correspond to economic sectors, labour inspectors responsible for industry and commerce may have hardly any contact with colleagues responsible for agriculture, who may be attached to the Ministry of Agriculture, or Mines (often attached to the Ministry of Industry, Energy or similar). The isolation of special branches of the inspection system is inexcusable when they are all part of the same government department or ministry; in these circumstances, there seems to be no obvious reason for a lack of central coordination. Even if the isolation does not lead to rivalry about fields of influence or competence, it is bound to be harmful to the standing of the labour inspection system as a whole.

Other divisions within a department/Ministry of Labour

All divisions of a labour department have certain common interests and a common field of action. This fact favours close cooperation and effective mutual assistance. Cooperation may take place at various levels and assume a variety of forms. Within the central authority, the units dealing with technical matters, legal questions and documents should be consulted by other divisions of the department. Exchange of information among divisions is very useful; for example, the labour inspection service is certainly able to put to good account the results of surveys undertaken by the manpower division. The labour inspectorate, in turn, can make an appreciable contribution to these surveys. Besides this, all divisions will be able to save resources by pooling facilities such as typing and document reproduction, equipment and transport.

Cooperation must be effective at the local level. Even when there is no provision for formal contacts between labour inspection and public employment services, informal contact should nevertheless be continuous. Thus, the office looking after foreign workers and migrant labour will maintain frequent contact with the labour inspectors, whose task is often to ensure that these workers have been recruited in accordance with the law, and to enquire into the conditions of employment offered.

Where there is a special service for industrial relations, it must cooperate with the labour inspectorate and exchange information on subjects such as industrial relations, policies followed by enterprises visited by labour inspectors, or perhaps the deeper causes or circumstances of industrial disputes. In the same way, there must be close cooperation between labour inspection and other technical divisions of a department of labour, for example, vocational training or the rehabilitation of people with disabilities.

Social security bodies

Because the labour inspection service and the social security authorities complement each other's efforts in certain important respects, the relations between them are of special relevance. Accordingly, at headquarters, the labour inspection management and the authorities responsible for social security policy decisions and implementation, in particular in the area of occupational accident and disease insurance and prevention, should be able to hold regular exchanges of views. Thus, when in any particular sector of the economy a programme is being devised for the prevention of occupational accidents and diseases, the technically responsible authorities cannot afford to do without the knowledge accumulated through the labour inspection system on subjects such as conditions of employment and workers' attitudes.

In some countries (Spain and certain Latin American countries), the labour inspection service exercises a certain amount of supervision over social security funds. Relationships between offices at various levels outside the national headquarters largely take the form of an exchange of information and a certain amount of mutual assistance. Where relations are good, a social security inspector will inform the labour inspector of facts brought to light by an enquiry that are likely to prove of assistance at some later stage. Conversely, the labour inspectors may have occasion to appeal for help to the specialized inspection branches of the social security administration, who may be better equipped to refer to accounts.

Under Article 14 of Convention No. 81 and Article 19 of Convention No. 129, industrial accidents and cases of occupational disease must be notified to the labour inspectorate. Sometimes the employer is required to inform the inspectorate directly, but often this information reaches the inspectorate through social security institutions, particularly where compensation for industrial injuries is paid from social security funds.

Social security funds are chiefly engaged in making payments to beneficiaries. They generally possess figures unavailable to the labour inspectorate and access to computer programmes, which enables a systematic use to be made of assembled data. Arrangements for cooperation between labour inspection and social security authorities should, if possible, provide for common interests to be taken into account in the processing of data drawn from declarations of occupational hazards. On that basis, it should be possible to plan joint action, especially in the following fields:

- selective checks on safety and health conditions;
- studies of major occupational hazards, their incidence and trends;
- the identification through claims of new occupational hazards not yet covered by existing regulations, with a view to prevention;
- the provision of advice and information to employers and workers and their organizations; and
- sharing in the activities of safety and health committees.

Article 19 of Convention No. 129 also provides for cooperation of another kind, specifying that "as far as possible, inspectors shall be associated with any enquiry on the spot into the causes of the most serious occupational accidents or occupational diseases". This cooperation is eminently desirable, and should occur whenever the accident calls for action by both labour inspection and social security authorities.

Planning agencies

It is important that the central labour inspection authorities remain in close touch with the bodies responsible for drawing up the national plan or regional plans. In some countries, effective relations already exist and these may range from consultation in its simplest form (a question about wages, for instance), all the way to a situation in which the labour inspection authorities are brought into the work done by planning committees and subcommittees (e.g. dealing with workforce planning and vocational training). Central labour inspection authorities should take the initiative in demanding that they be given a say in these matters in countries where they do not participate in the national planning process, a point which has been repeatedly stressed at international meetings and conferences on labour administration.

Employers' and workers' organizations

Under Article 5 of Convention No. 81, "the competent authority shall make appropriate arrangements to promote collaboration between officials of the labour inspectorate and employers and workers of their organizations". In addition, para. 6 of Labour Inspection Recommendation, 1947 (No. 81), advocates that collaboration between officials of the labour inspectorate and organizations of employers and workers should be facilitated by the organization of conferences or joint committees, or similar bodies, enabling a dialogue to be established among the various parties. In one country, a biennial conference of labour inspection bureaux is held, to which employers' and workers' representatives are invited.

In some countries, employers and workers or their representatives habitually and independently consult the labour inspection service about their problems. However, it is chiefly within joint or tripartite committees that the labour inspectors have contact with employers and workers. These committees may be set up spontaneously, or in accordance with some procedure laid down by law, or they may be advisory bodies set up nationally, regionally, sectorally or locally, for example, advisory labour councils, collective agreements supervisory boards, and national safety and health advisory councils. Where the government provides the secretariat for these bodies, the aim should be to organize regular meetings with meaningful agendas, and to ensure that decisions made are brought into effect. Poor administration will result in loss of interest by the employers' and workers' representatives, and ineffectual committees will become mere talking shops – if indeed they meet at all.

Labour inspectors collaborate with trade unions in workers' education activities, giving courses and lectures or taking part in seminars and occupational safety campaigns.

Other public or private bodies

In the course of duty, labour inspectors work with other organs and institutions in accordance with national procedure; the organization of justice and the courts; and the police, when an inquiry is being made into an occupational accident, or perhaps when the inspectors have to call upon them (to exercise their right of entry, for instance).

The labour inspector is constantly in touch with the municipal or district authorities responsible for public health and town planning. In systems that do not require a permit from the labour inspection service to open new industrial establishments, an agreement may be reached whereby the office responsible for supervising building submits applications for industrial-premises planning permission to the labour inspection service. Sometimes, this practice is recognized by law. The labour inspector can also have an important role in advising planning authorities on whether to permit residential or other developments in the vicinity of high-hazard factories. Conversely, advice may also be given on whether to permit additional facilities at, or extensions to, such factories already established in the vicinity of residential or commercial properties.

The labour inspector also maintains close relations with officially recognized bodies that are called upon to undertake the inspection of plant in cases when inspection is, by nature, highly technical, or when the labour inspection staff does not have the requisite technical experts. These bodies (specializing in the inspection of boilers, lifting appliances, electrical equipment and so on, or in the prevention of fires) usually have to be officially recognized by the Ministry of Labour, and this recognition is given only after the labour inspection authorities have been consulted. The inspectorate can call on these bodies for assistance, and may be entitled to comment on their activities. This right is sometimes extensive and in one country the labour inspection service is represented on the separate supervisory committees for each of the technical subjects regarding which "recognized bodies" carry out the inspection. These recognized bodies are obliged to report their activities and financial management to the committees. The committees are entitled to propose that recognition be withdrawn, or continued.

17.3 Specialization of inspectors

The various functions within an inspection service may be performed by all officials at a particular level, or only by those called upon to perform them, under a system referred to as either technical or horizontal specialization. There is also vertical specialization, since duties allocated to particular officials vary according to their rank.

In a number of countries, specialization is according to the subject of inspection. There may be:

- inspectors to ensure compliance with safety and health regulations;
- inspectors appointed specifically to ensure compliance with conditions of employment established by law or recognized collective agreements;
- wages inspectors;
- inspectors to enforce laws on the employment of women or children; or
- medical inspectors called upon to ensure that health and sanitary regulations are duly complied with.

In addition to medical inspectors, some inspectorates employ occupational nurses, hygienists, chemists, microbiologists, radiation specialists, and mechanical, electrical and chemical engineers. While they may have the same powers as labour inspectors, they generally act as technical advisers to the latter, as well as reviewing developments in their specialization, and drafting guidelines. However, sometimes inspectors dealing with all aspects of labour conditions are confined to certain economic sectors, in which case they are often attached to other government departments.

Some countries carry specialization to such lengths, both by aspect of employment and by economic sector, that one enterprise may be inspected by a number of different inspectors from separate inspection units, for example, units specializing in explosives, safety, health, the application of laws and regulations or the effect given to arbitration awards. At the other end of the spectrum, more and more countries have a single (integrated) inspection service (as discussed earlier) responsible for inspection throughout the economy; within it, inspectors are empowered to handle any of the problems under the service's mandate.

In some Latin American countries, but also in Austria, France and Germany, specialized inspectors deal with agriculture. The construction industry, the metallurgical and textile industries, and the transport sector, like agriculture, may, from the technical or employment point of view, be so different from other industries as to justify assigning inspection duties in these sectors to specialized inspectors. This arrangement allows for a greater familiarity with the problems of the particular sector, and hence more coherent and competent action, but it also has its drawbacks in that, having been recruited from the sector in question, these inspectors tend to have an insufficiently critical and questioning attitude to long-established practices. In the United Kingdom, the largest inspectorate (field operations) is responsible for factories, and for the construction, agriculture, education and health sectors. The chemical and hazardous installations division is responsible for the chemical industry, explosives and pipelines, and the HSE also includes the nuclear, offshore, railways and mines inspectorates. While these exist as separate units, they report to a single deputy director and benefit from common policies, procedures, support services, and the exchange of experience and information.

A further example of specialization by technical field, special duties can, under ILO Convention No. 81, be assigned to women inspectors. In this respect practice differs in many member States. In most countries, women inspectors perform exactly the same duties as their male colleagues. Elsewhere, their work is different. In Austria, women inspectors have special responsibilities in the field of general conditions of work, living conditions, and inspection of enterprises where women and minors are in the majority. In some Latin American countries, female social workers or welfare inspectors perform similar duties, although they do not always enjoy the same status or have the same authority as male labour inspectors.

The other form of specialization equates an official's functions to rank, officials being given special responsibilities commensurate with their position, both for the operations of the service and for representing it in relations with external departments or other public and private bodies. This level of specialization can also be justified by the diversity of the tasks entrusted to the inspection service; not all of them call for the same degree of experience or skill.

The management of the inspectorate is responsible for the overall operation of the inspection system: it is expected to ensure that the methods used and the interpretation of statutory provisions are uniform and reflect a unity of purpose. It must decide what programmes or problems are to have priority, and how they are to be carried out, and assess the results obtained. By analysing regular reports and by personal contact on the spot, it must keep track of the activities of officials stationed outside headquarters, and must support them with its authority whenever required.

Officials at management level usually deal with external relations, and will be called upon to share in the activities of advisory bodies at the highest level, deal with senior officials of other government departments (concerned with planning, the labour force, social security, health and so on). They often provide the government with draft laws and regulations, and with budget proposals to improve working conditions in the service or to make them more efficient.

In many countries, the management of the inspection service is the authority to which any appeal against a labour inspector's decision will have to be submitted. It is responsible for giving binding rulings in relation to an employer, or authorizing prosecution when subordinates are not empowered to do so. In matters of a technical nature, it can call on the assistance of specialists in areas such as safety and health, wages, the labour force or industrial relations.

Immediately below the directorate come the heads of the regional or provincial offices, with similar responsibilities for matters in their jurisdiction. These officers serve as a link between a regional or provincial branch and the central authority, to which they report any matter requiring a central ruling. They supervise subordinates and try to supplement reports with personal contact. In fact, they learn more about employment conditions in their area by visiting an enterprise than from the perusal of numerous reports. (The Deputy Director-General of the United Kingdom's HSE, for instance, accompanies one of his inspectors on an inspection visit once a month.) Regional directors give rulings on points referred to the authority (other than matters which require a ruling from central office), such as problems arising with particular employers, or disputes involving enterprises operating in different branches of industry within their area. In some cases they may be required to supervise or inspect other administrative units in the area of their responsibility.

Local branch offices are usually directly in charge of an inspector, who may have the assistance of one or more subordinates, although in extreme cases, a local office may consist of a sole inspector. When they have subordinates, the inspectors will supervise their activities, advise and support them, occasionally accompanying them on visits to enterprises in connection with special problems, or to check their inspection techniques. Inspectors examine inspection and investigation reports, particularly those designed to lead to legal proceedings, and should deal with more difficult issues and attend, in person, meetings held by the safety and health committees of the larger enterprises. Inspectors should investigate serious occupational accidents personally, preferably in conjunction with specialist staff, where they are available, and they should seek advice from the central or regional offices on matters creating a legal precedent or on points they cannot deal with alone. The inspector must submit the local office's periodical progress reports, which should include matters of interest contained in the reports of assistants. These line management functions already call for a certain degree of (additional) specialization. That is why more and more inspectorates provide not only technical and administrative training for their inspectors, but increasingly and repeatedly expose them to different forms of management training.

17.4 Workers' cooperation in inspection functions

As noted earlier, at the beginning of the twenty-first century in a number of former centrally planned Central and Eastern European countries (e.g. Czech Republic, Hungary, Poland, Slovakia and many countries of the Commonwealth of Independent States – CIS), workers' organizations were still closely associated with the exercise of inspection functions. A growing number of other countries with transition economies, such as Albania, the Baltic States, Bulgaria and Hungary, have abolished this dual system. In countries that have retained the system, the state inspectorate works in parallel with a second labour inspectorate administered by the trade union, and the activities of the state inspectorate are supplemented at the level of the enterprise by the activities of social inspectors. These trade union inspectors still have, among other things, the right to inspect the manner in which enterprises fulfil their obligations regarding occupational safety and health, and to make regular inspections of workplaces and installations. They also have the power to verify whether enterprises have undertaken investigations of occupational accidents, to participate in investigations and to investigate themselves in appropriate cases. They can also call on enterprises, by means of instructions of a binding nature, to remedy shortcomings in the operation of machinery and equipment and, in the event of imminent danger, to order a stoppage of work. Such measures may, at the request of the enterprise, be subject to appeal to the State Labour Safety Inspectorate, but the order remains in force until a final decision has been taken.

However, in a market economy system, trade unions cannot act as an agent of the State with quasi-executive powers if they are to properly represent the interests of workers. It is illogical for the State to pay trade unions to employ inspectors in addition to state inspectors, of whom there are generally too few, or for them to act as the sole employer of labour inspectors, as is still the case in some CIS countries. What confidence can employers have in the objectivity and fairness of inspectors if they are employed by trade unions? Impartiality and independence are essential elements for any inspectorate considered to be fulfilling the conditions of ILO Convention No. 81. There is also the danger that as trade unionists concerned with the protection of jobs or the level of wages, they will not be sufficiently demanding in requiring the improvement of working conditions. This can occur to the extent that they condone bad conditions, thereby failing the workers they are meant to protect and undermining the demands of the state labour inspectors.

One of the most important roles of a trade union in a market economy is to instruct and advise its members on employment and labour protection. Trade unions in these countries employ specialists in labour law, industrial relations and safety and health, and they provide advice to local units, shop stewards, safety representatives or even to individual members. They are specialists paid by membership subscriptions to provide a service to their members, and are not acting as an enforcement arm of the State. The trade unions' role (either through its specialist advisers or locally elected officers) is to draw the attention of the State's labour inspectors to perceived contraventions of employment and protective law, to complaints and deficiencies, as well as putting pressure on the labour inspectorate to be more responsive, more active and more effective. Trade unions are, of course, able to make representations directly to employers and this may achieve a quicker result, while still keeping an appeal to the labour inspectorate in reserve.

Trade unions must be able to demonstrate success in defending their members' interests, and labour inspection can assist in this process by responding sympathetically and effectively to legitimate complaints and, by going from the particular to the general, amending inspection policies, procedures or priorities in order to prevent similar abuses or problems occurring elsewhere.

It is in this way (not by seeking to replace or even supplement the work of the State in labour inspection, but acting instead as the eyes and ears of the inspectorate at enterprise level, reinforcing and targeting the state inspection presence and stimulating it into effective action to protect the interests of workers) that trade unions can best use their knowledge, experience and influence, and demonstrate their value to their members. Workers will not pay to become or remain members purely out of sentiment. They have to be attracted and convinced that the cost of membership is worth it in terms of service and support. This applies, in particular, to the area of labour protection, and the important role of trade unions and their representatives in making labour inspection work effectively.

Note

[1] The operative paragraphs of Conventions Nos. 81 and 129 are reproduced in Annex I.

REPORTING POLICIES AND PROCEDURES

18

18.1 Standardization

The importance of adopting standard forms and procedures, and of selecting common criteria to ensure comparability of information and statistics, cannot be overemphasized.[1] When uniformity is not established as a matter of policy, a great deal of valuable information material of undoubted practical utility cannot be put to use in furthering the overall policy objectives of an inspection service.

As a first step, the management of the labour inspection system should ensure that ordinary and special inspection reports, occupational injuries and diseases notification forms, statistical tables relating to injuries, official reports submitted to the legal authorities on contraventions, records of conciliation proceedings, and so on, conform to a standard format throughout the service. These forms may cover only the bare essentials or may go into great detail, depending on the degree of industrialization and development of a given country, on the administrative and financial resources that are available and on a host of other factors. An essential requirement of all forms and procedures is that they be designed in such a way as to make it easy to extract and collate the information they contain, particularly if the data are to be subsequently processed with electronic data processing (EDP) equipment.

Whenever necessary, other bodies should be called in to advise on the design of reporting forms. Statistical offices, medical experts and social security institutions can be profitably consulted on the forms used, for instance to notify employment injuries, and on the presentation of the tables concerning them. Industrial tribunals or others responsible for dealing with disputes may wish to draw on recorded information on contraventions, accident investigations, litigation or disputes included in the relevant records. The main point is that every national report should contain all the data required under the terms of Article 20 of the Labour Inspection Convention, 1947 (No. 81), and that these data should be presented in a uniform and comparable way.

However, similarity of material presentation does not in itself guarantee comparability: the criteria used when collecting data must also be identical. For instance, it is very difficult (however desirable it would be) to make international comparisons of occupational accident data, because in some countries the figures include all accidents reported, whereas in others they include only accidents that result in the inability to work for one, three or four days. Moreover, certain activities may be classified in different economic sectors subject to different definitions, and accidents to and from work may or may not be included as occupational.

This shows how important it is to use international standard classifications whenever they exist. With the spread of EDP it becomes more and more necessary to adopt standard classification systems to facilitate coding. The advantages of doing so include:

- easier collection and utilization of statistics at national level;
- increased confidence in the statistical information furnished by the labour inspection services to other departments (for example, to development planners);
- improved comparability of data from countries which form part of major geographical regions (e.g. Latin America, English-speaking Africa);
- the possibility of using data of worldwide comparability to help inspection system managers in other countries, or international organizations and institutions, in deciding on their research or technical cooperation priorities.

It is therefore recommended that the economic and social data contained in annual reports of inspection services should be compiled and presented on the lines laid down in two sets of international classifications:

- the International Standard Industrial Classification of All Economic Activities issued by the Statistical Office of the United Nations Department of Economic and Social Affairs; and
- the classifications of occupational accidents according to type of accident and according to agency, which were approved by the ILO's Governing Body at its 273rd Session in November 1998.

Finally, not only do the criteria and the presentation of data vary from one country to another, but also the period covered by the reports. In some cases there are even variations between regions or provinces within the same country, particularly in federal States. The value of the reports, especially as a source of information on the activities of the inspection system, as proof of its effectiveness and impact, and an aid to planning (within the service and in other bodies) is inevitably diminished by these variations. It is therefore essential that the inspection management should issue clear instructions fixing an identical period to be covered by periodical reports from decentralized or field units. In the absence of such arrangements, it is extremely difficult to use the information and data in the reports for countrywide (let alone international) comparisons.

Obviously, the need to standardize reporting periods also applies on the international level in terms of the obligations contained in the Labour Inspection Convention, 1947 (No. 81), and Labour Inspection (Agriculture) Convention, 1969 (No. 129), to submit annual reports to the International Labour Office. The use of national reports by the ILO is hampered by the fact that the financial year used as a reference period for the collection of data can vary considerably from one country to another. While in most countries the period chosen runs from 1 January to 31 December, others use 1 April to 31 March or 1 July to 30 June, and sometimes reports cover two years (contrary to the provisions of Conventions Nos. 81 and 129). This problem can only be solved by making sure that all annual reports refer to a standard base period, preferably the calendar year from January to December. This is already current practice in a large number of countries.

18.2 Individual inspection reports

The importance of adopting a standard inspection report form to be used by the entire inspection service in a given country has been mentioned; only if this is done will it be possible to aggregate and interpret the data on a national (and subsequently international) basis.

Although the presentation of reports varies widely from one country to another, certain traits can be distinguished. A report form of three or four pages appears to be common. It is easier to fill in and read the forms if the sheets are divided into numbered sections, each designed to show specific information. The following information is usually included on the forms:

- designation and main features of the establishment: name of employer, trade name, nature and description of the business (industry, commerce, agriculture); name of the enterprise to which the establishment belongs; number of workers broken down by sex and by occupational category, with a separate indication of the number of young people employed;
- conditions of work: hours of work, wages and other allowances paid; weekly rest periods and holidays; safety and health conditions (sometimes according to a separate form or checklist); classification of the enterprise in terms of occupational hazards; medical services;

- labour relations and welfare: the state of labour relations; whether there is a collective agreement; trade union or staff representation (shop stewards, etc.); frequency of strikes; composition of negotiating committees, safety and health committees or welfare committees;
- occupational safety and health: very often this is evaluated according to special procedures, often using detailed checklists, sometimes tailor-made for specific branches of industry;
- details of inspection: nature of the inspection (routine, targeted, partial, or in answer to a complaint); contraventions noted: laws or regulations contravened and nature of the contravention; action taken (advice, warning, formal notice, instructions to take immediate remedial measures, prohibition notice, report to legal authorities, including any recommendation for prosecution);
- names of principal managers and workers' representatives seen;
- name of the specialist(s) of the (external) occupational safety and health services; and
- date of the next (follow-up) visit.

The report should also include the date of the visit, and the name and signature of the inspector.

A report on the first visit to an enterprise should contain all the information listed above. On subsequent visits, the report might refer to information in the previous report that is still valid and include only entries relating to the current visit, or to any new situation that may have arisen since the previous one. However, for statistical purposes, the number of workers listed, according to occupational category, should be stated every time a report is made. In the design of labour inspection reporting forms, the use of tick boxes for precoded responses will guide inspectors on the level of detail required and will facilitate processing and tabulation.

A different type of form should be used for a special inspection visit. This form should give the following information only:

- name and address of the enterprise;
- the reason for the inspection, for example, special inquiry, follow-up inspection after formal notice has been served, or investigation of a complaint;
- the inspector's findings;
- an account of the way in which previous orders have been executed and of any action to be taken in connection with the current report.

Reports investigating occupational accidents should be more detailed and should include information on:

- the causes (direct or indirect) of the accident and its consequences;
- the state of occupational safety and health management, and the application (or not) of prescribed safety and health measures in the enterprise;
- any recommendations made by the inspector;
- the findings of the investigation; and
- action taken (official report, prosecution).

To facilitate subsequent use of statistical material, the same international classifications should be used for these forms and the forms used to notify accidents.

There is, however, a tendency for inspectors to become so interested in the causes and so anxious to demonstrate that they have carried out a comprehensive investigation that they write unnecessarily long and detailed reports which are simply filed, once action has been taken. Full reports will of course be required if legal action is contemplated or if the accident reveals a new hazard, or technical or medical problem. One highly computerized inspectorate requires normal accident reports to be drafted in 85 words. The entire database of accidents investigated in the past few years can then be subjected to a free text search.

Inspection reports provide the basis for the compilation of statistical data and the submission of information. However, the way the information and data are collated should make it possible to ascertain whether the provisions of the law are being applied:

- in a given branch of industry;
- in the geographical jurisdiction covered by a particular inspection office; or
- to produce information on conditions in a given branch of activity, for instance the incidence of accidents involving a particular type of machine, or explosions or poisonings associated with particular processes.

At intermediate (region, province) and national levels, inspection reports enable an assessment to be made of the work of subordinate units and, where necessary, instructions to be issued to them. However, any documents containing the inspector's personal appraisal of an enterprise and any notes or reports on conditions that would allow easy identification of the enterprise locally or regionally should be treated as confidential. Inspectors are bound to treat information acquired by them in the course of duty as confidential under Article 15(b) of Convention No. 81, and Article 20(b) of Convention No. 129, the provisions of which are frequently reflected in national laws and regulations. In other countries, not subject to the aforementioned articles, their position as public servants should suffice to restrain inspectors from divulging the contents of inspection reports or similar documents, other than statistical information, which should be presented in such a way that individual enterprises cannot be identified.

18.3 Annual reports

Article 19 of Convention No. 81 and Article 25 of Convention No. 129 require that local labour inspectors or inspection services submit reports on their work to the central authority at intervals and along the lines laid down by that authority, which may also indicate any special subjects to be covered.

The wording of these Articles allows ILO member States considerable latitude in the choice of the form and contents of these reports and the intervals at which they are submitted. Frequency varies widely from country to country, ranging from one week to one year, but in most cases reports are submitted monthly or quarterly. Depending on the mandate of the inspectorate, they may cover the following points:

- work carried out during the period covered by the report: number of inspections; journeys away from the office; establishments visited more than once; other activities such as participation in the negotiation of collective agreements, conciliation or dispute settlement; conferences or meetings attended, and training courses and seminars held;
- any important events which have taken place in the territory: strikes and threats of strikes with an indication of their gravity (duration, number of workers affected), their causes, their consequences for the workers (terminations, claims satisfied) and their economic consequences (number of working days lost, probable effect on the enterprise or enterprises concerned and any repercussions in the region);
- any particularly significant occupational accidents, with the inspector's own findings and conclusions;
- relevant data on all activities in regard to occupational safety and health, in particular regarding prevention of accidents and diseases;
- the outcome of any legal proceedings or appeals against enforcement orders;
- the results of any inquiries ordered by a higher authority and of any priority projects scheduled for the period covered by the report;
- the results of participation in national action programmes or campaigns;
- significant new risks or technological problems identified;
- particularly positive managerial or preventive initiatives taken by individual enterprises.

Monthly and quarterly reports that normally include statistical information also provide the basic information needed by headquarters for the annual report on the work of the inspectorate.

The preparation of periodic reports can, however, absorb excessive time on the part of inspectors that would be better spent on the ground in enterprises. Some inspectorates therefore only require local or regional reports once a year. Interim reports may be submitted monthly, tabulating the number of enterprises visited and the number of workers each employs, follow-up action taken and a summary of activities undertaken during the reporting period.

The obligation to prepare an annual report of the inspection service and to communicate it to the ILO is expressly stated in Article 20 of Convention No. 81 and Article 26 of Convention No. 129. The intention is to enable an assessment of the effect that the ratification and the application of Conventions have had on the efficiency of national inspection services and to obtain as clear a picture as possible of the work done by these services in ILO member States with ratified Conventions. But just as much importance is attached to the effect these reports have in the countries concerned. The obligation to publish the annual report and make it available to the public, especially to employers and workers, is part of the labour inspectorate's information responsibilities.

While the advisability of matching the form of the annual report to the needs of the country is acknowledged, the main purpose is to provide a comprehensive picture of the performance, indeed the usefulness of the inspection service. Therefore, the uniformity of essential content and its presentation is just as important here as for the other reports already mentioned. The international labour Conventions include provisions on the content of annual reports, and the advantages of receiving government reports in a homogeneous and comparable form are evident. The Conventions do, however, impose certain obligations regarding the period to be covered and the information to be included in the annual report. The minimum information to be supplied under the terms of Articles 21 and 27 of Conventions Nos. 81 and 129 respectively is listed below in the order in which those items appear in the Conventions.

Laws and regulations relevant to the work of the inspection service

It is not necessary for all reports to include a complete list of the laws and regulations enforced by the labour inspection service. For international obligations, it is enough for the first report, transmitted to the ILO following acceptance of the Convention, to contain a complete list of all these provisions, and for subsequent reports to mention only the changes that have occurred since the previous report, such as any new provisions adopted or any provisions annulled. It might, however, be advisable for official reports to contain or to review all the provisions from time to time – say every five or ten years.

It should be noted that the Articles of the Conventions which define the duties of the labour inspectorate refer to securing the enforcement of "legal provisions", which also includes arbitration awards and collective agreements. In the case of the annual report, only "laws and regulations" are mentioned. This reflects a reluctance to burden governments unduly by requiring them to supply numerous texts of limited scope. However, in countries where conditions of work are in a large measure determined by collective agreements – some of which cover hundreds of thousands of workers – it is necessary to name at least the most important agreements so as to avoid giving a false impression of the powers of the labour inspectorate.

Staff of the labour inspection service

This item should take into account the provisions of the international instruments. These stipulate that "the number of labour inspectors shall be sufficient to secure the effective discharge of the duties of the inspectorate" (duties which may differ considerably in volume and nature from one country to another). There is no need to supply a list of all members of staff; however, a table should be included giving the number of inspectors employed, both in the central office and in the local branches, classified according to grade and, whenever possible, by duties when these are shared out among specialist inspectors.

This raises an interesting question: What standard could be considered "an adequate number of staff" (in the sense of Article 10 of Convention No. 81)?

The ILO itself has not set such a standard. However, the European Agency for Safety and Health at Work presented some preliminary research (at a meeting in Warsaw celebrating the tenth Anniversary of the Polish Labour Inspectorate) showing that in about one-third of its member States, the ratio is approximately 1 inspector for every 7,500 workers; in another third it is approximately 1 to 10,000; and in the rest it is between 1 to 12,500 and 1 to 15,000.[2] Much as any such attempt to set a standard is fraught with (political, technical, methodological) difficulties, it does provide a thought-provoking benchmark. Based on these figures, similar threshold "standards" could be advocated for industrializing and transition economies, for instance, 1 inspector per 20,000 workers; and for developing countries, not less than 1 inspector per 40,000 workers (in both the formal and informal, urban and rural sectors). Again, this could merely be a benchmark. However, for a country such as Viet Nam (with a total active working population of some 34 million people), it would imply a minimum of approximately 1,000 labour inspectors (as distinct from the present number of 350); for a country like Kenya (with some 12 million workers), it would imply at least 300 labour inspectors (as distinct from the present 150); and in a country such as Hungary, that has an active working population of perhaps 4.5 million, the 220 labour inspectors presently in office could, in fact, constitute an acceptable minimum.

Statistics

Several categories of statistics are required of the labour inspectorate:

- enterprises subject to inspection and the number of workers employed in them;
- inspection visits;
- prohibition and enforcement notices issued;
- legal proceedings taken, and penalties imposed;
- occupational accidents and their causes;
- occupational diseases and their causes; and, possibly,
- the number and type of breaches of labour law (or the number and type of enterprises where such laws are breached).

From the reports received by the ILO, it would seem that no special difficulties have so far arisen in compiling these figures. However, occupational disease statistics often do not appear at all in annual inspection reports, or appear incomplete.

There are various reasons for this. In some countries occupational health, and hence occupational disease statistics, is the responsibility of a separate (medical) inspectorate of labour (or of occupational hygiene), while occupational safety and occupational accidents are matters for the labour inspection service. Owing to inadequate coordination, the service responsible for drawing up the annual report (in the final analysis, the ministry responsible for labour inspection) often has no access to the statistics relating to occupational diseases. In some countries each service publishes a separate report.

When questioned on the absence of statistics of occupational diseases, governments sometimes reply that no cases have been notified during the period under review. This is not surprising in developing countries, where detection and diagnosis of occupational diseases are often not yet carried out systematically. This should be clearly stated in the report. Another difficulty in the interpretation of occupational disease statistics is that the number and nature of diseases classified as being occupational in origin differ considerably from country to country. Variations occur according to the stage of development, the financial and medical resources available, the social security schemes in operation, and the types of industrial, agricultural and commercial activities carried out. It is also increasingly the case that the conditions concerning inspectorates such as asthma, upper limb disorders, dermatitis or stress are multifactorial and may or may not be due to occupational causes. In some countries, the law does not make provision for notifying the labour inspection service of cases of occupational diseases, whereas notification of employment accidents is usually compulsory. In these areas, it is not always easy for the labour inspectorate to obtain the information needed for the report. Inspection service managers should give thought to remedying this state of affairs.

One industrialized country used its 1995 labour force survey to ask a random sample of 40,000 individuals whether they had suffered from any illness, disability or other physical problem caused or made worse by their work in the past 12 months. Of the 7 per cent who answered "yes", 70 per cent agreed to a follow-up interview and to their doctor's records being consulted. A few cases were excluded because of uncertainty as to whether they were in fact related to occupation. If this scale of unacknowledged occupational disability, in a country which has been targeting good health at work as a major priority, is in any way typical of other countries, then labour inspection services indeed face a major challenge in the twenty-first century.

Presentation

All the abovementioned information may conveniently be presented in tabular form. The communication of statistics may be enough to satisfy the requirements of Conventions Nos. 81 and 129, but there can be no doubt that, even at an international level, a commentary summarizing the main trends and the most important events of the year, interpreting the figures, drawing conclusions from past experience and pointing the way to future developments would be an important and helpful addition to the tables.

At national level, too, it is much better if these basic facts are accompanied by additional information on the work of the inspectorate itself and by the results of inquiries into special problems and reports on the implementation of priority projects during the reporting period. The report might also include information and proposals relating to certain economic and social questions, such as:

- comments on the economic situation and its effect on conditions of employment (terminations and unemployment following the introduction of new methods of production or the decentralization of certain industries; manpower shortages in a given sector and so on);

- reports on any progress made in occupational safety and health and in the prevention of accidents, and an account of any assistance received from employers' and workers' organizations in these respects; any gaps in the corresponding regulations;
- the extent to which managers of enterprises are acknowledging the positive benefits of actively managing safety, health and industrial relations, and treating them as an essential element in total quality management (TQM);
- comments on the state of labour relations, with a note of any improvement or deterioration; this could include information on the activities of joint advisory bodies; the introduction of union representation in the enterprise; and any major strikes or lock-outs during the period, their causes and consequences.

The style of the report should be clear and concise. The economic and technical information contained in it should be detailed enough to interest the specialist, but at the same time the report should be intelligible to the general reader. It should avoid repeating year after year vague generalities on the subject of administration or on the need for social progress.

The report would be of only limited usefulness if it were merely to give an account of historical activities. The aim should be to provide information on which political authorities and managers can base their decisions and make use of past experience to stimulate reflection and action, thereby contributing to the development of future policy.

18.4 Reports to the ILO

The intention of international labour Conventions that the report should be public in character is quite clear from the provision under Article 20 of Convention No. 81 that "the central inspection authority shall publish an annual general report on the work of the inspection services under its control". However, the way in which the report is to be made public is not laid down in the Conventions, and practice differs from one country to another. Most governments publish a separate printed report which is obtainable, on payment or free of charge, from the government department concerned. In other countries, the report on labour inspection is contained in a single chapter of an overall report by the Ministry of Labour. Some countries publish their reports annually in an economic or social journal, or in a review of labour statistics. This method is not always satisfactory: the information given is often incomplete, and publication may be postponed from issue to issue or even dropped for several years. In certain countries, the report is published as a document for

Parliament and discussed in that form – usually an excellent way of highlighting the achievements (and deficencies) of the inspection system.

Particular problems arise in federal States. If the competence for labour inspection lies exclusively or in parallel with the federated units, each may produce its own annual report, often with considerable variations in time span, coverage, content and presentation. This makes comparison difficult, if not impossible, even at the national level. As a result, a comprehensive national report is often not established at all.

Finally, some countries (with more limited resources) publish their reports in the form of a duplicated document: and as long as enough copies are produced to reach a fairly wide public, this fulfils the country's obligations under the Conventions. But this is not the case when reports are issued in the form of internal departmental documents, since the purpose of the reports is to keep management, labour and the authorities informed of the inspection work carried out during the previous year.

The annual report must be transmitted to the ILO within three months of publication, and at the latest within 15 months after the end of the year to which it relates (Article 20, Convention No. 81 and Article 26, Convention No. 129). These deadlines should be strictly adhered to so that the ILO may be sure of obtaining information that is still of current interest.

Notes

[1] Further guidance is available in ILO/EASMAT: *Labour statistics based on administrative records: Guidelines for compilation and presentation* (Bangkok, 1997).

[2] European Agency for Safety and Health at Work: *Economic impact of occupational safety and health in the Member States of the European Union* (Bilbao, 1999).

EVALUATING IMPACT AND PERFORMANCE

19

19.1 Introduction

Every labour inspectorate will be familiar with the process of audit, at least as its object or recipient. Certainly there will be financial audits of various sorts, and almost certainly some overview of the inspectorate's personnel and appointments, policies and practices. Many governments have efficiency units which scrutinize the activities of departments in turn. Some cases will attract the attention of the ombudsperson or national equivalent, and from time to time a parliamentary committee of inquiry may focus its attention on some aspect of the labour inspectorate's performance.

This chapter deals with audits that the labour inspectorate initiates to evaluate its own impact and performance, systematically question the effectiveness of what it does in every department or activity, and review the efficiency with which it does it. It is all too easy for a labour inspectorate to become complacent, make appointments, set up systems, initiate policies, give instructions, issue reports, and respond to politicians and the public without being certain that what has been initiated or ordered is actually having the intended effect. An audit is designed to evaluate such procedures.

The chapter examines:

- which aspects of internal procedures merit examination;
- the various ways in which such evaluations may be undertaken;
- who might be involved; and
- how often the process should be repeated.

The purpose here is not to provide the "right" answers or to be prescriptive, but rather to suggest questions, areas, lines of inquiry and possible approaches to the audit process, which labour inspectorate managements may find useful to develop.

19.2 Evaluating the impact externally

A labour inspectorate exists fundamentally to improve working conditions, a phrase incorporating many different elements, but the emphasis here is on measuring the improvement in occupational safety and health, as being the one function common to all labour inspectorates.

While statistics of fatalities, accidents, ill health, incidence rates and absenteeism provide a rough indication of trends, they have serious limitations because of possible under-reporting, failure to identify occupational causes and the fact that they only measure failure, not success. For smaller enterprises, accidents are in any case a relatively rare event.

The obligations on management today to prepare policies, carry out risk assessments, develop action plans and undertake training not only give enterprises the means to audit their own performance, but also provide the labour inspectorate with a new tool to measure the performance of enterprises against fundamental legal requirements. The extent to which an enterprise has developed a comprehensive policy, undertaken risk assessments, prepared action plans, implemented those plans, undertaken internal audit inspections and reviewed its total performance gives a reasonable indication of its commitment and competence, and provides a baseline against which to assess progress at the next visit.

Does the labour inspectorate do this in respect of its own activities? Does it provide some indication of the labour inspectorate's impact? Are there ways of improving the impact?

Assessing compliance with specific requirements

From time to time, an inspectorate will want to know how satisfactory the level of protection against a particular hazard is, and how successfully it has publicized and advised on how to comply with new regulations. It will want to know how well it has succeeded in its campaigns or initiatives to eliminate or at least reduce accidents or ill health of a particular type or in a particular industry. Such programmes, or special or sampling visits are not simply evaluative, but have a practical purpose in bringing new pressure to bear on employers who have failed to act. This can in turn result in legal action which, if given publicity, puts pressure on enterprises not visited and raises public awareness of the inspectorate's impact. These inspection programmes may be necessary to establish the baseline for both prospective and retrospective cost–benefit analyses.

Problem areas

One of the perennial problems faced by labour inspectorates is that the more effective they are in reducing the incidence of accidents and ill health, the less obvious justification there is for maintaining or increasing their resources. Regrettably, it has sometimes taken high-profile disasters to galvanize political will.

One of the areas in which it is particularly difficult to demonstrate effectiveness publicly is in the control of major hazards. Part IV, Chapter 27 of this book makes it clear that the audit of a safety report requires considerable resources, yet the outcome generally involves intensive questioning and negotiation rather than visible legal action.

One labour inspectorate studied 23 formal reports on major incidents, 10 of which involved major fires in storage facilities. Common management failings included:

- the failure to carry out risk assessments when plant or process changed;
- lack of competence in many storage facilities;
- failure to maintain and control plant instrumentation;
- inappropriate design and location of occupied buildings nearby; and
- inadequate means of fighting fire.

The study indicated the areas in which the inspectorate could improve ts surveillance by focusing more directly on them when carrying out its inspections. It also led to the development of an investigation manual covering:

- the need for an inspection management structure appropriate to the level of the incident;
- guidance on the formation of multidisciplinary teams with the necessary expertise for the investigation;
- the inclusion of an independent element as a means of quality control; and
- a predetermined format for gathering information and reporting incidents.

The SMEs, including agriculture, are at the other extreme. Chapters 23 and 24 describe the particular challenges they present. The evaluation of the labour inspectorate's impact is equally problematic in view of this diffuse scenario.

One possible approach is to set objectives in relation to a specific policy or operational initiative, whether in terms of the number of enterprises reached, their awareness of specific hazards or other issues, or the extent to which this has resulted in action. These "measurements", even if they are sometimes subjective, can also be used as a baseline against which to gauge future progress and demonstrate effectiveness.

Assessing the relative effectiveness of various activities

An inspectorate's external activities may be divided into:

- the proactive: the inspection of enterprises as a total entity or some particular aspect of their activities;
- the reactive: the investigation of incidents, accidents, ill health and complaints, and the assessment of safety reports;
- the presentational: the use of the media, participation in conferences,
  seminars and briefing sessions, and the involvement of social and professional partners in the process; and
- the administrative: in terms of licensing, permitting and approving.

There are scant research data to guide an inspectorate's management on the
most effective way of making an impact. Managers generally have to control
reactive work that could otherwise overwhelm inspectors' time. Fatalities and
major incidents demand attention, because in serious high-profile cases the
public will expect some form of retribution. Where a serious contravention is
alleged, which may have provoked a relatively minor accident, it is usually too
resource intensive to investigate more than a small proportion of the violations
reported. After high-profile incidents, priority must be given to any indications
of a new hazard, or a higher risk from an established hazard, so that the investigation will modify current policies.

An audit might therefore review the accidents selected by a unit for investigation over a certain period and the value of the reports subsequently
produced. This in turn gives a valuable indication of the appropriateness of
current management guidance, and the field inspectors' understanding of those
guidelines, and provides evidence for possibly amending or retaining aspects
that can be politically sensitive in investigation.

19.3 Evaluating the performance internally

Making the best use of inspectors' time

While the previous section dealt with the effectiveness of the labour inspectorate
in terms of its impact on reality, this section is concerned with the efficiency with
which that impact is achieved, the relationship between input in terms of cost and
time and output in terms of productive activity, and the achievement of targets.
No labour inspectorate ever has enough resources to do everything it would like
to do, so it is vital that none of those resources, whether in terms of money, people
or effort, are wasted. It is therefore useful to pose a number of questions (it being
understood that these are only a sample of one of several possibilities). Some
countries, (for instance, Austria) have opted for a TQM approach, based on the
ISO 9000 Quality Management Series, but not detailed here.

The checklists given below are intended to help labour inspectorates evaluate their own performance.

Personnel management

- Are we now recruiting inspectors with the right knowledge and qualities for the demands of the future?
- When was our inspector training programme last reviewed and updated?
- Is our in-service training comprehensive in scope and adequate in terms of number trained?
- Have we access to appropriate specialist advice in technical and scientific disciplines?
- Are the staff deployed according to today's needs?

Administrative procedures

- Are instructions to inspectors easily accessible and are they all really necessary?
- Can we simplify or eliminate some forms, returns and procedures?
- Do we make full use of our office support staff? With briefing or training, could they relieve inspectors of some tasks?
- Are our travel arrangements both as efficient and as economical as possible?
- Is full and efficient use made of computers, e-mail and internet facilities?

Proactive inspection

- Does the basic programme focus on real priorities in terms of risk, poor performance, and particular sectors, for example?
- Do inspectors have the incentive/discretion to terminate an inspection once the main issues are identified, so that they visit, monitor and motivate as many enterprises as possible in their working day?
- Are special programmes of inspection or campaigns used to focus on particular risks and obtain publicity for particular initiatives?
- Are there effective arrangements for ensuring consistency in the interpretation and application of regulations and standards across the country?

Reactive inspection

- Is there clear guidance on the selection of accidents for investigation?
- Is too much time spent on excessively long and detailed reports which are not really used?

- Are inspectors alert to the causes of ill health, and do they have access to hygiene and medical advice?
- Are requests for advisory visits dealt with as economically as possible, for instance by telephone, guidance leaflets or e-mail at the initial stage?

Promotional activities

- Are requests to inspectors to address conferences, seminars and training sessions carefully evaluated – and accepted only if the inspectors' presence is justified?

Management style

- Is the checking or sampling of inspectors' work more detailed than necessary, but still sufficient to give confidence?
- Does top labour inspectorate management regularly visit field units to listen and learn, as well as to speak?
- Does top management consult staff on new proposals and welcome comments, suggestions and new initiatives?
- Is such positive feedback acknowledged?

19.4. Evaluation: How, by whom and when?

External evaluation: For and against

The choice essentially is between an external and an internal arrangement. Of course government audit and efficiency units may force their inquiries upon the labour inspectorate, in which case the best policy is to attempt to extract as much value as possible out of the process, given the input costs of inspector time. Generally, an external consultancy can be used to answer fundamental questions.

The main disadvantages are that external evaluation costs money, and involves detailed briefing and/or the attachment of an inspector to the team. The labour inspectorate is committed to the contract, although there is no guarantee that it will be successful or useful.

The advantages are that external evaluation has greater objectivity; takes no account of "received wisdom", untested assumptions and traditional approaches; and brings a new perspective, often applying experience gained analysing and solving similar problems in similar or even disparate organizations.

Internal evaluation: For and against

This is particularly useful for relatively limited evaluations that require particular inspector knowledge or are part of a pilot project for an external commission. The disadvantages are that it uses inspector resources; those selected to carry out evaluations may not be adequately trained for the job; and the results may not be statistically sound. The advantages are that it can be set up reasonably quickly; can be terminated if it does not appear to be making progress; and if well done can be immediately useful, as well as being a valuable piece of career experience for the individual or team concerned.

A cautionary note

Labour inspectorate management should be self-disciplined and not require endless special returns and inquiries, which are often deeply resented for wasting the time of inspectors in the field. Top management should, as far as possible, undertake its monitoring and evaluations by using and collating the data which field units collect routinely and find useful for local management purposes.

Alternatively, as described above ("Assessing compliance with specific requirements"), information gathering may be combined with special enforcement initiatives. When this is not possible, the inquiry should be fully justified and its purpose explained to field units.

How often?

This will depend on the subject. Progress in completing the annual programme is best reported on quarterly. More frequent reporting imposes an unnecessary burden, while less frequent reporting leaves too little time for corrective action if things are going wrong.

Most labour inspectorates have to produce an annual report, and this will inevitably include an appraisal of activities in the field. The more fully this can describe and justify the impact of special initiatives, the more useful it is likely to be to ministers, as well as ensuring that they have a favourable view of the labour inspectorate.

Reviews on the deployment of staff, the training syllabus and inspection policies should probably be undertaken at longer intervals, as these changes take more time to make an impact.

INFORMATION, PUBLICATION AND DOCUMENTATION SERVICES 20

20.1 General observations

The ILO's Labour Inspection Convention, 1947 (No. 81), Article 3, para. 1, makes it very clear that ensuring compliance with national legislation enforceable by labour inspectors is a principal function of labour inspection, as is giving advice and information to employers and workers on the best way of complying with legislation. Indeed, ongoing advice and consultation on the occasion of an inspection visit or other contacts with the "client system" are part and parcel of the daily work of inspectorates (although there are some notable exceptions, under certain circumstances, for instance the OSHA in the United States and the Netherlands Labour Inspectorate).

This chapter deals with the way information and advisory services can be organized as a strategic management instrument for any modern, prevention-oriented labour inspection system. Information, publication and documentation services (IPDS) play a central role in any labour protection policy or strategy aimed at prevention. There are a number of reasons for this, the main one being that lack of information on labour protection standards and how to comply with them in a satisfactory manner is a major contributor to poor working conditions.

IPDS is a strategic tool for labour inspection's central function, promoting its mission and its policies, and a supportive function in promoting its image and results to interested actors: other government agencies, the social partners and the general public. It has a particular role in labour inspection's impact in the SME sector, acting as a conduit informing employers, workers and their representatives about new legislative initiatives and safety and health developments within sectors of industry, and about how to integrate occupational safety and health management with the general business management of the small or medium-sized company.

While IPDS is reasonably developed in Australia, Canada, Japan, New Zealand, Western Europe and the United States, other countries including

Argentina, Chile, Tunisia, Ghana and Zimbabwe, and Eastern European countries are becoming more proficient in its use.

20.2 Different types of organization

The provision of IPDS in ILO member States can be generally divided into four categories:

- IPDS is not organized as a major function, but generally plays either a very subordinate role or is practically non-existent within the state labour inspection system; in such cases, another body may be responsible for IPDS;
- IPDS responsibility is distributed amongst several, sometimes many different government, parastatal and/or non-governmental bodies and organizations;
- IPDS responsibility is centralized and organized primarily within the Ministry of Labour for all functions of labour administration, including labour protection and labour inspection, but also employment policy and social security;
- IPDS is a primary responsibility of the labour inspectorate itself, independent of other labour administration functions.

These approaches are illustrated in the following sections.

20.3 IPDS outside labour inspection

In some countries with a very competent and effective labour inspectorate, IPDS may be provided by another body. In Austria, for instance, the General Accident Insurance Association has a legal mandate for prevention and produces information and publications on safety and health. However, the Central Labour Inspectorate has recently established its own public relations unit and is preparing occupational safety and health documents for enterprises.

In France, the bulk of practical material on occupational safety and health is produced by the National Institute for Safety at Work (*Institut national de recherche et de sécurité, INRS*) and by the social insurance system, the *Caisses régionales d'assurance maladie (CRAMs)*, of which some 20 or more are under the national authority. However, information for employees concerning the risks they run and the protective measures they should take is considered to be very important. Employers are expected to present an annual action plan to the enterprise safety and health committees, and the INRS sets aside 35 per cent of its budget for supplying information and education to employees and students at technical schools.

20.4 Many players, vague coordination

Denmark, Germany and Switzerland are examples of countries where the IPDS responsibility is distributed among quite a number of players. The labour inspectorates themselves have little or no influence over most of these activities, or do not make a contribution to them.

In Germany, the situation is exacerbated by the fact that the development of labour protection policy and law is essentially the responsibility of the Federal Ministry of Labour and Social Affairs, while administration, or executive implementation, is the sole responsibility of the federal states or *Länder*. Furthermore, the German labour protection system is characterized by separate individual and publications responsibilities. The coordination and coherence of IPDS are therefore a major problem.

In Denmark, even though the labour inspectorate, the Danish Working Environment Service (WES), has a major responsibility for IPDS, it is not the only player in the field. The Danish Working Environment Fund (WEF) is also a major producer of materials and documentation. The WEF undertakes to provide information, training and research in the field of the working environment. Other actors include the National Institute of Occupational Health and Sector Safety Councils. Despite the multitude of actors there is a relatively clear pattern of roles. The Danish system is of considerable interest to international observers, as much of the IPDS work is funded – at least to a large degree – from outside the government budget through the WEF.

In Argentina, insurance underwriters have a legal obligation to deliver publicity, training and technical assistance. They are aided by the Supervisory Agency on Occupational Hazards, which have similar responsibilities and have funds allocated for the purpose in primary legislation.

20.5 Competition with other functions

The Netherlands and Finland appear to represent typical examples of the third category of centralized responsibility.

In the Netherlands, a Central Department for Public Information is responsible for publishing information documents, studies, guidelines and periodicals. As the labour inspectorate has to compete for funds with other departments/functions, it often loses out to issues which generally have more political priority. However, budget provisions have been made for the core activities of the inspectorate:

• to support the enforcement task; and

- to strengthen the inspectorate's capacity to respond to complaints, and to requests for information and accident reports.

At present, the situation in Finland is similar to that in the Netherlands.

20.6 A strong role for IPDS

Among countries where IPDS for labour protection is a central function of the state labour inspectorate, Ireland, Norway and the United Kingdom merit particular attention.

Ireland categorizes its IPDS under the following:

- information and training;
- legislation and resources;
- specialized services; and
- operations.

While the overall policy highlights the importance of access to information and advice on labour protection matters, another core factor is seen as the need to generate the data which enable governments, employers and trade unions to become aware of the economic costs of accidents and ill health at work.

Norway, although its overall situation is in some ways comparable to that of Denmark, has in the main placed responsibility for IPDS with the Directorate of Labour Inspection's Department of Public Relations.

The Department's responsibilities are:

- media relations;
- data provision;
- central answering service;
- internal information;
- information material;
- publication of a magazine;
- an internet website;
- an information plan; and
- special campaigns.

This last category is best illustrated by reference to the United Kingdom's system. Responsibility for IPDS in occupational safety and health within the state labour protection system lies primarily with the Health and Safety Executive (HSE). Within the HSE, there is a Directorate of Information and Advisory Services (DIAS). It is interesting to note that the aims and objectives of DIAS are to help other directorates and divisions of HSE achieve their planned objectives "by adding value to their communications and information activities through a high-quality, professional and expert information and advisory service ensuring value for money and exercising control on behalf of the Executive".

More specifically, the aims of DIAS as a central instrument of the HSE leadership to promote its main strategy, "Good Health is Good Business", are:

- to have a primary role in fulfilling the requirements of the Health and Safety at Work Act 1974;
- to make the public aware that the Health and Safety Commission (HSC) and the HSE are the independent national authorities responsible for the safety and health of everyone at work, and to inform them how these responsibilities are being discharged; and
- through a sustained programme of publicity, information and publishing, to make all those concerned conscious of the importance of proper safety and health standards, to tell them what those standards are and what they should do to maintain them.

DIAS achieves this by organizing its work under the following groupings:

- the press office;
- the publications sector;
- the publicity sector;
- information services; and (as supporting unit)
- the financial and planning sector.

These sectors prepare a annual plan, which is presented for confirmation to HSE management.

Demands for the service are driven by HSE's business needs – internally by the organization's need to keep up to date, project its message and maintain a high profile with a coherent and cohesive corporate image.

The most important external audiences are:

- employers and trade associations, including small firms;
- employees (and trade unions);
- the media;
- professional institutions and organizations;
- safety professionals;
- safety representatives
- opinion formers;
- local authorities (and environmental health officers); and
- international partners.

Finally, HSE's statement on its publications provides an interesting example of a concise "corporate mission" on IPDS:

> We have a duty to ensure that risks to people's health and safety from work activities are properly controlled, and our publications have an important part to play in our overall strategy. Very often we know what must be done to comply with the law, but as a regulator, we have a duty to ensure that our knowledge is communicated to others clearly and simply so that they know what they need to do. We publish a great deal about guidance, and we should be certain it is: necessary; relevant; concise; informative and accurate. To be of optimum value we should ensure that our advice is expressed in terms that are relevant to the audience. We want people to read what we publish, understand what they need to do and be able to act on the advice that we give.[1]

Note

[1] HSE: *Enforcement policy statement* (Sudbury, Suffolk, 1995).

LABOUR INSPECTION AND OCCUPATIONAL SAFETY AND HEALTH MANAGEMENT SYSTEMS STANDARDS 21

21.1 Introduction

In the final decade of the twentieth century, more and more market economy countries began progressively to adopt a different style of occupational health and safety (OSH) intervention for medium-sized and large enterprises. In some countries this was stimulated by legal provisions which specifically required enterprises to prepare a written statement of their policy, organization and arrangements for achieving safe and healthy working conditions, and in some cases prepare annual plans of how this was to be achieved. An increasing number of countries amended their legislation to place a comprehensive obligation on employers to ensure the safety and health of their employees in all circumstances.

Up until then, most national legislation had a very large number of specific obligations (and many still do), either in the main legislation or in supporting regulations, decrees, ordinances and schedules. The emphasis was on achieving compliance with specific, often very narrow or limited requirements, rather than adopting a holistic, prevention-oriented approach to OSH. In many countries, if things went wrong or if there was a lack of compliance, it was the unfortunate supervisor, foreman or employee who was held responsible and often punished, and the charges always related to contraventions of very specific requirements.

With the spread of generalized and comprehensive obligations, exemplified by the ILO's Occupational Safety and Health Convention, 1981 (No. 155), and in the European Union (EU) by the provisions of the Safety and Health Framework Directive (89/391/EEC), this approach to OSH was no longer adequate or appropriate. This new approach to legislation made it unequivocally clear that top management was primarily responsible for achieving acceptable standards, and the only practical way of discharging such a comprehensive obligation successfully was by using a systematic approach.

In 1999, government representatives and the social partners of the EU Member States agreed on the European Guidelines on the Organization of

Occupational Safety and Health. In April 2001, a tripartite meeting of experts formally adopted the ILO *Guidelines on occupational safety and health management systems, ILO-OSH 2001*.[1]

21.2 The analogy with quality and environmental management

It was quickly realized that a systematic approach, similar to that required for quality management (and subsequently for environmental protection), was required. In the 1990s, a number of countries developed guidance to help management create a robust, logical, practical and self-correcting system for achieving and then maintaining acceptable standards of OSH and, indeed, for promoting continual improvement. In most cases these systems were advisory rather than mandatory, but compliance with them tended to help management in its dialogue with inspectors.

In a few countries, this system of self-regulation or internal control became mandatory, and towards the end of the twentieth century there was increasing pressure for OSH management systems to be aligned with quality and environmental management systems, and easily implemented in an integrated fashion. Some saw advantages in systems enabling voluntary certification by a third party, a development which would also lead to the option of accredited certification, whether voluntary or mandatory.

Quality management and quality assurance standards

Since their publication in 1994, the ISO 9000 series of standards on quality management and quality assurance have become increasingly important, not only to purchasers looking for reassurance that they will actually receive the product or service which they have ordered, but also to manufacturers, suppliers and contractors of services, anxious to demonstrate and promote their own efficiency and commitment to quality. Thus, as government regulators have increasingly promoted the view that achievement of high standards of OSH is simply another aspect of any successful and progressive company's commitment to efficiency and competence, there has been increasing interest in the integration of OSH management into quality management system approaches.

In essence, such standards require documented systems for quality policy, and the organization, planning and procedures to achieve a quality system: contract review; document and data control; verification of the end product; process control; inspection; and the testing and control of non-conforming products. In addition, the quality records themselves have to be maintained, internal quality audits carried out and arrangements made for appropriate training. Simply listing the major elements of a quality assurance (QA) system shows the relevance of a close relationship with OSH management.

Environmental management systems

Similarly, since its publication in 1996, ISO 14001 detailing appropriate environmental management systems has been seen as having a close parallel with occupational safety and health management systems (OSHMS). The ISO 14001 approach involves six elements:

- an initial status review of the organization's efficiency and effectiveness in terms of environmental (or OSH) management systems in the light of relevant legislation, existing guidance and best practices in the sector;
- a policy recognizing environmental (OSH) management as an integral part of business performance, and a prime responsibility of line management from top to bottom, thus ensuring understanding and implementation at all levels in the organization, with employee involvement and consultation, and a periodic review of the policy, a management system and a compliance audit;
- planning, both in terms of the enterprise's overall plans and objectives, and its operational plans, to implement arrangements for control of risks identified through risk assessment and the measures necessary to comply with legal and other requirements;
- implementation and operation, including making people aware of their responsibilities, and ensuring that adequate training has been given, and that there are effective communications, systematic documentation and authoritative operational control;
- corrective action, involving proactive measurement of performance, monitoring compliance through surveillance, and active measurement of performance that monitors accidents, ill health, incidents, etc. In addition, a periodic audit should critically appraise all the elements of the management system; and
- management review of the overall performance of the environmental (OSH) management system, the findings of audits and internal and external developments.

Environmental Management and Audit Scheme

The EU's Environmental Management and Audit Scheme (EMAS) regulations came into force in April 1995. They are related to ISO 14001, but contain stricter requirements concerning the use of best available technology and the external communication of the company's environmental performance. The central focus of the EMAS regulations is to:

- promote environmental management in industrial companies;
- foster the management of continuous (environmental) improvement;
- promote the implementation of cleaner technologies;
- foster external auditing and verification of the environmental management system; and
- promote greater communication by companies with the public.

All these considerations are directly applicable to occupational safety and health, and clearly have a close relationship with the revised EU major hazards directive of 1996[2] and with internal control legislation as practised in Scandinavian countries.

21.3 Recent developments

BS 8800

This standard, published in the United Kingdom in 1996, sought to improve the occupational safety and health performance of organizations by providing guidance on how the management of OSH may be integrated with the management of other aspects of business performance. It shares common management system principles with ISO 9000 ("Quality management") and ISO 14001 ("Environmental management"). It is also compatible with the United Kingdom's HSE guidelines, *Successful health and safety management*, as described in section 21.4.

While the publication contains guidance and recommendations, it does not provide specifications which can be used for third-party certification purposes.

A universal assessment instrument

In 1997 the University of Michigan developed a OSHMS assessment instrument, comprising five categories, 27 sections, 118 OSHMS principles and 486 measurement criteria. A central aspect of the analysis included an assessment of the presence or absence of 27 common OSHMS variables (in some 24 modules and approaches examined). In addition to four non-auditable standards or guidance documents, including the Australia/New Zealand standard AS/NZS 4804 and the British BS 8800, the analysis identified some six auditable OSHMS standards, including ISO 14001, even though this was not, strictly speaking, an OSHMS standard, but is used as a template by many organizations for OSHMS development.

Internal control and other management systems

In many ways, the internal control (IC) system is analogous to the ISO 14001 environmental management standard. Could IC not be equally well integrated into a management system such as the ISO 9000 series in terms of quality assurance (QA)? There is no clear-cut answer, since QA is not a prerequisite for IC or vice versa, although the QA concept has had a significant impact on the introduction and design of IC.

The most important reasons for integration are the similarities of the two concepts in that:

- IC and QA are built upon the same type of requirements, laws, regulations, standards, norms, requirements by the customers and requirements of the enterprise;
- the consequences of not complying are similar in that failure will, in the end, weaken the enterprise;
- IC and QA are built on the same basic principles – prevent, investigate and correct – and IC is therefore often referred to as the QA of OSH; and
- both IC and QA require similar closed audit loops.

The objections to integration are that:

- in many enterprises QA concentrates on contracts, products or services and the ISO 9000 series does not cover IC satisfactorily;
- those operating the QA system are not usually competent in safety and health, which are overseen by specialist personnel, and this might lead to confused responsibility and a decline in efficiency;
- QA is not accepted by the authorities as proof of compliance with IC requirements, principally because it does not take into account the psychosocial working environment, involve the obligatory participation of employees, or make provisions for using occupational health services;
- for enterprises not already operating a fully functioning and documented QA system, the introduction of an integrated system from the beginning would be very resource intensive.

Towards an optimal solution

Rather than integrating the systems, an optimal solution might be to utilize the knowledge, experience and monitoring techniques of quality oversight in applying IC. The crucial elements in IC and similar approaches must remain the process of risk assessment and the preparation and implementation of action plans to mitigate such risks.

As noted, at least two key variables are missing from the QA standard: employee participation and adequate occupational health/medical programmes and surveillance, which, it is felt, would need to be included in any international document.

In the above analysis of systems, most models were found to be strong in addressing traditional management issues such as hazard control, training, evaluation and risk assessment. However, there was a general weakness throughout the models in areas often considered central to management system approaches aimed at integrating preventive OSH strategies in company management: management commitment; resource allocation; continual improvement; OSHMS integration; and management review.

From this analysis it is apparent that there is still some way to go before there is international agreement on a comprehensive, integrated standard for OSH, quality and the environment.

Towards a comprehensive OSHMS standard?

In 1996, discussions took place between ISO, the ILO and other stakeholders such as industry and trade unions, leading to the overall conclusion that ISO should not start OSH management systems standardization. The main arguments against this were the widely varying regulatory and institutional frameworks of OSH in different countries and the fact that it was not a business-to-business relationship, or indeed a matter of international trade. ISO was considered less suitable to develop this standard than the ILO with its tripartite structure, in which those most directly concerned – employers and workers – had a strong say in standards development. In 1997, ISO decided to defer the issue.

In 1998, the ILO began work on the preparation of non-mandatory *Guidelines on occupational safety and health management systems*. These were to provide basic requirements for the development and implementation of national and enterprise policies and principles; address key elements of internationally existing OSHMS standards; correspond to the system approach of ISO management standards; and engage the process through the ILO's tripartite structure.

One of the fears of industry was that if ISO started developing yet another standard incompatible with existing management systems standards, this would lead to difficult implementation processes and additional third-party certification demands. It was not, however, a universal view and, in the meantime, in response to market demands for OSHMS certification, several certification organizations and standards bodies took the initiative to develop a harmonized "de facto standard" called "Occupational Health and Safety Management System Specification", Occupational Safety and Health Assessment Series (OSHAS) 18001. This was followed in early 2000 by the publication of OHSAS 18002, providing guidelines on the implementation of OHSAS 18001.[3]

Although the precise format of any final integrated OSHMS system is uncertain, the value of this approach is indisputable in that it:

- aligns OSH objectives with business objectives;
- integrates OSH programmes with, and into, business systems;
- establishes a logical framework upon which to base an OHS programme;
- establishes a universal set of more effectively communicated policies, procedures, programmes and goals;
- is applicable to and inclusive of cultural and country differences;
- includes continuous improvement within the concept; and
- provides an auditable baseline for performance worldwide.

21.4 Examples of OSHMS standards at work

Successful health and safety management (United Kingdom)

The publication *Successful health and safety management* by the United Kingdom's HSE (substantially revised in 1997) is aimed at directors and managers of enterprises, as well as safety and health professionals and workers' representatives. It describes the principles and management practices which provide the basis of effective OSH management, sets out the issues to be addressed, and can be used for developing improvement programmes, self-audit or self-assessment.

The principles are universal, but how far action is needed will depend on the size of the organization, the hazards presented by its activities, products or services, and the adequacy of existing arrangements. Some of the actions advocated go beyond what is strictly required by legislation (for example, there is no general legal requirement to audit), but it has been well received as providing guidance on good practice in OSH management in all types of enterprises.

The document suggests that there are five major elements of a successful system: policy, organizing, planning and implementing, measuring perform-ance, and reviewing performance, each element in turn being subject to systematic audit.

In the case of policy, the key messages are that effective OSH policies contribute to successful business performance by:

- supporting human resource development;
- minimizing financial losses arising from avoidable unplanned events;
- recognizing that accidents, ill health and incidents result from failings in management control and are not necessarily the fault of individual employees;
- recognizing that the development of an OSH prevention culture is necessary to achieve adequate control over risks;
- ensuring a systematic approach to the identification of risks and the allocation of resources to control them; and
- supporting quality initiatives aimed at continuous improvement.

Effective safety and health policies can have an impact on:

- corporate strategy and social responsibility in terms of the company's image or its environmental impact policy;
- financing, for example in loss-control and cost-reduction strategies, insurance, and investment decisions;
- human resources in terms of recruitment, training, development and structuring of the organization to promote a positive safety and health culture;
- marketing, product design and product liability to comply with safety and health standards and legal requirements;
- manufacturing and operating policy in respect of design selection, construction and maintenance of premises, plant, equipment and substances, procurement policies, including the selection of contractors; and
- the information management system.

The four "Cs" can be achieved in terms of the following structures and processes:

- establish and maintain management *Control* within the enterprise;
- promote *Cooperation* between individuals, safety representatives and groups so that safety and health becomes a collaborative effort;
- ensure the *Communication* of necessary information throughout the organization; and
- secure the *Competence* of employees.

Control needs to be exercised by line management, with specialists acting as advisers. Successful organizations actively encourage and support *cooperation* involving employees in setting performance standards, devising operating systems and procedures, and monitoring and auditing. Effective *communication* about safety and health involves information coming into the organization, flowing within it and emanating from it. *Competence* must be achieved through the systematic decisions on objectives and methods, identification of training needs, the effective delivery of this training and the evaluation of its effectiveness.

Planning is essential for the implementation of OSH policies so that a system will control risks, react to changing demands and sustain a positive prevention culture. A systematic approach is necessary to answer three key questions:

1. Where are we now?
2. Where do we want to be?
3. How do we get there?

The answers to these questions will indicate what needs to be done to implement and sustain effective risk-control systems.

Reviewing safety and health performance involves both "active systems" which monitor the achievement of plans and the extent of compliance with standards, as well as "reactive systems" which monitor accidents, ill health and incidents.

Finally, there is a need to audit the structured process of collecting independent information on the efficiency, effectiveness and reliability of each element in the total safety and health management system, and to draw up plans for corrective action.

Internal control

In 1992 Norway, and in 1993 Sweden, introduced systems of IC or self-regulation (sometimes also called "self-inspection" regimes). The Netherlands followed suit a few years later with its own "system control" concept, containing some variations on the Nordic countries' approach. In Norway, IC became mandatory, with regulations requiring the employer to identify goals, responsibilities and safety and health activities, carry out risk analyses, develop plans of action and monitor how the system worked. The enterprise has a clear operational responsibility for carrying out IC locally, while the state labour inspectorate not only checks that the system has been implemented but also motivates the enterprise when necessary. The regulatory agency therefore has both a policing and a teaching role in the process of system audit. Inspectors primarily examine the documentation prepared by the enterprise for its plan of action, organization and procedures for monitoring safety and health.

The system practised in Switzerland is similar to that of Norway. Swiss enterprises also have to implement a prevention concept that implies internal control. Inspectors likewise give priority to a "systems approach" (control of the smooth functioning of the labour protection system) rather than a traditional, detailed inspection. In this context, resorting to branch- or sector-specific solutions opens interesting possibilities in terms of synergies, rational utilization of resources and effectiveness. This approach would seem to be particularly suitable where a given sector is made up predominantly of SMEs.

The basic philosophy is that promoting a healthy working environment is primarily a question of management. Safety, health, welfare and productivity should all be integrated into the organization and management systems of the enterprise. If the working environment is an integral part of the life of the enterprise and, as such, an important part of the production line, it should also be a part of the QA system of the enterprise.

A system for assuring quality, and accordingly occupational safety and health, must:

- be based on and explicitly refer to values and goals defined in the culture, ethics and philosophy of the enterprise, laws and regulations, and pro-grammes and instructions;
- encompass reliable and accepted norms, standards, criteria and measuring methods;
- be built on the best available technology, methodology and equipment;
- be run by competent and motivated personnel; and
- be efficiently managed.

The Norwegian Working Environment Act 1990 makes it obligatory for the employer at each workplace to work systematically to improve the working environment of the enterprise and implement the concept of internal control. This requires the employer to:

- organize systematic measures to ensure that the requirements of the authorities are complied with; and
- document the measures established to provide a sound working environment.

In this way the Norwegian authorities gave priority to a "systems approach" rather than the traditional on-site detailed inspection. The effect of this change was to move from detailed inspections to a self-regulated working environment, with monitoring undertaken by the employer. This required systematic and continuous action at the enterprise level to undertake the activities described in administrative procedures. There was also particular emphasis on adequate documentation.

To ensure success, employers had to commit themselves to total engage-ment in promoting the IC system, and the process demanded a democratic dialogue with employees to promote involvement and participation. As a result, however, by 1999 a total of 64 per cent of enterprises with more than 100 employees had implemented the IC concept, while only 34 per cent of those employing 10 employees or less had done so. It was in a sense understandable that larger enterprises with more resources, better systems and more familiarity with QA systems were more able to adopt and better comprehend the advantages of introducing these systems, to the benefit not only of safety and health, but also productivity and efficiency.

The main barriers to the wider adoption of IC were that:

- it was perceived as a large and complex system where enterprises had difficulty identifying the rules and regulations to be complied with, and which created a lot of paperwork;
- the authorities, especially the inspectorate, did not introduce, explain and promote IC, nor did they really understand the realities under which the enterprises were working; and
- where neither management nor employees were committed and did not see any advantage in the system, there was no internal motivation.

In 1996, because of the difficulties smaller enterprises experienced in implementing the regulations, the Government simplified the requirements while retaining the concept of self-regulation and the responsibility of the employer to organize systematic work on safety and health.

The main changes were that:

- the regulations were simplified to make them more accessible to enterprises, and explicitly to state that the IC system should be adjusted to the size, activities, risk and type of the enterprise in question;
- more emphasis was put on the importance and value of IC as a useful and relevant tool for enterprises, and there was an explicit requirement that they carry out risk assessment; and
- the documentation was made less demanding, although it had to include the enterprise goals for safety and health, a description of the organizational set-up and allocation of responsibilities, the measures to be taken to safeguard the safety and health of employees based on risk assessment, the procedures for internal monitoring and the systematic surveillance of the IC system to ensure that it was functioning as expected.

In addition, measures were taken to strengthen the input of the inspectorate, insurance companies and the social partners. The result has been that over the past few years, the IC concept has become more widely accepted in the SME sector.

In many cases, the legal framework is still inadequate and needs to be adapted to atypical forms of work and the flexibilization of working hours. Switzerland, for example, has very recently introduced a new law covering not only the physical, but also the mental health of workers, and fixing employers' obligations with regard to ergonomics, work organization, and psychological and sexual harassment. This new legislation is considered a powerful tool for the preventive work of labour inspectors.

The Swedish experience

In 1992, the Internal Control of Work Environment Ordinance came into force in Sweden. Since then, the aims of the Government have been to:

- induce companies and administrations to achieve a substantial reduction in the number of work accidents and work-related diseases;
- induce companies and administrations to create and maintain an efficient IC system; and
- ensure that improvements occurring in the working environment are of an enduring nature.

Similar in many ways to the Norwegian system, experience in Sweden also led to a simplified approach to implementation of the ordnance in SMEs, the so-called "IC-small" project. However, acceptance and full implementation of the IC concept and integration of OSH into company management in the SME sector in Sweden still appears to be disappointingly low.

The experience of the Land of Hessen in Germany

The German *Land* of Hessen selects different forms of intervention for the degree of risk, for a particular defined objective, or in relation to cause. This is known as a "bottom-up" approach, (the Industrial Safety Checks in Works (ASCA) Programme conducts a cause-related form of audit), whereas a "top-down" (systems audit) approach is geared to the long-term improvement of working conditions. (The Bavaria State Labour Protection Office has developed a similar system, called OHRIS, Occupational Health/and Risk/ Management System.)

The ASCA programme works by tackling company management systems and checking long-term compliance. It helps companies build up internal management systems to prevent safety and health shortcomings, and looks for deficiencies, which are the underlying causes of infringements. The apparatus used includes:

- checklists for site inspections;
- questionnaires for managers and others responsible within the enterprise for safety and health; and
- various tools for assessing the internal organization.

By classifying various organizational aspects according to structure and operations, a detailed assessment of the internal safety systems and their origins can be made by cause analysis, allowing the organizational deficiencies which have triggered these shortcomings to be identified.

Because the ASCA apparatus is modular, it can be applied to businesses of any size, sector or structure. In some organizations it simply requires some refining of the existing safety management systems, while in others fundamental restructuring may be required.

A handbook has been published to help businesses with the implementation of safety management systems. The close link between the handbook and the ASCA apparatus means that the collection of information, analysis and the planned improvement of the internal safety organization can go hand in hand, significantly reducing the causes of accidents and ill health. It has been found to result in a qualitative and quantitative improvement in the work of the regulatory authority in Hessen, and monitoring can be carried out in a more systematic, effective and efficient manner. ASCA allows inspectors to advise companies so that they are able to create the most suitable OSH management system.

A systems control approach in the Netherlands

Government policy on working conditions must rely on employers taking an active approach and cooperating with their employees to introduce an OSH system into company management. In the Netherlands, every employer is obliged by law to comply with many technical safety and health standards, and to formulate and implement a safety and health policy. Employers are not responding just because there are obligations laid down in laws. Indeed, systematic integration of labour protection management in the employer's general management is stimulated tremendously (in the Dutch experience) when employers are convinced that it is in their own interest to do so. The Netherlands Labour Inspectorate has developed a list of "seven good reasons" for an active approach:

- safe and healthy workplaces to avert accidents, avoid damage to workers' health and prevent disability; and for ethical and financial reasons;
- better motivation of workers leading to better-quality work. The more employees can organize their own work, the better their motivation;
- good labour relations in the enterprise;
- a better image, not only for better relations with customers and clients, but also to obtain and keep good, qualified employees;
- attention to quality control of the working processes, and the adjustment of these processes and machines to those who operate them in order to prevent

accidents and lead to better, more efficient and more environment-friendly production, and thus to better products or services;

- avoiding damage and claims: accidents, catastrophes and incidents lead to damage of goods, damage to the environment, loss of production, loss of market share and damage to the company's reputation; and
- less sick leave, with a view to preventing the occurrence of production disturbances and thus saving expenses.

Over and above the "seven good reasons", Dutch employers appeared to require further incentives. In the Netherlands, the absenteeism rate used to be the highest in the Western world. To push employers to reduce sick leave as a financial necessity, the Dutch Government chose to place a higher financial burden on enterprises with higher sick-leave rates. From 1996, every employer in the Netherlands had to pay the wages of sick employees during the first 52 weeks. This has turned out to be a strong trigger for prevention. Another financial incentive was a fiscal one favouring employers who invest in worker-friendly machines and tools. (A similar subsidy scheme is operated in France by CRAM, the regional OSH insurance and inspection body.)

The Dutch approach emphasizes that good management, in the area of OSH and sick-leave prevention, is a matter of organizing and clarifying to all employees their employer's labour protection objectives, how they will be attained, and what financial and technical means are available for that purpose.

In formulating the objectives and making plans, the employer has to take into account three important points:

- to consult and to cooperate with the company's works council on such items as new investments, new premises, new materials or working methods, and plans based on risk assessment;
- to assign supervisory tasks to employees, particularly managers. The employer is also under a legal obligation to give these employees the powers and means necessary for the proper performance of these tasks;
- to enlist advice (usually external) from safety and health experts. In the Netherlands, there is a covering system of advisory consultants (*Arbodiensten*) to provide these services. In the past four years, over 100 *Arbodiensten* have been certified by the State Labour Inspectorate. The qualification process is not easy, as the quality and performance requirements of these advisory services are very high.

The Netherlands approach is a cyclic process consisting of four steps: gaining information, making plans, implementation and checking. There are five important items requiring systematic and constant attention:

- systematic regulation of the workplace;
- responsible behaviour on the part of workers;
- effective supervision;
- responsible purchase of materials; and
- responsible design of workplaces.

In this process, the Government's role consists of applying a well-balanced mix of instruments. This mix – beyond regulation – must be composed of:

- *Guidance:* a good advisory infrastructure, aimed at outlining the benefits of good working conditions, and at promoting and stimulating labour protection management systems.
- *Financial incentives:* fiscal incentives; financially supported covenants; penalties for high sick-leave levels.
- *Cooperation:* between the Government (labour inspectorate) and the social partners at national and branch level; and between employers and workers at company level.
- *Enforcement:* systematically checking the effects of the policy at the workplace, and focusing on unwilling employers and direct penalties to emphasize impact.
- *Monitoring:* this must be continuous and consistent, in order to follow and document the effects and consequences of this policy.

21.5 Implications of OSHMS for inspection

"Top down" or "bottom up"?

The introduction, by many countries, of either a mandatory requirement to adopt internal control, or highly persuasive guidance to the management of medium-sized and large enterprises to adopt OSHMS, has had a profound impact on the process of inspection. The traditional approach whereby inspectors aimed simply to identify legal irregularities and then give advice or impose sanctions, depending on the seriousness of the offence, is increasingly discredited. In some countries the labour inspectorate is formally prohibited from giving advice, and in many the obligation is on management to find its own solutions or pay for independent advice.

While small enterprises present a different case (see section 21.6), labour inspectorates do not have the resources, or often the detailed knowledge of the process, to act as unpaid safety advisers to the whole of industry and commerce.

The new approach to management enables, indeed obliges, labour inspectors to adopt a different approach, often called "systems audit". This means a comprehensive, systematic and structured evaluation of the enterprise's systems for the identification, assessment and control of risks. It involves examination of the enterprise's management organization, the competence of its staff and arrangements for planning, implementing and monitoring the effectiveness of risk-control systems.

Auditing can be very effective at a corporate level in looking at high-level management systems and can apply pressure at key points. It is, however, a resource-intensive technique and raises the question of whether it should be undertaken "top down" or "bottom up".

The "top-down" approach

The top-down approach is exemplified by the Swedish procedure whereby proactive enforcement is undertaken in pedagogical or instructive terms. Progress in the adoption of effective internal control is seen as a four-stage staircase starting at level 1, where no internal control has been established. Level 2 denotes that it has been accepted at a theoretical level, that risks have been charted, an action plan has been prepared and tasks have been allocated, but the routines have not yet been implemented. At level 3, they have been implemented, the policies are in place, risk assessment has been carried out, routines established, actions planned and the first audit completed. At level 4, it is evident that internal control is actually having a positive effect on the physical and psychosocial environment, reducing the number of work injuries and absences due to illness.

The process of "systems inspection" involves two inspectors meeting the management and safety delegates in a round-table inspection. Normally two to three months' advance notice is given, resulting in a considerable amount of activity immediately before the inspection. The purpose of the meeting is to stipulate the demands to ensure progress from the theoretical to the implementation stage.

As the process of internal control develops, the role of the inspector changes. Around level 3, the purpose is to verify whether the system functions or not. At this stage inspectors undertake individual interviews with management representatives and safety delegates. This type of inspection is announced in advance, normally a month before the event, and the interviews give inspectors a chance to compare the answers from the managing director with those from supervisors and safety delegates. They are thus easily able to discover whether the system is a reality or not.

Similarly in Norway, "system audit" primarily involves the inspector in the examination of documentation prepared by the enterprise describing its organization, plans of action and procedures for monitoring safety and health. Here the inspector is not only checking that the procedure is implemented but is also motivating the enterprise as to what action is needed. Effectively, the inspector acts both as police officer and teacher. It is a time-consuming approach and, because of the pressure on inspectorate resources, the result is more emphasis on risk-based inspections, prioritizing them according to the degree of occupational risk in the enterprises.

Any such process must be supported by physical examination of the plant, premises and equipment on the ground, by review of processes and other documentation, and by the questioning of managers, supervisors and workers, even if this is done only selectively or by sampling. The experienced labour inspector knows that what is said to exist, even what management honestly believes to exist, whether in terms of plant, procedures or understanding, is often very different from reality.

The "bottom-up" approach

The "bottom-up" technique is illustrated by the Swedish labour inspectorate's approach to the investigation of serious accidents, which can also be described as a four-level process. After the inspector has traced the course of the event (level 1), and through interviews and examination of the actual workplace has found the causes of the accident (level 2), he or she starts looking for the underlying causes (level 3). Underlying causes include not only conditions specific to the individual but more general working conditions, including methods, substances and tools. Level 4 represents deficiencies in management and directly related deficiencies in internal control at management level.

The "bottom-up" approach is equally valid for proactive inspection, and perhaps particularly for follow-up inspections. Using this approach, the labour inspector makes a relatively rapid examination on the ground, concentrating on departments, plant, processes, procedures and individuals which are particularly crucial to the maintenance of safety and health, or which were found to be lacking or defective on the previous visit. Any irregularities can then be discussed with top management as evidence that OSH is not being managed effectively. However, the emphasis is not on the immediate causes (for example, lack of protection or human-factor failure) but on identifying the underlying cause in terms of inadequate risk analysis, planning, corrective effort, training, supervision or monitoring.

A failure is seen not just as a contravention of the law, which it may be (and attract a penalty) but as a failure of the enterprise to follow its own system. In this scenario, what are the implications for its marketing, quality or financial systems? Management must take action.

Stimulating self-motivation

The traditional approach to inspection will never raise standards quickly, since management does the minimum to satisfy the labour inspector and then sighs with relief that he or she will not return for a few years.

The contemporary approach is to appeal to the commercial (or, in the case of state bodies, the political) self-interest of management and, by demonstrating the benefits in efficiency and effectiveness, make management self-motivating. Once convinced, an intelligent management will ensure that the OSHMS is self-sustaining and the labour inspector can adopt a variety of low resource cost methods to sustain awareness and audit by publicity, conferences, surveys and letters of enquiry. These systems may also be certifiable by a third party and, in the future, the certification body itself may become qualified for accreditation in these fields.

21.6 The relevance of OSHMS to small enterprises

Experience with mandatory internal control

The Norwegian experience suggests that there are practical difficulties in persuading small-enterprise employers to adopt internal control (IC). Usually the employer is personally responsible for every aspect of the enterprise and simply has no time or energy for any system, unless it is extremely simple. Even the most basic documentation may well result in the employer in practice taking sole responsibility for all the issues listed.

The Swedish labour inspectorate takes the view that in the case of small enterprises the best method of inspection is still the traditional approach. It has, however, sought to define what IC means for small enterprises by stipulating five minimum elements:

• access to the Internal Control of Work Environment Act 1992 and relevant ordinances;
• knowledge of actual risks and legislation;
• routines for continuous risk assessment;
• routines for the investigation of work injuries; and

• action plans for remedial measures.

In order to activate small enterprises prior to inspection, brochures are sometimes sent to them describing the purpose of IC and listing these minimum requirements. Information dissemination meetings are also held to reinforce the inspection process.

Experience where OSHMS is not mandatory

It is likely that many other labour inspectorates will agree that the traditional approach is appropriate to most small enterprises, but they will at the same time adopt a wide range of supplementary techniques for improving standards in such enterprises (see Part IV, Chapter 23).

21.7 Implications for the inspectorate's management

If the introduction of IC or OSHMS systems audit has direct consequences for the inspection process described in section 21.3, it also has fundamental implications for the management of the labour inspectorate in terms of recruitment, initial training, in-service reorientation, knowledge building, and the management of discretion and internal monitoring.

Implications for recruitment

If the role of the labour inspector is increasingly to require, persuade and convince management to adopt a comprehensive OHMS approach, then the ability to explain the key elements of what this involves, and to monitor management's understanding and implementation of these processes and procedures, will not necessarily call for inspectors to be engineers, chemists or lawyers.

All front-line inspectors will have to be able to speak convincingly to enterprise management about management systems and their relevance to OSH. Labour inspectors will still have to be able to inspect a wide range of small enterprises effectively and provide appropriate advice, but this is what they have always done and, of course, the inspectorate will still have to have access to engineers, chemists, lawyers and specialists of every sort.

The type of person the contemporary inspectorate will seek to recruit is one with the appropriate basic knowledge, but also with the ability to persuade and convince and, only as a very last resort, to compel.

The implications of training and orientation

The implications of training are self-evident. Few recruits will have studied business administration, but the principles are well established and a full understanding of them in the context of modern enterprise management – and not only safety and health – is an essential part of the inspector's knowledge base. The greater challenge for inspectorate management may well lie in the need to reorient the thinking of inspectors, particularly of those in mid-career, or who are reluctant to change their methods. They need to be convinced of the validity of the new approach and be empowered with the confidence in their ability to adopt it. This confidence can only come from additional in-service training and from positive experience of the effectiveness of the method.

A wider discretion

Finally, the inspectorate management may well have to redefine the limits of inspectors' discretion. It would be counterproductive to be rigidly prescriptive as to the method to be adopted. While there will be large and even some medium-sized companies with a good understanding of management systems, and who will readily appreciate the benefits of integrating their management of safety and health into those systems, there will be others, even quite large organizations, where the immediacy of the risk and the inadequacy of current management will call for a much more traditional approach in the first instance.

Conversely, while most small enterprises may well be dealt with in a traditional fashion, supplemented by other techniques, there will be some that are responsive to a management system approach and will be able to sustain a self-motivating and self-auditing system. At the end of the day, the inspector will only be able to tell by experience whether to continue to pursue a management line, or when to abandon persuasive efforts and revert to a "bottom-up" approach.

The management of the inspectorate must ensure that the staff has the discretion to operate as they judge best.

Notes

[1] ILO: *Guidelines on occupational safety and health management systems, ILO-OSH 2001* (Geneva, 2001).

[2] Council Directive 96/82/EC of 9 December 1996 on the control of major-accident hazards involving dangerous substances.

[3] OSHAS: *Occupational health and safety management systems. Guidelines for the implementation of OHSAS 18001* (Hitchin, Herts., 2000).

PART IV

LABOUR INSPECTION: SECTORAL ASPECTS

"However advanced it may be, a country's labour legislation is liable to remain a dead letter if there is no system of labour inspection to enforce it."

Report of the Director-General,
International Labour Conference, 71st Session, 1985

LABOUR INSPECTION AND CHILD LABOUR

22

22.1 The scope and nature of the problem

The scale of child labour

Some light work can be an essential part of a child's socialization and development process, and a means of transmitting acquired skills from parent to child. Children might be involved in craft workshops and small-scale services, assisting their parents in ancillary tasks, acquiring skills and gradually becoming fully fledged workers in family establishments or trades. Work of this kind is not risk free, in terms of children's health and safety and their schooling, but this is not what is generally meant by child labour.

The concern is for children who are denied a childhood and a future: children who work at too young an age, who work long hours for low wages, who work under conditions harmful to their health and to their physical and mental development, who are often separated from their families and who are frequently deprived of education. This kind of labour is invariably carried out to the detriment of the child and is in violation of international law and, usually, national legislation.

According to the ILO's latest estimates, about 250 million children between the ages of 5 and 14 are working full or part time in developing countries. Almost half, some 120 million, work full time, every day, all year round. Some 50-60 million are between 5 and 11 years old.

Available data suggest that more boys than girls are economically active, but girls who are denied educational opportunities because of their role in household tasks and care of siblings may not be accounted for in these statistics. Working in the early childhood years may have a more significant impact on girls, reinforcing gender discrimination and resulting in a denial of life chances. Moreover, girls are often engaged in work that exposes them to sexual and other forms of exploitation.

The nature of child labour

Many children work in extremely hazardous occupations and in dangerous industries such as construction, mining, quarrying and agriculture. In many parts of the world, a large number of children are trapped in virtual slavery. They are bought and sold across national borders, and the commercial sexual exploitation of children is on the rise. The employment of very young children and girls presents a particularly alarming problem. The younger the children, the more vulnerable they are to hazards at the workplace and to economic exploitation. ILO surveys show that up to 20 per cent of child workers are under the age of 10 in some areas. The situation of the girl child deserves particular attention for various reasons, particularly because of the nature of their work and the conditions under which they work. Much of their work is hidden from public view. For example, domestic service is a major sector of child employment. Girls working as child domestics are largely "invisible" workers, dispersed and mostly ignored. Isolated from their homes and sometimes virtually enslaved, they are frequently exposed to violence and sexual abuse. Many children work in the informal sector, or on the streets.

The worst forms of child labour

"The strengthening of labour inspection services can obviously be an important measure, and preventive labour inspection strategies offer considerable promise in the case of eliminating forced labour."

ILO: *Stopping forced labour, Global Report under the Follow-up to the ILO Declaration on Fundamental Principles and Rights at Work, 2001*

The above quotation very much applies to eliminating the worst forms of child labour, which comprise:

- all forms of slavery or practices similar to slavery, such as the sale and trafficking of children, debt bondage and serfdom and forced or compulsory labour, including forced or compulsory recruitment of children for use in armed conflict;
- the use, procurement or offering of a child for prostitution, production of pornography or pornographic performances;
- the use, procurement or offering of a child for illicit activities, in particular for the production and trafficking of drugs; and
- work which, by its nature or the circumstances in which it is carried out, is likely to harm the health, safety or morals of children.

Other potentially harmful work

Activities in this category comprise:

- work which exposes children to physical, psychological or sexual abuse;
- work underground, underwater, at dangerous heights or in confined spaces;
- work with dangerous machinery, equipment and tools, or which involves the manual handling or transport of heavy loads;
- work in an unhealthy environment which may, for example, expose children to hazardous substances, agents or processes, or to temperatures, noise levels or vibrations damaging to their health; and
- work under particularly difficult conditions, such as work for long hours or during the night, or work where the child is unreasonably confined to the premises of the employer.

Even where children do not suffer the worst forms of abuse cited above, or extremely dangerous conditions, many are allowed insufficient rest, or work in cramped conditions with inadequate seating or unsuitable tools, and without appropriate welfare facilities.

Finally, many millions of children traditionally work in agriculture as part of the family unit, but are exposed to risk because their home is a workplace which presents a wide variety of hazards.

22.2 Inhibitions to effective labour inspection of child labour

Lack of political will

Notwithstanding obligations under international standards, a major obstacle to labour inspection in many countries is the lack of political support. This is often expressed in state budget allocations. In many developing countries, the whole labour administration system receives less than 1 per cent of the national budget; sometimes it is a mere 0.1 per cent. Labour inspection services in turn receive only a fraction of that sum. This is in stark contrast to the fact that the cost to the State of poor labour protection in the form of accidents, illnesses, absenteeism, abusive exploitation, industrial conflict and the like is in excess of 5 per cent of total GDP in numerous countries. There is substantive evidence that an effective and efficient labour inspection system can significantly reduce these losses. For instance, strong political support for labour inspection and commitment to standards in many industrialized market economy countries in the last decade has made a measurable difference in the performance of their labour inspectorates and, therefore, in the reduction of socioeconomic losses at both macro and micro levels.

Although labour inspectors may be convinced of the usefulness of their work, they have no control over the political and social environment in which they operate. It is hard for them to single out child labour abuse in workplaces where other labour regulations are being ignored. Labour inspectors are often frustrated because, on the one hand, they are asked to enforce the rules while, on the other hand, the underlying message is not to disrupt the economy. Lack of political will and therefore political support for inspectors when they meet resistance and defiance inevitably undermine their morale and their confidence, as well as weakening their determination to achieve improvements.

Shortcomings in the law: The need for reform

Political will and commitment must not only translate into adequate resources; it must first and foremost provide an appropriate policy framework and legal base for labour inspection. Large volumes of outdated, fragmented and increasingly complex regulations effectively impede labour inspection services in the functional and rational execution of their duties. In some countries, the labour code alone contains several thousand articles, supplemented by even larger numbers of parallel or subsidiary regulations. This is true of child labour provisions, which are often found in several different laws and are sometimes inconsistent with each other. Inspectors may be required to master thousands of technical and legal standards in the area of safety and health alone, an impossible task that often results in inertia or stagnation.

Many countries have streamlined their regulatory framework, weeding out contradictory, often overlapping or outdated regulations and standards. Others have mandated all their regulatory agencies to make the legislation more easily understandable, more relevant and more "user-friendly". This has, in no small way, contributed not only to a better understanding by employers of what is required of them, and thus improved compliance with the law, but also to more effective supervision of compliance by labour inspectors.

For labour inspection to be effective, clarity in legislation and administrative regulations is very important. With inconsistencies and gaps in the law, varying minimum ages, a range of different age thresholds in different areas of child labour, and confusing definitions (if any) of hazardous and non-hazardous work, enforcement of the law becomes virtually impossible. The situation is not helped by standards that should govern labour inspection but are often scattered and complex.

Strengthening inspection of children's working conditions is only possible if a rational distinction is made between "hazardous" and "non-hazardous" work, on the basis of clear guidelines which ensure that a child's developmental needs are not prejudiced and that there is a real prospect of protection from abuse and exploitation. Using the guidelines on "hazardous work" in the Worst Forms of Child Labour Recommendation, 1999 (No. 190), instead of prevailing broad generalizations such as "dangerous to health", can certainly help to make the legislation more workable. Introducing a clear age limit conforming to the Minimum Age Convention, 1973 (No. 138), below which no child may work, can also help to rationalize child labour laws, and thus facilitate inspection and standard setting.

Some countries prohibit work during school hours, but do not have accompanying compulsory education regulations, or they have minimum ages for child labour and education that do not coincide. Others have compulsory education laws but still charge even low-income families school fees, or do not provide equitable access to schools. Consistency between law and policy is critical for effective child labour inspection, a requirement that some countries have not yet achieved.

The commitment to eliminating child labour must be clearly established in national laws and policy. This requires the political will to eradicate child labour and place it as a priority on the national agenda. States must establish comprehensive and clear bodies of legislation on child labour and labour inspection. The complexity and limitations of the law can be a serious barrier to effective law enforcement. The absence of a comprehensive and rational set of standards at the national level on both child labour and labour inspection makes the work of the labour inspectorate difficult, if not impossible.

Education, attitudes and economics

Even given the political will and unambiguous, comprehensive regulations and standards which clearly state that child labour will not be tolerated, strict enforcement alone is unlikely to be successful. In addition to the practical problems of inspection discussed in this chapter, it is self-evident that, where child labour has proliferated without sanctions over a long time, there is work to be done concerning the approach to education and attitudes. Employers and parents have to be educated and persuaded of the need for change.

The imposition of sanctions, while aiming at compliance by employers, might unintentionally drive the children into more dangerous or degrading forms of work, and into even more "invisible" workplaces. Inspectors are likely to be sympathetic to parents in extreme poverty who appear to have no alternative than to put their children to work. However, preventive measures are also likely to raise awareness throughout society of the desirability of eliminating child labour once and for all. In the context of child labour, it is necessary to develop, within the inspection services, a clear, considered, coherent and consistent policy establishing the balance needed between the two broad categories of labour inspectors' methods of intervention, "sanctioning" and "prevention".

22.3 The authority of labour inspectors

Defining the authority of labour inspectors

The authority of labour inspectors must be clearly defined. There must be an unambiguous definition of the role and functions of the labour inspectorate, as well as of its authority in relation to child labour. The legislation must establish the general principle that labour inspectors may enter and search premises, and specify sectors or areas where this power is limited. The mandate of the labour inspectorate must be established not only to guide its own action, but also for the sake of other government agencies, employers' and workers' organizations, and NGOs with a role to play in securing the rights of children, as well as the children and their families themselves, so that they all understand the role of the labour inspectorate and utilize it effectively.

With clear authority to enter and search workplaces, special provisions must regulate inspectors' access to places where child domestic workers are employed or where children work in private homes. They also have to be protected against acts of intimidation by third parties or senior officials. The obstruction of the work of inspectors must incur severe penalties or sanctions. If labour inspectors have a direct or indirect role in prosecution, they need to network with other agencies connected with law enforcement, such as the office of the state prosecutor or attorney-general, judges and the police. They will also require training on how to investigate complaints, conduct inquiries at the workplace or in their own office environment, initiate prosecutions and give evidence.

The qualities of labour inspectors

The labour inspectorate must have an efficient and trained body of permanent staff with the necessary status within the public service to perform their responsibilities. They need to know the law, the industrial and commercial environment, and the measures that have to be taken to protect workers in general and working children in particular. They must be able to maintain records, collect statistics, analyse data and write reports. The inspectorate must also have an infrastructure of support services for record keeping and maintaining the confidentiality of information. The impartiality and authority of labour inspectors has to be ensured through the system of recruitment, their conditions of employment and, most importantly, their expertise and conduct.

Given their protective and preventive responsibilities, labour inspectors must be able to interact with workers and employers and obtain their cooperation in upholding the law. In so far as they have a role to play in conflict resolution, they need to have conciliation skills and considerable sensitivity. They must be trained in communication skills, as their responsibilities require that, in addition to employers and workers, they collaborate with a range of government officials and technical personnel. Networking with medical doctors, engineers and other professionals concerned with safety and health and other labour protection issues at the workplace may also be necessary.

However, developing countries generally have a great shortage of human and material resources to carry out labour inspection functions. There may perhaps be genuine intentions to apply the law, but performance fails to measure up to these intentions. Posts exist, but qualified inspectors cannot be found and there are insufficient funds for training and purchasing equipment.

Training inspectors in child labour issues

In order to make labour inspection more effective in the fight against child labour, labour inspectors must be familiar with the problem and aware of the possible consequences for children. The appropriate training of inspectors is a critical dimension of effective enforcement. Positive country experiences and best practices, as well as international standards, must be applied to improve the quality of training so that the inspectorate can respond to its dual role of prevention and protection. The experiences of past inspection visits should be introduced as case studies in the training process. There is an urgent need to improve skills in collecting data, maintaining records, writing reports and conducting the various interventions in order to ensure effective monitoring. Practical exercises in this regard should be introduced into training. Inspectors need to be made aware of the intrinsic value of abolishing or regulating child labour as part of the broader dimension of guaranteeing children's rights. Knowledge of international standards and reporting procedures must therefore be integrated into the training of labour inspectors in order to help them fulfil their role in identifying the shortcomings of laws and policies.

Any significant role in combating child labour inevitably requires labour inspectors to be trained in a number of additional areas, starting with the phenomenon of child labour itself, its incidence and range, and the desirability of its abolition, as well as the relevant international standards and national regulations. In view of the sensitive nature of child labour, there is a need for training in the psychology of handling intimidated and bewildered children, whose only experience is of poverty, insecurity and often violence, and who have no knowledge of their rights or the functions of labour inspectors. Employing women labour inspectors when dealing with cases involving child labour can be helpful, as they are perhaps perceived as less daunting to the children involved. They are certainly more acceptable where only girls are employed or where religious and cultural attitudes require that women talk to girl workers and inspect their working conditions.

Labour inspectors engaged in combating child labour often have considerable sympathy for the child workers, their families and the impossible dilemmas they face. For many parents, especially lone mothers and parents in situations of extreme poverty and deprivation, there is simply no alternative to putting their children to work. Working children mean survival of the family unit and there is no perspective before them other than immediate physical survival. Training is the appropriate way for inspectors to acquire the necessary professional understanding in such emotionally demanding situations. A clear policy and effective methods need to be developed on this aspect of the work.

Resources for and the status of inspectors

The role of labour inspectors in combating child labour raises considerations of their status and working conditions. Inspectors' status needs to be enhanced and their working conditions improved, if labour inspection is to be carried out in the most effective and efficient way. Labour inspectors regularly find themselves under considerable undue pressure not to perform their tasks properly because of the threat they appear to represent to important economic interests, whether corporate or local. They therefore need recognition, respect and support at the political level and from the community, but this is difficult to achieve if their independence is threatened, their status low, and their salaries and working conditions inadequate. Unfortunately, this is often the case and, in such circumstances, results in low motivation and poor performance and, at worst, a serious risk of corruption, and further lowering of status. The problem of attracting new entrants to the inspectorate in some countries is a measure of these general problems. It is necessary to improve salaries and conditions in various ways, and possibly, but not necessarily, increase the number of inspectors, for labour inspection involves far more than simply visiting all workplaces – which would be impossible anyway.

22.4 Managing the inspection of child labour

A clear policy

A labour inspectorate must have a comprehensive national enforcement policy including clear policy instructions on labour inspection and child labour, which should, at least:

- emphasize prevention as the main aim and develop prevention-oriented methods of intervention;
- address the need to balance advisory and supervisory elements, unannounced inspections and the considered use of sanctions; and
- address the use of complementary inputs such as birth registration and school attendance records, information services, use of the media, voluntary compliance programmes and codes of practice, credible monitoring systems, and collaboration with other organizations and authorities.

The policy should in particular include methods aimed at informing, persuading, influencing or stimulating employers of children to comply with the law on a sustainable basis.

Clear strategies are necessary to:

- establish priorities in those situations which are most abusive or most hazardous to minors;
- define clear objectives for intervention, such as:
    - the elimination of the illegal employment of children;
    - the establishment of preventive measures to improve the working conditions of young people who are legally employed;
- extend intervention to all types of workplaces:
    - urban and rural;
    - registered and unregistered;
    - visible and invisible;
- adopt concrete measures, bearing in mind that the purpose of inspection is to ensure compliance with the law and not just to apply sanctions.

Planning and setting priorities

Provided there is both a clear policy and the political will for action, the central inspection authority can organize inspection programmes that either include child labour among other aspects to be investigated, or are dedicated specifically to combating child labour.

Sometimes inspection plans are based on campaigns, or special national or sectoral action programmes aimed at problems that are already serious, or expected to become serious – for example, problems related to a particular substance or process used in an industry or to particular categories of workers (including child workers), or problems which have been assessed as particularly serious throughout a given industry. Priority might be given to searching out and eliminating the worst forms of child labour prevalent in a given country.

Special inspections, investigations and follow-up visits

Besides ordinary or regular inspections, there may be special inspection visits, follow-up visits or team visits, each of which has its own set of prerequisites, methods and consequences. Inspection may deal with specific issues (safety and health), or it may address all aspects of workers' protection. An integrated approach is obviously more cost-effective, but it is also more demanding and requires a higher level of competency. Special visits may concern the investigation of accidents or complaints or the collection of data; they may also be ordered specifically to detect and deal with cases of illegal child labour. Often, inspections for the purpose of investigating illegal forms of employment are organized on a teamwork basis, involving agents from outside the inspectorate such as labour administrators, other government agents, representatives of labour market organizations, experts or monitors from NGOs, and possibly other bodies.

Efficient inspection also depends on the rigour with which follow-up visits are undertaken. These visits must be made if an employer has been ordered to take certain action within a specified period, after which he or she faces legal charges. Follow-up visits are also useful when a new regulation or policy has been introduced and the inspector wishes to ascertain whether the requisite action has been taken. In programming child labour inspection activities, it is important to give them due priority and a specific allocation of time or "inspector days", to prevent the work being squeezed out by other functions.

Complaints

Inspection visits to workplaces may be initiated by the inspection service itself or prompted by complaints from the public. Normally, complaints are made by those affected – the victims – or by their representatives. However, child workers or members of their family do not normally report instances of child labour (except perhaps in cases of forced labour), because their circumstances are such that they see no alternative and therefore have an interest in perpetuating it. They may not even know whether there are laws against it.

Members of the public, as individuals or as members of an organization, could play an important role in reporting child labour. In most countries where child labour is prevalent, specific abuses are rarely reported, but heightened public awareness and better training of inspectors can increase the number of complaints.

Coordination and cooperation with other authorities, and workers' and employers' organizations

Labour inspection alone cannot solve the problem of child labour, but it can certainly make a very valuable contribution. This means cooperation with the ministries of education, health, and social affairs whose mission it is to protect the safety and welfare of the public in general, and of children in particular. It means cooperation with local authorities, who can help locate the establishments employing child labour and facilitate access for the labour inspectors.

It is essential to establish good working relations with employers and workers' organizations and others, such as the community, who can assist labour inspectors in carrying out their duties. The importance of cooperation and coordination has to be emphasized, because it creates an atmosphere where the labour inspectorate is viewed not only as reporting on violations, but as working together with all the actors involved towards the elimination of child labour. Working with government agencies, employers and workers, and other concerned groups such as NGOs is particularly important, as these groups are often well placed to identify instances of abuse and to support children once they have been removed from employment.

Inspection procedures should specifically include cooperation with the police, social services and juvenile courts. The use of intermediaries has proved particularly useful in dealing with sensitive aspects of child labour, and they should encourage collaboration with employers' and workers' organizations through collective negotiation, structures representing workers, and other arrangements for dialogue at the level of enterprise.

Collection of data

Inspectors should also contribute to the systematic gathering of information on the nature and extent of child labour, for instance on a sectoral basis, data which can be then used in policy development, to plan monitoring and for publications and research.

22.5 Dealing with particular inspection problems

Finding and gaining access to premises

One of the difficulties in eliminating child labour or improving the working conditions of minors is that the work often takes place in the informal sector. If labour inspection activities are planned solely on the basis of the official registers of businesses, they will cover only a fraction of the establishments in the country. It is not often that any significant number of child workers will be found in these officially registered businesses, at least in industrializing countries.

In some countries only registered, established, large or medium-sized and, in many cases, exclusively urban enterprises are monitored. In such cases, inertia and limited resources may inhibit inspectors from fulfilling their advisory and enforcement function elsewhere, particularly in small businesses in the informal sector of the economy. Given these circumstances, it is often difficult to track down cases of child labour. If inspectors are able to extend their action beyond registered businesses, however, they are more likely to succeed in identifying areas employing child workers.

Since most cases of child labour occur in the informal sector in both urban and rural areas, in home-based activities carried out by the children's families or, as in the case of domestic service, in "invisible" workplaces such as the child's own or someone else's home, they are very difficult – often legally impossible – for inspectors to reach. Inspectors face problems of legal intervention in these informal work situations, not to mention the practical difficulties of gaining access to shifting workplaces in the informal sector (e.g. the streets).

In most countries, the law states that when workers live and work on the same premises, the occupier's permission is required before those premises may be entered. If permission is refused, there is usually little the inspector can do, despite the fact that a large number of people may be involved whose conditions of work could be quite unsatisfactory. Indeed, this requirement is often abused for the very purpose of hiding illegal forms of employment, including child labour, from the inspectors' intervention.

Lack of understanding of the inspector's role

The difficulties involved when people are living in scattered private dwellings provide considerable scope for fraud. It also happens that the people whom the inspector is there to protect do not fully understand what inspection is about, or are too frightened to cooperate. In these circumstances, the inspector must rely on tact and the powers of persuasion to win their confidence, obtain information and then take the necessary remedial action.

The mere presence of a stranger, meaning the labour inspector, may alert children working in agriculture and other sectors to disappear from the worksite. Labour inspectors therefore often need to act very quickly in order to be effective. However, parents often need to have their children near them while they work, because where work is scarce parents have to take advantage of whatever opportunities are on offer.

Lack of children's cooperation

A common problem for inspectors is the uncooperative attitude of child workers themselves (often forced on them by their employers) and their parents, for whom the negative connotations associated with child labour are not immediately obvious. It provides them with an income, however small, and, sometimes, the chance to obtain some minimal training – which could be, in some cases, more attractive than the apparent alternative of inadequate schooling followed by unemployment – and thus they do not perhaps appreciate the intervention of labour inspectors. Apart from the difficulty of facing such potentially negative reactions, inspectors often also have no choice but to resort to some legal or even physical force in order to fulfil their obligations. This is unseemly in professional terms, and also raises the serious issue of the personal safety of inspectors. This in turn highlights the broader issue of the limitations on the proper conduct of labour inspection in dangerous and violent conditions, and emphasizes the need to enhance and improve the status and working conditions of labour inspectors generally (as mentioned earlier). Where children do not cooperate with the inspectors, there has been some success using a multidisciplinary approach working with, for example, the juvenile police, the labour courts or the social services.

22.6 Enforcing compliance and applying sanctions

The difficulties

The application of sanctions in this area of labour inspection is by no means straightforward, and the hurdles to be overcome can be summarized as follows:

- proving the child's age;
- the difficulty – already referred to – of actually discovering illegal child labour;

- the economics of the family in poverty;
- the attitude of parents and the children themselves; and
- the considerable expenditure in inspector time and resources to bring just one case to court.

The low status of inspectors in some ILO member States seriously weakens their determination to press for any enforcement measures. However, these difficulties cannot be allowed to excuse inaction or half-hearted enforcement.

The essential sanctioning policy

In the final analysis, inspection without determined enforcement and enforcement without the visible application of available and effective legal sanctions will not reduce the scale of child labour. Unless laws prohibiting the exploitation of children are seen to be vigorously and equitably applied and enforced, well-intentioned and compliant employers will become disillusioned for being put at a competitive disadvantage, while ruthless and uncaring employers will continue to benefit from defying the law with impunity.

While clear legislation and political support are important, the effective programming of various types of inspection and investigation is also vital. Then, when serious cases of illegal exploitation of children are discovered or when children are found to be exposed to major mechanical, chemical or psychological risks, and particularly where the employer fails to cease such practices immediately, the application of sanctions must be swift and certain.

Inspectors must be encouraged and supported by their hierarchy in ensuring that serious contraventions are taken to court and effectively prosecuted. Equally important, these cases must be widely publicized, not only as a warning to other non-compliant employers, but also as an encouragement to cooperative employers, and as a signal to society at large that the exploitation of children cannot be tolerated.

LABOUR INSPECTION AND SMALL AND MEDIUM-SIZED ENTERPRISES   23

23.1 Justification for a special approach

Small and medium-sized enterprises (SMEs) have historically been defined against various criteria, including:

- the number of people employed;
- the volume of output or sales;
- the value of assets used;
- whether the owner of the enterprise works alongside workers; and
- the degree or not of specialization in management.

The significance of the criteria may vary according to whether the promotion or protection of SMEs, the application of labour legislation or other special measures are under consideration. In practice, the numbers of people employed is probably the most common criterion, and is used in this chapter.

SMEs include a medium-sized enterprise in the formal sector with 150 workers, a small enterprise with no more than 50 workers, family businesses engaging three or four family members, cottage industries, artisanal enterprises, micro-enterprises (less than 10 workers) and self-employed workers in the informal economy. The term covers all types of ownership, including limited liability companies, partnerships, cooperatives and sole ownership. It includes manufacturing businesses engaged in small-scale building and road construction, transportation, maintenance and repair services, trade and professional services. Generally, coverage extends to all enterprises where the major operational and administrative management decisions normally rest with one (or at most two) person(s). The perception of enterprise size is that, for example, a medium-sized enterprise with 150 employees will distinguish itself less from a large enterprise than from a small one with only 20 employees.

Problems of SMEs: Productivity and working conditions

The performance of small enterprises, whether in terms of efficiency, working conditions or degree of social protection, is mixed. In many countries there are SMEs that are highly profitable and productive, and provide good working conditions and wages, but in other parts of the world, particularly in developing countries, productivity, efficiency, wage levels and social standards are poor, and in many cases unacceptably low.

There are some indications that the generally inferior employment conditions offered by SMEs can, at least in part, be compensated by non-financial advantages. Some workers consider that SMEs offer better understanding of the importance of one's work in the company, better personal control of one's work, a higher likelihood of having one's ideas accepted and easier relations with other workers in the workplace.

Generally speaking, however, low wages, poor working habits, lack of resources, and a relatively hazardous work environment are the norm. Hours of work are long. A 12-hour work shift and a seven-day week are not uncommon in some developing countries. Young children may be employed in heavy work. Machinery used may be obsolete in design, not properly maintained, and there may be exposure to hazardous chemicals. Worksites may be situated in family dwellings, posing hazards not only to the workers but to other family members as well, or in slum areas where overcrowding, heat, dust and poor ventilation are perennial problems. Standards of sanitation, hygiene, fire safety, protective devices and first aid are generally low. Workers who have accidents may not be covered by workers' compensation. To make it worse, not only are wages generally lower in these industries, but workers may also not even be paid on time. These prevalent conditions contribute to the generally poor working environment. Working conditions and occupational safety and health problems seem to be closely related to production problems, but solutions to inadequate conditions can pay for themselves in terms of better enterprise performance, and even generate substantial gains in productivity and competitiveness.

A growing body of evidence available at the ILO indicates that improvements in working conditions and the environment, equitable income distribution and the security of social protection can be key ingredients for business efficiency and competitiveness. In innovative enterprises, the quality of work and products or services are elements of the same strategy; workers' involvement and commitment are an integral part of the functional development of the enterprise, and social and environmental efficiency go hand in hand with economic efficiency. This is the challenge to labour administration, and labour inspection in particular: how to promote small-enterprise development which combines economic efficiency and job creation with adequate social standards, working conditions and labour protection. Evidence indicates that sound policy and regulatory environments, effective service delivery systems, and the creation of collaborative structures and tripartite arrangements can play important roles in achieving this objective.

If it is true that the biggest problems are often encountered in small enterprises, it is likewise true that a considerable number of SMEs are very well organized in terms of occupational safety and health, and certainly in many industrialized market economy countries.

Labour standards

National legislative provisions give effect to ILO standards (and sometimes supranational norms) and reflect national policies for the protection of working people. In principle, this body of national and international labour legislation applies to all workers, whatever the size of the enterprise. SMEs, however, may plead exceptional circumstances, since they may lack the capacity to meet the labour standards expected from large enterprises. Many international and national instruments of labour law therefore already contain exemptions and specific provisions designed to reflect the economic circumstances of SMEs and seek a balance between, on the one hand, fostering this potentially important source of employment and, on the other, maintaining acceptable and equitable labour standards. The ILO opposes any kind of deregulation which abrogates the most essential protective legislation or opens the way to unsatisfactory or exploitative conditions. It does, however, accept both the elimination of unnecessary provisions (or their replacement by others producing desired results with less bureaucracy) and a more flexible application of regulations, such as extended time for compliance, if balanced by other acceptable measures.

SMEs sometimes face special difficulties in applying labour legislation because it was not conceived with their specific characteristics in mind. This is why employers, workers and policy makers tend to express concern over undifferentiated regulatory arrangements. The current worldwide expansion of the SME sector demands a regulatory framework that is adapted to the specific character of SMEs. This framework reconciles the fragility of many SMEs with the need to secure reasonable rights for their employees, while not contributing to the erosion of standards in enterprises strong enough to meet them. What is required is a means of adjusting national and international labour law to the characteristics of SMEs.

Reducing regulatory constraints on SMEs

Small firms are moving out of the shadow of large companies. They are increasingly being viewed as a form of organization that requires specific policies and institutions tailored to its needs. SMEs are not scaled-down versions of large firms. Many public agencies are now examining the appropriateness to small firms of policies geared essentially to large firms and organizations.

Furthermore, many countries have established high-level advisory committees, often including representatives of the private sector, to evaluate existing policies and regulations and, if necessary, recommend improvements. Attention has been focused on the need to reduce administrative burdens on all enterprises, and in particular on small and medium-sized ones, with strategies for reviewing existing regulations, rigorously evaluating new regulations and maintaining a rolling review of regulations in the future. Another important strategy is the simplification of administrative procedures. Special attention has been paid to the reporting requirements of SMEs.

In 1999, EU countries were using at least three of the following approaches:

- information and advice concerning requirements and administrative procedures;
- simplification of administrative forms;
- creation of special rules for SMEs;
- replacement or simplification of existing laws;
- evaluation of possible effects of new legislation;
- research into administrative burdens on SMEs; and
- greater user-friendliness of the regulatory framework.

23.2 Priorities for the future

A better understanding of SME needs

There is no question that much of the experience which labour inspectorates have accumulated in dealing with larger enterprises is relevant to SMEs as well. However, there seem to be certain, possibly inherent limitations in applying some approaches first developed for (and often with) bigger enterprises of the formal industrial sector to different kinds of SMEs, particularly in the informal sector. Important innovative concepts, such as internal control (IC), or auditable safety and health management systems, have usually been designed with the larger, organized type of enterprise in mind. If, for instance, there is no management "system" whatsoever, as is very often the case in SMEs, it is difficult to conceive how an OSH management system can be effectively established. It can, of course, be imposed by law, and followed up by more or less severe sanctions of questionable impact; but such a regime will not ensure "ownership" by the SME entrepreneurs – a precondition for acceptance and sustainability, and therefore overall policy success.

In view of the hesitancy, for instance, of Swedish SME employers to adopt the legally prescribed IC regime, a new method was devised, based on three actions, which small companies were thought to be able to accept:

- to survey the work environment with a checklist, and make a plan to reduce the risks and correct deficiencies;
- to have a meeting with the entire personnel once a year and discuss (eight) ready-made questions, which cover different aspects of internal control in the regulations;
- to check that, when this is done, labour protection of a higher quality is in practice part of day-to-day business.

Perceived needs, objective needs, and demand

Just as, to be successful, businesses require knowledge of the needs of their customers, labour inspectors have to develop a very accurate understanding of the situation of SMEs so that they can respond appropriately to their needs and develop relevant services for them.

In 1998, the Committee of Donor Agencies for SME Development suggested that the starting point for the design of any intervention intended to reach SMEs was an assessment of their needs and perceptions. Central to any such approach to SMEs is the belief that their performance can be improved by changing the various factors affecting them. These include demand-side factors, as well as supply-side factors (including networks, availability of information, government regulations and policies). ILO experience from many developing countries shows that SMEs respond positively, and are even willing to pay for service opportunities which meet an immediate felt need.

This leads to the conclusion that inspectorates should also develop interventions and services for which there is a demand from SMEs. However, SMEs do not always know what is in their best interests and do not necessarily have a complete knowledge of all the factors pertaining to their business. Interventions based on an external analysis of SME needs may therefore have to educate them as to the potential benefits of the service offered.

Meeting the challenges

The central issue is how one can meet and reconcile the two major challenges facing labour inspection: first, the many new legal, technical and conceptual requirements of the first decade of the twenty-first century; and, second, the growing pressure from governments, workers' and employers' organizations and, in particular, the SME community to control costs and reduce the "burden of inspection" within an overall policy of favouring SME development and, in consequence, all important employment growth.

The following topics are of relevance:

- awareness of SME needs;
- review of regulations;
- alternatives to regulations;
- building strategic partnerships;
- new vectors for the message; and
- mentoring.

23.3 Six possible initiatives

Developing an understanding of SME needs

First, the real and perceived needs of SMEs have to be assessed and understood by both policy makers and inspectors in the regulatory agencies. A sector-specific approach can be useful in this respect.

In 1996, an Australian Government task force described the needs (both perceived and real) of SMEs as follows:

> The small business community is frustrated and overwhelmed by the complexity, and cost of dealing with government regulation and paperwork. Small businesses often do not understand their compliance obligations and have an underlying fear of penalties from doing the wrong thing. Government departments and agencies must implement a broad and sustained programme of action to reduce the burden and give small business operators more time to operate and grow their enterprises. There needs to be a substantial change in the culture of government, as a precondition for the development of a prevention culture in SMEs. Governments must remove unnecessary regulation and improve the quality of administration. Proposed regulation needs careful scrutiny to ensure the burden on small business is minimized. Departments and agencies responsible for regulation must monitor the impact of their paperwork and compliance requirements on small business and report annually on their progress in reducing the burden.[1]

"Burden" is defined as all the additional paperwork and other activities that small business must complete to comply with government regulations. It represents the time and expense outlaid over and above normal commercial practices. The burden includes lost opportunities and disincentives to expand the business. Small businesses (not only in Australia) spend valuable time finding out what its obligations to governments are, and then spend more time providing the same basic information to different government agencies, often at federal, state and local levels. The most time-consuming information exchanges for a small business occur during the start-up phase, or when its circumstances change and when it provides periodic reports and returns to government. One major problem is the lack of coordination at various levels of government, as well as among different government agencies. Small businesses want a "one-stop-shop" where they can conduct their business transactions with all the government offices concerned, and receive all the relevant information and guidance.

These initiatives would simplify dealings with a range of departments, resulting in lower compliance costs for small business. The initial establishment costs would largely be recovered in the medium term from savings by participating agencies. Furthermore, the culture of policy makers and regulators must change in order for long-term improvements in regulation to be maintained.

There are therefore a number of key messages from small business in relation to the compliance burden:

- While SMEs accept the need for a degree of government intervention and are prepared to meet their fair share of the burden, people in small businesses feel habitually overwhelmed and unable to cope with government requirements. Importantly, small business operators are afraid of doing the wrong thing and will let business opportunities pass rather than take issue with government authorities.
- There is a difference in perception between government regulation reformers and small business. While the former point, with some justice, to significant reforms, small business believes, rightly or wrongly, that the situation is getting worse.
- SMEs say consistently that there is a need to change the culture of regulation; it is often the behaviour of regulators, as much as the regulation itself, which is the cause of concern.
- Policy makers, often unconsciously, are the root of many of the problems, as they generally determine the requirements small business must meet in an environment isolated from practical operating experience. Policy makers need to be more accountable for the decisions they make and need to understand the impact of those decisions on small business.
- Small business wants certainty and simplicity from government, and is prepared to give up some equity to get it.

- Wasted time is the clearest message of all. For small business people, time spent complying with government requirements is time lost from running and expanding the business.

Reviewing the regulatory framework

Second, the regulatory framework has to be thoroughly reviewed. The United Kingdom's Health and Safety Executive (HSE) research and analysis, for instance, has highlighted the need for:

- keeping the law up to date and clear;
- developing good, simple, reasonable guidance; and
- helping small firms to meet their (minimum) legal requirements on the part of the inspectorate.

The Australian report referred to above has developed the following basic useful principles:

- there is a legitimate and understandable role for industry regulation (and information collection) in a modern society;
- regulation and data collection should be the minimum required to achieve the stated objectives;
- regulation should be developed in consultation with the groups affected and in a transparent manner;
- regulation should be administered by the sphere of government most directly concerned;
- regulation should be designed, administered and enforced in a manner which minimizes the compliance burden on SMEs;
- the provision of clear and simple information about obligations and compliance requirements must be freely available;
- regulators should have a good understanding of the circumstances of small business in developing and administering regulations; and
- there must be a clear delineation of regulatory responsibilities and effective accountability mechanisms.

In short, the regulatory framework should be up to date, comprehensive, user-friendly and as simple as possible.

Developing complementary regulation approaches

Third, alternatives to regulation must be more actively explored and developed. Alternatives include self-regulation or co-regulation, or codes of conduct or practice. These are usually developed as part of an industry self-regulatory scheme. They can be in the form of a charter of ethics, principles of good practice, a service charter or other. Co-regulation applies when industry self-regulation is made mandatory, as is the case for compulsory codes of practice. Voluntary compliance programmes, such as the "employer model" developed by the German Mutual Accident Insurance Associations (*Berufsgenossenschaften*) as an alternative to statutory inspection, also fall into this category.

Often, these schemes represent genuine alternatives to prescriptive regulation. Potential advantages include:

- **relevance** – because the code has been developed by those intimately concerned with the sector or the problem;
- **acceptance** – for the same reasons;
- **flexibility** – the code can be responsive to changing industry conditions or business practices;
- **efficiency** – reduced costs associated with complaints mechanisms that might otherwise have resulted in court action;
- **comprehensibility** – even if dealing with compliance with legal obligations, texts can be drafted in ordinary non-legal language;
- **choice** – employers are free to choose other solutions; they tend to acquire "ownership" of the solution or model of their own choosing;
- **certainty** – if they follow the code, they can be certain of having done what is required (in the case of conflict, there will often then be a shift in the burden of proof);
- **reduced compliance costs** – self-regulation, while not without cost, should be a cost-effective alternative to prescriptive regulation;
- **effectiveness** – improved quality of products or standards of service delivery; enhanced customer satisfaction; and higher levels of employee safety and health.

Supporting the building of strategic partnerships

Fourth, in view of the structural weakness of the traditional social partners in the SME sector, new strategic partnerships must be built, or existing ones redefined and revitalized. The inspectorate must look beyond the traditional social partner organizations. In Germany, district artisan associations have proved to be very effective in introducing labour protection awareness and simple, relevant concepts to SMEs with support and guidance from the inspectorates, either by external multidisciplinary services or by establishing a common service to be used by all associated craft establishments.

More importantly, labour inspection must link up with the growing number of state- or donor-funded programmes for job creation and employment growth through SME development. Many countries organize these programmes using the public employment services. Logically, labour protection concepts pointing to the synergy between better conditions of work and higher productivity could and should be introduced into employment promotion programmes. Different departments, which in the majority of countries belong to one and the same labour administration system under one minister, should cooperate on such a vital issue, although this does not always happen in practice. The start-up phase of SME development is, however, the time when future employers tend to be most receptive and accessible.

Other new strategic partners are to be found in social security institutions, workers' compensation organizations or insurance bodies. Sometimes this cooperation is time-honoured, while sometimes it is non-existent, even though inspectorates and accident insurance coexist and serve the same client system. Where OSH inspectorates have merged with the workers' compensation authorities, the enforcement agency has a much more solid resource and database, thus allowing for better access to, and penetration of, the SME sector.

Cooperation of labour inspectorates with public (and possibly private) occupational health services to improve OSH in SMEs is another case of a potentially successful strategic partnership. In Finland, there are 1,080 occupational health units with 700 physicians, 1,500 occupational health nurses and 200 physiotherapists (counted as full-time employees); and 11 district labour protection authorities with 400 labour inspectors. Both organizations have a common inspection target of 225,000 enterprises (and public sector establishments). Of these enterprises, 94 per cent are very small (less than 10 people), and only 60 per cent of these small enterprises are covered by the OSH. Enhancing healthy and safe working conditions is a common statutory aim of both OSH and the labour inspectorate. Both visit working premises. Following a study, both agencies saw improved structural cooperation as very important, but more formal agency agreements and, in particular, guidelines from the top administrations were urgently needed.

Similarly, in Japan, a major cooperation project has been undertaken to reinforce the existing industrial health promotion centres, establishing a centre in each prefecture to strengthen consultation and information services, as well as to impact on small workplaces.

The structural weakness of enterprise-level social partner representation in the SME sector is notorious. In Sweden, the Government has contributed to overcoming this weakness by helping to set up a system of regional safety representatives. These people are employed in one enterprise, but are responsible for a significant number of enterprises in a particular sector or region. The Government covers roughly 70 per cent of the costs of operating this system. A similar scheme operates successfully in the United Kingdom on a pilot basis, using a sector approach, but without government subsidies.

Devising new ways of getting the message across

Fifth, new ways have to be developed to explain to the SME target group that it is unnecessary or even inappropriate to choose between productivity and labour protection. These two should be mutually reinforcing and ILO experience shows that it is essential to pursue these two objectives simultaneously. This positive dynamic between productivity and occupational safety and health provides the basis for some of the most successful strategies for improving working conditions. The United Kingdom's campaign "Good Health is Good Business" is a case in point. Although mailing campaigns to SMEs is a possible technique, the United Kingdom experience is that sharply focused seminars are more effective.

Since all management decisions are usually made by only one person – certainly in so-called micro-enterprises – the small enterprise owner is the key player in any strategy to "get the message across", and to improve working conditions. The enterprise owner will tend to think, "What does this mean for me?" Therefore, it is pivotal to establish the link between productivity, quality and working conditions.

Some concepts of how increasing productivity and profitability in small enterprises can be achieved while improving working conditions have been developed by the ILO. Work Improvements in Small Enterprises (WISE) is one of its longer-running international programmes. It is based on the concept that working conditions, product quality, productivity and competitiveness are interlinked to strategic issues for small businesses. The use of local "best practices" and bringing business managers together in groups have proved highly successful in generating solutions of simple and low-cost improvements that link productivity with a safer and better workplace. This training is effective when it focuses on:

- a multifaceted approach building on local practice;
- positive achievements and feasible solutions which are locally attainable, including low-cost solutions; and
- learning-by-doing, which directly involves managers through group work.

A typical training course consists of a checklist exercise, group discussions of low-cost examples collected from the participants' enterprises, group work on proposing and implementing (during the course) simple improvements, and group presentations of the results. Many practical improvements have been carried out in WISE training courses in almost 100 developing countries. By providing real workplace opportunities, it is adaptable and effective in varying local conditions. The "six principles" of WISE, which are seen as the key to successful participatory programmes in SMEs, are as follows:

- build on local practice;
- focus on achievements;
- link labour protection with other management goals (quality, productivity);
- use "learning-by-doing";
- encourage exchange of experience (in groups); and
- promote workers' participation.

Although WISE was originally created with developing countries in mind, it has now been adopted, sometimes slightly modified, in developed countries as well. It has become the central strategy of the Danish Working Environment Service in dealing with SMEs.

Start and Improve Your Business (SIYB) is an ILO management training programme for small businesses. It develops and strengthens basic management skills in areas such as marketing, costing, accounting, planning, logistics, production and personnel management. The programme provides a comprehensive set of training materials for small-enterprise managers. The focus is on business management skills, but a special module on working conditions has now been developed to raise the awareness of small-enterprise managers of the positive relationship between productivity, occupational safety and health, and improved general conditions of work. It gives them a range of practical tools to enable this.

The InFocus Programme on Boosting Employment through Small Enterprise Development (IFP/SEED) expands on the ILO's small-enterprise promotional activities. It works with local partners to promote comprehensive, integrated, high-impact and cost-effective interventions to help small enterprises develop their job-creation potential. An important component of IFP/ SEED focuses on how to ensure the mutual reinforcement of competitiveness and an improved working environment.

Labour inspectorates should establish constructive relationships with all those providing support services to SMEs, since these agencies and companies are spearheading the development of the SME sector in many countries. Supporting services include financial services, such as credit and insurance schemes; they also include a wide range of non-financial services, increasingly referred to as Business Development Services (BDS). BDS include, for example, training, business advice, information and counselling. Concepts such as WISE and SIYB can be propagated through national networks of BDS providers, including government, non-government and for-profit organizations, since these networks usually organize extended outreach to the SME community.

Of course, the inspectorate can organize this outreach itself. In 1995, in New Zealand, a major strategy was launched to assist small employers understand their responsibilities under the legislation and to describe "how to do it" in a simple manner with information kits, guidelines and handbooks. Training was given to all OSH officers on the delivery process of this information and how it interacted with the enforcement side of the business. The kits were not designed to be merely given away. The OSH inspector has to work through the material with the employer. The "employer model", originally developed by German Accident Insurance Associations (who run their own inspection services under the "dual system"), follows a similar approach. It is being introduced in a greater number of EU Member States, such as Austria and Portugal.

In the United States, OSHA (federal) funds "on-site consultation services" run by state government agencies. With the Federal Government providing 90 per cent of the funding, state consultancy bodies visit an enterprise and advise it about hazards in the workplace, and methods to eliminate or reduce those hazards. The service is free. Information obtained during a consultation visit is not used for inspection purposes. However, an employer who obtains a consultation visit and complies with the consultant's recommendations receives a lower priority for future inspection than does an employer who does not utilize the consultation service. Over the past five years, OSHA's on-site consultation services conducted more than 100,000 free visits, more than 50 per cent of which were with enterprises with fewer than 50 employees.

Promoting mentoring by large employers

Last, but not least, labour inspection can help build and influence partnerships between large companies and SMEs. Different approaches have been developed by different agencies. In the United Kingdom, work has concentrated on the important role of large firms in promoting action to raise safety and health standards at small firms that are their contractors, suppliers or neighbours; and on the crucial role of safety and health professionals in large firms in establishing and assessing standards in small contractor and supplier firms. Safety and health is one of a number of indicators of general managerial capacity used by large firms, as they strive for quality-management processes in response to customer pressure for excellence, and pay attention to better supply-chain management, loss and risk control. Many small firms, however, appear indifferent to the loss-control argument. However, approximately half of the United Kingdom's small firms work for larger firms as contractors or suppliers. These relationships can motivate small firms to go for better safety and health performance. Most big firms apply the same procedures to aspiring suppliers and contractors, irrespective of size, and insist on main suppliers and contractors "cascading" these procedures when taking on subcontractors. Small firms feature more in the subcontracting chain, rather than as direct contractors.

However, "quality management" pressures have led large firms to radically reduce the numbers of suppliers and contractors, and thus the bureaucratic procedures for recruiting and controlling them. This may reduce opportunities for small firms, which need to understand the increasing insistence by big firms on good standards of safety capability in both suppliers and contractors. Besides, big firms will communicate their experience of small firms to other potential employers, so bad labour protection records can give such firms a bad name. Thus, competitive and customer pressures, and quality management aims, tend to spread and standardize requirements down long chains of suppliers and contractors, and to exclude non-conformers permanently. The conclusion is that large firms seek high standards of safety and health internally and with business partners for "business-related" reasons, particularly loss control and quality management, rather than for compliance or moral reasons. Evaluation has shown that for both parties contractual obligations are more likely than fear of prosecution to lead to higher standards of safety and health. This scheme appears to resemble what in Canada (notably Ontario and some other provinces) is known as mentoring, and is actively encouraged with good results by the inspectorates there.

In Ireland, the labour inspectorate (HSA) launched its Good Neighbour Scheme in 1996. The objective of the scheme is to bring large and small companies together to promote greater awareness of workplace labour protection issues. Since larger companies, in the main, have the necessary infra-structure and specialist arrangements in place to deal with a range of related issues, they can offer a helping hand to smaller ones. Many of the larger companies found their participation in the scheme worthwhile. It provided them with an opportunity to discuss working environment issues with small companies with whom they usually enjoy a business relationship, and to highlight their expectations in relation to the standards to be adopted within the company in a user-friendly, non-confrontational way. The smaller (beneficiary) companies found the information, training and advice provided invaluable in coming to grips with safety and health issues in the workplace. The scheme does not seek to substitute or undermine the legal responsibilities of individual employers. Instead, it seeks to promote greater awareness of workplace safety and health issues through a pooling of information and knowledge between larger and smaller companies.

The scheme is said to be simplicity itself and much of its success to date has been as a direct result of this. There is no form filling, cost or indeed bureaucratic red tape. The companies were chosen following recommendations from the Inspectorate with first-hand experience of labour-protection management systems in practice in the selected enterprises. The participating companies were drawn from a wide cross-section of industrial sectors. A good geographic spread was also achieved. The feedback from participating companies has been entirely positive.

The Japanese system of Labour Accident Prevention Instructors is similar and has been established for longer. Its people are in full-time employment with medium or, usually, large companies, whether as experienced trade union members or perhaps as personnel managers or even as managing directors, who work as volunteer advisers and instructors to smaller companies. The scheme is organized by the Japanese Labour Standards Bureau (the labour inspectorate), which asks employers and trade unions to nominate suitable people for training as instructors; they then work in cooperation with local Labour Standards Inspectorates (LSI). They are volunteers, but are paid travelling expenses and a small honorarium from the budget of the Labour Standards Bureau. They have no formal right of entry to premises and no enterprise is obliged to receive such an instructor, but a refusal to do so could well result in the LSI making an early inspection. Their activities will in any case be directed at companies with a poor labour protection record.

23.4 Lessons to be learned

One of the most difficult problems state labour inspectorates, as regulatory and intervention authorities, face in the SME sector is having to reconcile two potentially competing policy demands for more and better labour protection in all enterprises, on the one hand, and unfettered growth, and thus increased employment, on the other. In many, if not most countries, these demands, though not necessarily opposed, collide within the competence of one and the same state authority, the Ministry of Labour (or the equivalent state labour administration system). This labour administration system develops and often manages job creation and other support programmes for SMEs. It also, as a rule, is responsible for regulation and inspection.

This chapter has suggested at least six specific initiatives a labour inspectorate can take to resolve this potential conflict, without accepting double standards. The standards to be met remain the same for all employers. The differences lie in the way obligations are presented to SMEs in terms of language, minimal bureaucracy, enforcement process, time-frames for compliance and so on. The process of meeting requisite standards can be made easier by codes of practice, developed by specialists in that sector or problem, in plain language, and the availability of helpful publications from a "one-stop shop", which also provides contacts with relevant government departments.

Labour inspectorates can ensure that programmes concerned with job creation, productivity, competitiveness or quality make the link with improved labour standards, and give all-inclusive advice. Any training must be highly practical, focusing on sectoral or local practice and concerned with attaining feasible, preferably low-cost solutions. Finally, they can promote mentoring and partnerships with large companies, not just on moral grounds, but as a matter of economic survival for SMEs in the contractor–subcontractor supply chain.

Note

[1] Commonwealth Government of Australia: *The Small Business Report* (Canberra, 1996).

LABOUR INSPECTION IN AGRICULTURE

24

24.1 A special challenge for inspectorates

The range of activities, employment conditions and hazards

The term "agriculture" covers an enormous range of activities from highly mechanized "prairie farming", or intensive rearing of livestock, to subsistence farming by family units in remote regions of the world (with forestry as a separate area of employment). Hazards include manual, mechanical and transport hazards found in industry and commerce, and the hazards arising from the use of a range of chemical products. There are hazards associated with animals, with buildings and when the workplace is also the home, with risks to the family themselves, and particularly to children.

Agriculture is considered to be one of the most hazardous sectors, next to mining and construction. It is in agriculture that the highest rates of fatal accidents are recorded, both in developing and industrialized countries. This is compounded by the whole range of diseases and injuries related to agricultural tasks which, despite their frequency, are not always diagnosed and notified to the appropriate authorities. In most countries only certain categories of agricultural workers are covered by national legislation. Thus a large number of agricultural workers, representing almost half of the world's economically active population, are deprived of any form of social protection.

Apart from the Labour Inspection (Agriculture) Convention, 1969 (No. 129),[1] agricultural workers are protected by the Plantations Convention, 1958 (No. 110), and agriculture is generally covered by the Occupational Safety and Health Convention 1981 (No. 155). Until 2001, however there was no comprehensive international standard dealing specifically with the problems of safety and health in agriculture. In that year, following a general discussion in 2000,[2] the 89th Session of the International Labour Conference adopted the Safety and Health in Agriculture Convention (No. 184) and Recommendation (No. 192).

According to ILO estimates, of an annual total of 335,000 fatal workplace accidents worldwide, some 170,000 agricultural workers are killed every year. The World Health Organization (WHO) estimates the total cases of pesticide poisoning as between 2 and 5 million each year, of which 40,000 are fatal. Developing countries consume more than 20 per cent of the world production of agrochemicals and are responsible for approximately 70 per cent of the total number of cases of acute poisoning occurring in the world, corresponding to more than 1.1 million cases.[3]

In the EU and many other regions or countries, agriculture ranks as one of the four most hazardous occupations alongside mining, fishing and construction. Many people in the industry do not consult a doctor unless they are seriously ill, so details of the extent of ill health are unclear. However, in one industrialized country it is estimated that:

- 80 per cent of agricultural workers have some form of musculoskeletal injury (aches, sprains or strains);
- the incidence of people affected by asthma is twice the national average;
- more than 20,000 people are affected by zoonoses (diseases passed from animals to humans) each year; and
- 25 per cent of the workforce suffers from hearing loss as a result of their work.

In developing countries the prevalence of common agricultural hazards is exacerbated by ignorance, especially regarding diseases with delayed effects, and compounded by factors such as illiteracy, unwillingness to complain or report ill health for fear of losing one's job, and perhaps one's home, malnutrition, lack of health care or adequate medical treatment, and the farm worker's economic vulnerability to exploitation.

For these reasons, the agricultural sector must be a priority for any labour inspectorate.

The law

Although Convention No. 129 has been in existence since 1969, and Convention No. 155 since 1981, by December 2001 only 40 ILO member States (out of a total of 175) had ratified Convention No. 129 and only 37 had ratified Convention No. 155.

While this does not mean that member States that have not ratified the Conventions have no appropriate legal provisions, it does suggest that legislation is not adequate to enable those States to implement the full provisions. Indeed, in some developing countries, only large enterprises and plantations are subject to labour inspection, and there are still countries where occupational safety and health legislation does not apply to agriculture.

The workers

While trade union representatives of agricultural workers do exist, trade unions, even in industrialized countries, have difficulty organizing because of the scattered nature of the employment and the small numbers of employees in each unit. As mechanization advances, so the number of agricultural workers declines. In developing countries the problem may be compounded by distance, the fear of discrimination by the employer against union members, ignorance of the law and employment rights, and illiteracy.

Traditionally, children have always worked on family farms, not always as a matter of economic necessity, but as a way of interesting them and involving them in the business. However, there are also many incidences of exploitative, illegal forms of child labour in this sector in both developing and developed countries. Furthermore, many people in agriculture work beyond the normal retirement age, putting them at risk of occupational hazards.

The employers

Employers range from large multinational or national enterprises to the smallest units employing casual labour at peak times. Many farmers are self-employed and may not be covered by legislation, trained in safe working practices or reached by inspection services, advisory activities or publications, even though they are exposed to the same hazards as employees. Farmers often work under time pressures because of the vagaries of the working environment, the market or the climate. Because of their work they tend to be self-reliant, and this encourages the adoption of ad hoc and unsafe practices.

In certain countries, inspectors' activities are obstructed, and threatened or actual violence is directed against them, sometimes associated with racial prejudice and often uncontested because of lack of support from the police or other authorities.

Coordination and cooperation between government departments

In some countries the labour inspectorate responsible for agriculture is part of the same organization as that responsible for safety and health in industry and commerce, in others they are separate and in still others there are separate inspectorates for employment conditions (wages, etc.) and for safety and health.

International discussions have identified another problem: inadequate coordination between the labour inspectorate and departments with parallel or related responsibilities in health, education or industrial and commercial development, and therefore a lack of coordinated efforts to tackle the structural causes of inadequate and hazardous working conditions.

24.2 Hazards in agriculture

In order to appreciate the size of the task facing labour inspectors, the range of knowledge they require, and the spread of medical or technical expertise they should be able to call upon, it is instructive to summarize the principal hazards to which agricultural and forestry workers are exposed.

Basic hazards

Agricultural workers are subject to many of the same dangers as industrial or commercial workers, including:

- manual handling of loads, including not only excessive weights and difficult lifting but also the special problems involved in handling livestock;
- injuries with hand tools of every description, especially knives, and in developing countries the use of heavy traditional tools for long hours;
- slipping, tripping and falling, especially from ladders and roofs, during unskilled maintenance work, or being struck, for instance during tree felling;
- power tools, including the risk of vibration "white finger" from chain saws;
- noise, which can exceed damaging levels, whether in the use of certain machinery or, for instance, where pigs are raised intensively;
- dust from the milling of rice and other products, which may cause respiratory problems;
- gassing or asphyxiation in silos.

Mechanical and electrical hazards

These include:

- tractors overturning without roll-over protection;
- all-terrain vehicles (ATVs) used in unsuitable locations and without protective headgear for drivers;
- power take-off shafts, which are notoriously badly guarded and a common cause of fatalities;

- specialist machinery of every conceivable kind with inadequate protection for transmission or dangerous operating mechanisms, which are often poorly maintained or misused;
- electrocution during installation, use and maintenance, and when diggers or specialized equipment are used under power lines.

Chemical hazards

Unlike in industry where chemical processes can generally be enclosed, or at least emissions can be controlled, pesticides, herbicides, fungicides and fumigants have to be released in order to take effect and they are, by design, intended to attack some form or aspect of a living organism. In some countries, certain chemicals are still employed contrary to WHO recommendations. All too often the user receives too little information about the hazards and precautions and, even if the user is not illiterate, the labels with instructions and precautions may be in a foreign language.

Indiscriminate use or misuse of agrochemicals are widespread. Often the workers are not provided with appropriate personal protective equipment, and even where protection is provided, its use is difficult to enforce in very hot or humid climates. In some societies it is traditionally unacceptable for women to wear this type of clothing, and children are rarely adequately protected. The position is made worse by the long latent period between exposure and the onset of symptoms in the case of some chemicals, or by sensitization which makes even the smallest further exposure unbearable. The reuse of inadequately cleaned containers presents a further hazard. Special problems include aerial spraying and work in enclosed buildings such as greenhouses.

Hazards associated with livestock

Apart from the physical hazards associated with the management and handling of livestock, zoonoses, including micro-organisms such as E.coli (O 157), present a serious hazard. Contact with animals, their carcasses and waste products, as well as with poisonous plants, may give rise to allergies, respiratory disorders and lung diseases.

Agricultural workers are also exposed to a variety of diseases such as brucellosis, parasitic diseases such as haemorrhagic fever and bilharziasis, and infectious diseases such as tetanus, rabies or Lyme disease. In some areas there is the risk of anthrax and skin disorders as well as fungal infections, and agricultural workers are generally exposed to a wide variety of conditions causing dermatitis.

Risks to children

For many children, the workplace in agriculture is their home and their home is the workplace. Quite apart from the problem of child labour (dealt with in Chapter 22), children on farms can be at risk even when at play. They are particularly at risk because of their inexperience, their lack of awareness of hazards and their immaturity. Hazards include:

- falls from heights, from trailers, stacks of material and buildings;
- being run over by tractors or other equipment;
- being crushed by falling gates, tractor tyres or unsafely stacked goods;
- drowning in tanks or slurry pits, and suffocation in grain stores or silos;
- contact with moving machinery;
- injury or disease from contact with animals.

The effect of these accidents and fatalities can be more devastating to families than accidents to the workers themselves, bad enough as these are.

Hazards and risks

A hazard is the potential for any tool, plant, substance or activity to cause injury or ill health. The risk is the chance, or likelihood, of that hazard actually causing injury in the particular circumstances under consideration.

In EU countries, and doubtless elsewhere, it is increasingly common practice to require employers to carry out risk assessment as the basis for precautions they adopt. It is important that, whatever the legislation, labour inspectors encourage employers in agriculture to do precisely the same in order to ensure that adequate precautions are taken to mitigate or eliminate the risks from the above hazards.

Ireland requires every farmer, including those who are self-employed, to prepare a safety statement in which workplace hazards are identified, and the risks assessed and recorded in writing with the necessary preventive measures clearly specified.

24.3. Problems facing labour inspectors in agriculture

The inspectors

First, even where legislation applies to agriculture, in developing countries there are often too few inspectors to assure even a token appearance at more than a tiny proportion of workplaces, and the larger the plantation and more remote the agricultural activity, the greater the problem.

Second, agricultural inspectors in developing countries often receive inadequate training. They may have a month or two of basic instruction, and then work in the field under supervision for another month or so before inspecting alone. It is clear, however, that given the need for familiarity with the law, with standards and with inspection methods and procedures, in addition to all the technical matters, these training periods are generally too short to adequately instruct inspectors in the hazards found in local agricultural and forestry activities. There is seldom provision for in-service refresher training, and the availability of specialist medical and technical support varies widely.

Third, many inspectors in developing countries complain of inadequate resources, particularly for transport, so that even if they have time, they are unable to afford to travel to more distant parts. One developing country in southern Africa has, however, passed a law requiring large employers to provide transport for the inspector from his or her base to their plantation, and if necessary to provide overnight accommodation.

Employers and workers

As noted above, widespread ignorance of the law, of employee rights, and of hazards and precautions is often prevalent, especially in developing countries. While advisory leaflets are essential, the many languages and dialects in some countries present a problem, even in the absence of widespread illiteracy.

Employers in some countries are positively adverse to providing reasonable working conditions and are hostile to inspectors. Where there is high unemployment and jobs are scarce, workers are not disposed to complain and the trade unions' priority is the level of wages rather than working conditions.

24.4 Strategies for improvement

An action programme

The strategies to be put in place depend upon the particular situation in the country concerned, political imperatives, financial capacity and practical possibilities. Nevertheless, the absence of political will, lack of finance or expertise should not excuse inaction. Unless an action programme is presented to the Government by the labour inspectorate, there is nothing to stimulate political will and the necessary resources will not be found. Unless clear priorities and an action programme are presented to inspectors, the inspection process will remain fragmentary. If efforts are not made to inform and motivate employers and workers, nothing will change.

Influencing governments

Ministers responsible for labour inspection in agriculture must influence their colleagues in government to:

- support tougher legislation to protect employees in all sectors and parts of the industry or activity;
- ratify and transpose into domestic legislation the provisions of the relevant ILO Conventions, and in particular Conventions Nos. 129 and 155;
- increase the funding of the labour inspectorate both to enable a sufficient number of inspectors to be recruited, and also to provide for adequate training and ongoing briefing, as well as the resources to enable them to actually do the job, for instance by providing an adequate travel budget;
- promote training and a system of qualifications, which include safety and health, for workers, farmers and farm managers; and
- encourage, and if necessary finance, relevant organizations, as well as the labour inspectorate, to produce and distribute concise guidance on hazards, risks and preventive measures in agriculture and forestry, including advice on measures to prevent injury to children on farms.

Coordination

Departments responsible for labour inspection must take positive steps to promote effective, results-oriented targets for cooperation with relevant government departments on occupational health promotion. Where necessary, economic incentives should be used that do not reduce standards but instead promote and improve working conditions.

Influencing those in agriculture

In general, safety and health at work is influenced by three main factors:

- the job:
    - how safe it is;
    - how well designed the equipment is;
    - whether the "hardware" or work systems are appropriate, etc.
- individuals:
    - their attitudes, skills and habits;
    - how well trained they are;
    - their perception of risks.

- the environment/organization:
  - the culture within which the individual is working;
  - the resources of the business;
  - working patterns;
  - "uncontrollable" factors such as the weather and behaviour of livestock.

Agriculture, more than most other industries, is a way of life. Consequently the cultural, social and economic environment in which it exists is very important. Given these complex influences and the great range of hazards, there can be no single technique for raising standards of labour protection in agriculture. Instead, the labour inspectorate must make use of both traditional methods and less conventional approaches.

24.5 Clear enforcement and promotional policies

A statement of intent

The management of the labour inspectorate responsible for agriculture must decide and preferably publicize its policy in respect of:

- its priorities in terms of intended results within a stipulated timescale;
- its priorities in terms of classes, locations or sectors for priority proactive inspection;
- special enforcement campaigns;
- its policies in relation to the investigation of complaints and accidents, in respect of the control of employment conditions as well as ill health, so that important preventive activity is not swamped by short-term demands on the inspectors' time;
- its policies in relation to the use of sanctions and the guidance it gives inspectors to maintain a balance between the provision of help and advice and the institution of legal proceedings;
- its intention to publish simple, informative guidance, preferably using relevant illustrations, and the use it intends making of publicity and the media, and participation in agricultural shows, training courses, seminars and conferences;
- its general policy for making a maximum input with existing resources through eliminating bureaucracy, shortening reports, limiting the time inspectors spend in the office, and its policy for the use of intermediaries such as suppliers, manufacturers' agents, clubs, employers' bodies and local employees' associations to transmit the message.

Inspection

Inspection is effective, but it is also resource intensive. Each inspector can only reach a limited number of businesses a day, and travelling takes time in remote rural areas. It is therefore important to target visits to businesses or employers where the visit can have most effect.

The inspector's job is not to look at every risk, but to assess how well safety and health are being managed, whether appropriate physical and procedural controls are in place, and then to judge how best to secure compliance. Some inspectorates target different specific risks every year, enabling them to visit more premises, and to gain an indication of how that business is managing safety and health generally. Inspection is also a useful opportunity to gather information to guide future policies.

These inspection campaigns targeted at specific risks or a specific geographical area, supported by good publicity locally or nationally, and backed by strong enforcement, have a "multiplier effect", influencing even those who were not visited by an inspector. One inspectorate sometimes targets influential farmers in a particular locality who have status among their peers. These tend to be the first to adopt new working methods, but if inspectors can persuade them to adopt improvements, this can have an indirect effect on their peer group.

Investigations

While the investigation of accidents, cases of ill health and other incidents is important, it is also resource intensive. Whilst investigations may reveal contraventions requiring legal action, they also tend to produce improvements because the employer has seen for himself what can go wrong. An inspectorate must, however, ensure that it maintains a balance between its reactive work and its proactive, preventive role, so that investigations are targeted on incidents where most improvement can be gained.

Advice

Although inspectors can give useful advice during inspections or investigations, a special visit to give advice is rarely justified. Much can be done by telephone or by having a wide range of advisory leaflets.

Enforcement

As in other fields of employment, inspectors usually try to obtain improvements in safety and health by advice and persuasion. However, it is important that the inspectorate has a clear policy on, and makes effective use of, its powers by notice or order to require specific action to be taken, and even to stop or prohibit particular processes. Although resource intensive, appropriate use should also be made of any punitive powers, such as prosecution, where the employer fails to comply with an order or blatantly disregards people's safety and health.

Work with manufacturers, designers and suppliers

One significant cause of injuries in agriculture is unsafe equipment, although many countries have standards to be met by designers, manufacturers and suppliers of articles for use at work, for the physical standards of the items and for safety and health information to be supplied to users. Inspectorates can therefore invest constructive time and resources in ensuring that businesses in the agricultural supply chain meet their legal duties, because good standards at this stage benefit safety and health in many agricultural businesses down the line.

Suppliers also have an important role to play in influencing the culture in agriculture because of their integration into the agricultural community. Suppliers or agents can build up relationships with their customers, and consequently farmers sometimes trust the advice they get from their suppliers more than the advice they receive from "official" sources.

Work with contractors

Contractors play an important role in some countries because many small farms do not have the specialist knowledge and/or cannot afford the latest equipment, and therefore buy in the services of specialist contractors. These contractors usually have relatively up-to-date (and therefore intrinsically safer) equipment, and should be trained and experienced in the work they do. However, they face other risks. Much of their work is, by its very nature, potentially higher risk (pesticide application, harvesting). They are often work in unfamiliar surroundings, and communication and cooperation between them and the business they are working for may be poor.

However, because of the peripatetic nature of this type of work, an inspectorate investing in regulating and advising contractors can improve standards in the workplaces visited.

Work with intermediaries and partners

Because of the great number of agricultural businesses, it is particularly important to interest those who can influence the culture in agricultural communities. A national association representing farmers can, for instance, be consulted and then invited to support a particular campaign affecting their members. Community groups, such as young farmers' or rural women's groups, can be encouraged to organize activities with themes related to safety and health. Competitions on "Efficiency with Safety" could be judged in relation to the practical outcome of some everyday farming task and how safely it was performed.

Work with trainers and educationalists

One of the best ways to influence attitudes towards the appreciation of risk and in relation to behaviour is through training and education. Whether working in schools or agricultural colleges or with other training providers, there is an opportunity to ensure that students and trainees receive the key messages about agricultural safety.

It is important to ensure that safety and health form an integral part of any vocational qualification in agriculture. Schools are increasingly being encouraged, and in some cases required, to teach the basics of safety and risk awareness, which can have a particular focus in rural areas. Story videos with a safety lesson and colourful leaflets, supported by information packs for teachers, can prove popular and effective.

Advertising campaigns in the press, television and radio can be used to inform and shock by sensitizing parents to the risks their children face.

Work with commercial partners

Some countries' inspectorates work with commercial partners such as insurance organizations, organizing campaigns, sponsoring guidance literature or sponsoring competitions, particularly in relation to child safety. Customer assurance schemes have the potential to enable supermarkets or marketing cooperatives to emphasize the fact that their produce is not only of good quality, but has also been produced with due regard to the safety and health of agricultural workers. A number of countries have "good neighbour" schemes in which large organizations with reliable systems for managing safety and health and expertise in that field provide help to their smaller "neighbours". In some cases, the smaller business has been a supplier or contractor to the larger one.

Information and advisory services and publicity campaigns

These services and campaigns are an essential element of any inspectorate's comprehensive approach to agriculture. In practice, however, the techniques are no different from those employed in relation to other sectors of employment and areas, as discussed in greater detail in Chapters 13 and 20.

24.6 Training and supporting inspectors

Labour inspectors' qualifications, training, staffing and resources

In order to enable inspectors to undertake these functions effectively, the management of a labour inspectorate responsible for agriculture must ensure that:

- it recruits staff, preferably with relevant agricultural experience, but also with the ability to benefit from and absorb training, and perhaps above all with the personality and independence of judgement which will make them effective in the field;
- the longest and most comprehensive training programme that the service can afford is provided, covering not only technical issues relevant to the region but also motivational skills and the psychology of employers, workers and society;
- some training capacity is available for updating or post-probationary training and, for more experienced staff, management training;
- a rational system is developed for the allocation of staff and other resources in order to make best use of them, given the inevitable limitations.

Medical and technical support

Since it is impossible for each inspector to be expert in every aspect of the job, it is important that the management of a labour inspectorate, responsible for agriculture, either has its own specialist advice (doctors, nurses, and specialists in mechanical and chemical hazards), or makes appropriate contractual arrangements with other government departments or with academic or private bodies in order to have access to specialist advice when needed.

International support

Labour inspectorate management should explore and make every effort to benefit as much as possible from the experience of other countries dealing with similar problems, by establishing links with international expert bodies such as the ILO or, in the case of developing countries, with donor countries willing to provide expertise and training as a service.

Notes

[1] The operative paragraphs of Convention No. 129 are reproduced in Annex I.

[2] ILO: *Safety and health in agriculture*, Report IV(2), International Labour Conference, 88th Session, Geneva, 2000.

[3] See ILO: *Encyclopaedia of occupational health and safety,* edited by J. M. Stellman; 4-volume print version and CD-ROM (Geneva, 4th edition, 1998).

LABOUR INSPECTION IN THE NON-COMMERCIAL SERVICES SECTOR

25

25.1 Introduction

The Protocol of 1995 to the Labour Inspection Convention, 1947 (No. 81), extends the application of the provisions of the Convention to all activities in the non-commercial services (NCS) sector, that is, categories of workplaces not considered to be either industrial or commercial.[1]

The definition may therefore include public administration (national, regional or local), the armed services, the police and other security services, prisons, fire brigades and other emergency services, which as a rule are neither industrial nor commercial. It may also include activities such as education, health services, post and telecommunications, railways, harbours and airports, as well as public utilities such as gas, water and electricity supply, waste collection and disposal, and other social, cultural or recreational public services as well as charities.

Subject to a number of conditions, individual ILO member States may exclude wholly or partially:

- the armed services' military or civilian personnel, or both of these categories;
- the police and other public security services; and/or
- prisons services, prison staff or prisoners performing work, or both of these categories.

The duties of labour inspectors in regard to these activities will therefore differ between countries.

25.2 Risks and special considerations

Exposure to risk

Irrespective of the financial or social purpose of their work or their employment status, whether as civil servants or as public or private employees, workers in the NCS sector are entitled to the same degree of protection against risks of injury and ill health to which they are exposed, or vulnerability to unfair employment practices, as those employed in industry or commerce.

This is no minor issue. The NCS sector employs between ten and 50 per cent of the labour force, depending on the country, which translates into hundreds of millions of people worldwide. Available information indicates that NCS employees, however defined, are often afforded a lower standard of labour protection than those employed in other sectors.

In the first place, because many commercial-sector occupations and most types of industrial, transport and agricultural activities are to be found in the NCS sector, employees in the sector are exposed, to a greater or lesser extent, to most of the same risks as those involved in these activities outside the NCS. These risks include inadequately protected machinery, hazardous substances, ionizing radiations, pressure systems, lifting and transport equipment, unsafe access and workplaces, and unhealthy working environments, as well as violations of labour protection legislation concerning other conditions of work.

In addition, many occupations in the NCS sector carry particular and unique risks, including exposure to:

- the effects of uncontrolled research in universities and institutes;
- HIV/AIDS, hepatitis B and viral infections in hospitals, and among police and prison officers;
- violence against the police, prison officials, health workers, social workers and teachers;
- animal attacks against postal employees;
- the risk of injury during training in unarmed combat, firefighting and rescues, riot control and military manoeuvres;
- the risk of gassing, fire and chemical burns to firefighters and to police in traffic accidents;
- injuries related to the lifting of patients and the elderly;
- needle injuries and exposure to anaesthetic gases, sensitizing sterilizing agents and cytotoxic drugs in hospitals;
- the strain of shift work, night work, work during weekends and holidays, and at antisocial hours for all professions with on-call duties;
- mental stress among education and health-care staff, and excessive hours worked by junior doctors and assistants;
- Weil's disease among sewage workers; injuries to refuse collectors and fumes from disposal of chemicals;
- the risk of railway line workers being struck by a train;
- the effects of de-icing fluids at airports;

and many others.

Budgetary constraints

Managers in the NCS sector not only work under most of the same pressures as managers in the private sector, but they also face some different and even unique constraints. Managers everywhere are subject to budgetary restrictions, but in the case of the NCS sector, financial provisions may be determined less by the "market demand" for the service than by political judgements on what the taxpayer is willing to pay, or even by macroeconomic national financial considerations. On the one hand, NCS managers cannot justify increased expenditure in terms of projected increased "sales", because individual members of the public do not benefit from services in direct proportion to what they pay, while, on the other hand, they cannot cease to trade and must ensure the continuity of the service.

Managers nearly always have fewer resources than they would like, and these resources must provide for the service itself and, among other things, for adequate labour protection of their staff and indeed sometimes the general public as well. This conflict of priorities, stemming from legal obligations, makes for hard choices, particularly as managers come under pressure to provide for more health services or more efficient policing. This can often lead to the deferral of what is not seen as urgent, as well as underinvestment in the improvements of buildings and other workplaces or facilities. In some cases, the need to provide adequately for residents in charitable institutions is used to justify poor working conditions because of the threat that the necessary protective expenditure would cause the institution to close, obviously to the detriment of the residents. Employment in the NCS sector therefore does not guarantee a high standard of labour protection; in fact, the reverse is very often the case.

Conflict between the needs of patients or pupils and those of staff poses difficult problems for the labour inspector, particularly when asked by a manager to weigh his or her demands, not against reduced profits, as in the case of a commercial company, but against fewer clinical operations or reduced educational facilities. These are arguments of a different order, and the consequences for inspectors are discussed later in this chapter.

A particular problem arises when labour protection legislation is fully applied for the first time to particular subsectors of the NCS sector. The experience of countries that have done this shows that there will invariably be deficiencies, some of which are serious, and that it will not be possible to rectify them all immediately: priorities will have to be set and resources planned within a programme. This is the moment when advice from the labour inspectorate might well be sought. One approach is to introduce the application of a law to particular subsectors within a stipulated time-frame.

Another approach is to apply the law globally from the outset, in consultation with employers and workers and in coordination with the labour inspectorate, using discretion in setting priorities and progressively ensuring full implementation.

Management considerations

Many organizations or institutions in the NCS sector are structured like industrial or commercial enterprises. However, there is not always the same clear hierarchical management structure through which decisions at the top are transmitted and compliance is monitored. Many scientists, academics or medical consultants working in the NCS sector hold personal appointments with limited accountability. In addition, they work in premises or with equipment for which they are not responsible and for whose standards they may have limited power to influence. They may also be working at the frontiers of knowledge, where precautions are guided by principle rather than established rules. Their lack of accountability and single-minded concentration on the objectives of their work may lead them to expose both themselves and others to hazards. Experience shows that it is not enough to rely upon professional self-discipline, not least because however brilliant such consultants or academics may be in their own field, they are seldom aware of what labour protection involves. Indeed, when told, they may be quite hostile and have to be persuaded into compliance by any means available.

National and internal security

Those responsible for the armed services, for police, internal security services and prisons are understandably concerned about preventing the unauthorized disclosure of confidential information. In applying labour protection to these subsectors of the NCS, countries have found that the problem is far less difficult to resolve than first appears, provided appropriate special arrangements are made. For instance, inspections may be made uniquely by appointment and by inspectors with an appropriate level of security clearance. Documents and reports can remain secure on the relevant premises. There may have to be restrictions on the inspectors' right to take samples of substances and materials. Inspectors may legitimately be precluded from inspecting front-line or active service units or manoeuvres in times of declared tension. Similarly, it may be impossible for them to carry out an inspection during a rescue or a police or prison operation, or the actual fighting of a fire. This would not, however, prevent the labour inspector from (periodically) reviewing, from a labour protection viewpoint, the procedures laid down after a particular incident and investigating what had occurred.

A number of countries currently distinguish between labour inspectors' right to supervise the labour protection of civilians working for the armed services and the rights (if any) of the uniformed personnel itself. In such cases, while military premises employing civilian personnel are open to labour inspection, usually by appointment, other premises and activities are not.

Some countries provide for the inspection of prisons and labour protection rights for prison officers, but this does not extend to the prison inmates themselves. Others provide for the inspection, by appointment, of both prison workshops and premises such as kitchens, laundries or maintenance shops where prisoners may be working.

Training for hazardous occupations

One of the recurrent problems in the NCS sector is how to train people to do a potentially hazardous job without exposing them to unnecessary risk. This problem arises with the armed services, fire brigades and other rescue services, as well as with the police, public security and prison services. On the one hand, training must be sufficiently realistic and thorough to ensure that lessons are learnt the easy way. On the other hand, there is a tendency for management in these services to simply take operational requirements into consideration, a practice which can expose trainees to quite unnecessary and unjustified risks, such as those involved in the use of other trainees rather than dummies when simulating rescues.

While inspectors may have to be precluded from inspecting during actual operations, this should not prevent their examining and discussing training and operational procedures to ensure that hazardous work is prepared for and undertaken with maximum efficiency and minimum risk.

25.3 Who inspects the labour inspectorate?

One consequence of applying Convention No. 81 fully to the NCS sector is that labour inspectorates are themselves subject to inspection. To ensure objective assessment, this should be done in a way that avoids self-inspection. A number of inspectorates have nominated particular field units to inspect the inspectorates' own premises and procedures, or have arrangements made for field units to inspect their neighbouring units in a progressive sequence. Countries with more than one inspectorate may have arrangements to inspect each other's premises.

25.4 The process of inspection in the NCS sector

The impact of changing inspection practices

The traditional approach of labour inspectors, practised over many years, has been to visit enterprises, identify deficiencies, provide advice that is confirmed by letter or notice, check by means of a repeat visit and, if necessary, resort to coercion or punitive action. This technique, however effective, can cast the inspector in the role of unpaid consultant, when, having obtained any necessary advice, it is in the first instance the employer's responsibility to comply. Inspectorates are therefore increasingly looking to industry and commerce to self-regulate and to exercise internal control. Providing free consultancy services on labour protection to every employer is far too costly. New legislation increasingly requires employers to make their own arrangements for access to appropriate advice on labour protection matters. Inspectors may well advise on the criteria for compliance, in other words, the most effective means of complying with legal provisions (Article 3(1)(b) of Convention No. 81), but avoiding technological detail, as their role is to ensure that protection under the law is actually provided.

The second major development has been in the presentation of labour protection to employers, not as a mandatory obligation to be unquestioningly followed, but rather as an essential component of efficient, cost-conscious, quality-oriented, modern management. The International Organization for Standardization (ISO) norms for quality management systems have provoked enormous interest worldwide, initially as a means of assuring satisfaction to the customer, but increasingly enabling the employer to meet working environment and safety and health objectives. It is an approach clearly reflected in some countries' concept of internal control or internal responsibility systems, and in enforcement policies elsewhere.

If the efficient management of labour protection and the working environment is seen as essential to economic and financial success in industry and commerce, it should bring equal benefits to activities in the NCS sector. The methods that any non-commercial service aspiring to efficiency should adopt are: analysing objectives and obligations; setting priorities and planning how to meet them; establishing systems and procedures to ensure quality and consistency; allocating responsibilities; providing for feedback and correction; auditing regularly; and from time to time reviewing the entire system. Labour protection fits neatly into this system as yet another important component that must receive due consideration and appropriate resources.

Seen in this way, the application of labour inspection standards to the NCS sector is not an imposition, but a contribution to quality and efficiency to the satisfaction of employees and the general public.

A time-consuming and complex process

Compared to the process in industry and commerce, labour inspection in the NCS sector tends to be more time-consuming and more complex, not because of its technical content – although, as indicated above, there are many unique risks – but because the inspector is often dealing with another branch of the administration. There are long, often inflexible budgetary processes, the need to note (even if not always to surrender to) political priorities, the public expectation of improved services, the professional independence and commitment of officials, consultants and academics who are reluctant to see funds diverted to the "lower priority" of labour protection, the lack of risk awareness and, lastly, national security.

The labour inspector has to fully possess the knowledge, understanding, diplomacy and determination to face these problems and objections and, if possible, overcome them. This might involve negotiating different timescales for general improvements, or for the removal of various hazards, compromising on physical solutions, or persuading senior officials that intelligent and properly resourced management of labour protection and the pursuit of progressive employment policies contribute to the overall efficiency of the organization, and to the quality of service. However, it is important that the inspector should have the necessary power to request improvements needed and the ability to use them. This may be the only way to influence the political process to make essential additional funds available or, at the very least, to reallocate existing resources. In this manner, the inspector, by giving an independent outsider's opinion, often provides welcome support and strengthens the hand of the NCS sector manager.

Because the use of remedial powers may not be as straightforward as in industry and commerce, and may cause embarrassment, inspectors try to achieve improvement by persuasion and agreement. If this fails, they must be prepared to use whatever coercive or penal instruments exist. For these reasons, labour inspection in the NCS sector is more time-consuming and more complex than in other sectors. Incidentally, it also demands particular skill. The combination of these issues presents labour inspection with a significant challenge.

"Internal" inspection

It is sometimes argued that labour inspection is unnecessary because a particular NCS has exceptionally effective "internal" inspection procedures, an arrangement widely adopted in the armed services as well as railways, postal services and sometimes other utilities. The arguments for this approach are that the relevant officers are usually technically competent, understand the technology and can take account of budgetary constraints and programmes, as well as security considerations. Against this it is argued that these inspections may not be objective enough and that the officials concerned do not have sufficient awareness of the broad range of labour protection matters. Often drawn from the ranks of the service they are called upon to inspect, and part of the line management, they may be insufficiently critical or too lenient towards serious problems. Their awareness of budgetary constraints may unduly influence their recommendations. It is also argued that there is little difference between such an arrangement and the internal labour protection organization of any large private enterprise – which is unquestionably subject to external independent state inspection. More seriously, the future careers of "internal" inspectors often depend on the very officials they must occasionally criticize if they are to be effective. It is therefore clear that these "internal" arrangements are an inadequate substitute for independent, external state labour inspection. Those responsible for labour inspection should remain alert to the weaknesses of these internal systems and the adverse consequences for labour protection standards.

Remedial powers, sanctions and alternative measures

In most countries remedial measures include a variety of mechanisms, such as formal letters pointing out the infraction, enforcement notices requiring action within a specific time or prohibition (stop) notices, or on-the-spot administrative or coercive fines and, as a last resort, criminal prosecution. Many countries allow the application of both administrative and criminal law. While some countries do not permit the criminal prosecution of NCS-sector juridical personnel, others allow prosecution of NCS personnel, including individual directors and managers. Whatever the system, it appears that an effective pattern of remedial notices and punitive sanctions must be in existence, even if sanctions are used infrequently. The absence of these mechanisms means that an NCS-sector establishment will be under far less pressure than private industry or commerce to comply with regulations and/or inspectors' findings, to the point of being able to disregard them at will. If nothing else, inspectors risk losing credibility if they require remedies which the establishment can regularly ignore with impunity. This greatly reduces the effectiveness of any inspection. Admittedly, the value of fining a government ministry or agency is often questioned, on the basis that this merely constitutes a transfer of taxpayers' money from one department to another. At the same time, some instances indicate that the publicity accompanying good example setting may have a strong promotional effect towards improving labour protection.

In almost every country, the recurrent question is: can one arm of the State prosecute another?

In the United Kingdom, the central Government, the armed forces and police can claim "Crown immunity" from prosecution. However, inspectors can issue "Crown enforcement notices" ordering an immediate stop to the work or compliance within a given period. These notices are discussed with trade union representatives and, if not complied with, are pursued by the department responsible for the inspectorate and the corresponding department in the NCS sector, at progressively higher levels, which may, if necessary, proceed all the way to the Cabinet. Even if the procedure seldom has to be fully invoked, its very existence serves to exert sufficient pressure on the NCS-sector unit to comply with the inspectors' requirements. Military personnel can sue the Ministry of Defence for negligence, which is also seen as a spur to improving labour protection management. In practice, the foregoing procedures have enabled inspectors to achieve their labour protection aims.

An alternative means of bringing pressure to bear on NCS bodies is illustrated in the Austrian system of combining administrative measures with publicity. Thus, all deficiencies noted under the federal Worker Protection Act 1994 (amended 1997) must be published, together with the official reaction of the relevant ministry. Serious deficiencies must be reported to the Labour Inspectorate's headquarters and to the relevant NCS-sector minister, who is obliged to comment to the Chief Inspector of Labour about the action taken. Formal demands, in the shape of prohibition notices, are also issued to the relevant minister if action is not taken.

In the United States, the Cabinet member responsible for the OSHA is required to submit an annual report to the President on the safety and health status of individual federal agencies, and continuing disagreements on action taken to implement inspection reports may be submitted to the President for resolution. In addition, federal agency managers' individual performance has to be assessed against their units' labour protection record. Canada appeals to financial self-interest by demonstrating the increased insurance and compensation costs of poor compliance. The Netherlands was able to obtain government agreement to the application of the full range of sanctions to the NCS sector by allowing a lengthy time period for the implementation of relevant legislation, from entry into force to actual application: for instance, some eight years in the case of education and hospital services.

25.5 Employers and trade unions in the NCS sector

Where the State is the employer, the trade unions are seen in many countries as having a particularly important role (as there is usually an above-average degree of unionization in that sector). In many countries, NCS bodies are required or encouraged to establish joint labour protection committees, usually when there are more than a specified number of workers. In Norway and Sweden, career members of the armed forces have trade union safety representatives (although conscripts' representatives have fewer rights). There are also safety representatives and committees in the Netherlands' armed forces. Safety representatives in the NCS sector may be elected from among the employees or appointed by the trade union. Denmark and the United Kingdom, among other countries, have joint sectoral councils or advisory committees to resolve problems and set standards, for instance in the health services, education and transport sectors. The inspectorate in the United Kingdom has a group which maintains a dialogue with the armed services, the fire brigades, and police and prison authorities, as well as the relevant trade unions. In the Netherlands, the Working Environment Subcommittee of the tripartite Social and Economic Council regularly considers labour protection and inspection policy issues, and there are routine requirements to establish safety committees, where more than 35 people are employed in the NCS sector, except that in the case of national, regional and municipal administrations, as well as education, the equivalent consultative bodies have fewer powers than other works councils. (For instance, they cannot demand that the head of a unit undertake expenditure on labour protection in excess of his or her budget and authority.) In the United States, federal agencies are given the opportunity to establish occupational safety and health committees, and where a committee meets OSHA requirements, the OSHA is precluded from conducting "unannounced" inspections. States and territories with OSHA-approved programmes must likewise establish joint committees.

The practice of structured NCS-sector employer/employee collaboration in the field of labour protection and of cooperation with the labour inspectorate (as promoted by Article 5 of Convention No. 81, and paras. 4-7 of Recommendation No. 81) can be perceived as widely accepted in different ILO member States. This cooperation appears to be particularly productive when, despite financial strictures, governments wish to make progress implementing the labour inspection instruments. Applying to the full the Convention's provisions for collaboration between labour inspectors and employers, workers and their organizations, will not only show ways to target limited inspection resources and facilitate inspection visits that take place in a positive and helpful manner, but will also determine rational priorities for government policies for the further development of inspection systems.

25.6 The need for action

The issues under review are therefore of obvious concern to the social partners, and many countries have given considerable attention to labour inspection in the NCS sector. Others, however, seem to have hardly considered the question. Even where legislation seems to apply, in practice little if any inspection is in fact undertaken. Inspections tend to be reactive to complaints or accidents rather than preventive measures. This may be due to a lack of resources or a perception that the NCS sector is not a high-risk area, and therefore not a high priority in the absence of effective powers of enforcement, remedies and sanctions.

The large number of workers involved and the large number of hazards often particular to this sector, the need for equal protection and universal application of existing international standards are reasons that clearly underline the necessity of providing effective labour inspection at all workplaces in the NCS sector. It is also vital that due priority should be given to programming systematic proactive inspection of workplaces throughout the sector.

Notes

[1] The operative paragraphs of the 1995 Protocol are reproduced in Annex I.

LABOUR INSPECTION IN THE CONSTRUCTION INDUSTRY 26

26.1 The problems presented by the construction industry

Characteristics of the industry

In spite of advances in mechanization, the construction industry in every country of the world is labour intensive. It does not lend itself in any significant way to automation, and even prefabrication off site has severe limitations. The greater the size and complexity of the building project, the greater the range of specialist and craft skills required. The amount of activity and the level of employment are directly affected by the local, national and international economic climate. While increased mechanization in terms of lifting and drilling, excavating and mixing has reduced some of the hard physical labour, it has also made possible unusual and innovative designs and introduced new hazards.

Whereas the building and construction trades were for many years a sector in which skill levels were not very high and in which experience and know-how could largely substitute for a lack of basic technical training, this is no longer the case (at least in industrialized countries). The proportion of unskilled workers is on the decline, and in a number of Western European countries is less than that of skilled or highly skilled workers. Overall, however, skill levels in this sector are still lower than their comparable categories in the manufacturing industry. This factor is not unrelated to the persistently high number and gravity of industrial accidents experienced by building and construction workers. From this point of view, unskilled workers are particularly at risk, as they do not have the opportunity to achieve correct mastery of the operational methods which take due account of safety regulations. Experience of trade practices and the required manual operations do not include adequate awareness of the industrial hazards involved. There is thus a serious need for safety training for these categories of workers.

Another contributing factor is the amount of casual and temporary labour employed in the construction industry, a prevailing feature of new forms of personnel management emerging in this sector. Workers are recruited on fixed-term contacts, the length of which is determined by the duration of the building site or the construction project. In industrialized countries, this form of employment, governed by a fixed-term labour contract, is both widespread and legal. In developing or industrializing countries, the proportion of casual workers is increasing and even becoming the main form of employer–employee working relationships. All this has a serious effect on collective labour relations. The high turnover of labour (recruited for the site) and the short service of employees prevent the setting up of normal arrangements for trade union representation at the worksite. The precarious nature of the employment does not allow workers, who might wish to do so, to surmount the legal barriers and set up a structured system of representation. This accounts both for a very low rate of unionization amongst these workers (who may also be afraid of non-renewal of their work contract) and a lack of dynamism in collective labour negotiations at the enterprise level in this sector.

Structure of the industry and employment practices

Generally, the number of large enterprises in the construction industry is smaller than in industry. Small firms, for various reasons, dominate this sector. It is easier for a small firm to respond to market demand by specializing in the service it offers than for a large or medium-sized enterprise to maintain its various departments in full activity, which presupposes the existence of a well-developed organizational structure. Small firms are thus better able to introduce themselves to technical areas of the construction industry and compete for specialized and simplified operations such as finishing work. They carry out minor work, and adapt to the planning and programming of main contractors on large worksites. In fact, the terms "small firm" and "subcontractor" are sometimes interchangeable, because many of these firms work for others. Another factor stimulating the development of small firms in the building industry seems to be the relatively modest amount of set-up investment required.

Self-employment occupies an important place in the building and construction industry. It is widespread in industrialized and developing countries, and those who work on their own account as contractors or subcontractors usually have a considerable part to play in the sector. The existence and development of small firms and self-employment are factors related to the various modes of subcontracting which have become commonplace in the industry. Self-employment and subcontracting are often closely linked, as the self-employed form a kind of extension to the activities of other small enterprises, which therefore avoid the need to take on permanent employees.

First of all, the technical character and divisibility of the various successive operations to be undertaken in a major building operation enable separate job lots to be allocated amongst different specialized enterprises. Secondly, the flexibility the system allows encourages enterprises to entrust work to subcontractors rather than seek out, engage and train employees who will have to be dismissed when the job comes to an end. This commercial bargaining between enterprises tends to restrict the scope of labour relations and frees enterprises from the need to take on personnel they would otherwise require. The drawback to subcontracting, however, is that the bargains struck about work to be performed are all too often based exclusively on considerations of financial profit, reflected in fixed wages and/or time limits for work performed, but prejudicial to the observance of safety requirements on the job.

The client's representative does not always exercise the direction or co-ordination of the multiple operations carried out in these circumstances by self-employed workers, piecework artisans or "licensed" independent workers with due authority. The various forms of subcontracting are themselves subject to evolution and can be practised to excess. From the practice, which has almost always existed in the industry, where main contractors delegate part of their operations to subcontractors for a global payment, there is a shift towards a form of subcontracting which can be described as "serial" or "pyramidal". In such scenarios, the subcontracting firm farms out the same job-lot to another firm, and so on. At the end of the line in this process of delegation, there may be a single self-employed person carrying out the subcontracted work, or several self-employed people working in isolation without any waged employees. It is not always easy to make a clear distinction between this type of work and waged employment, especially when the self-employed have been directly recruited as a result of subcontracting arrangements made between large employers. What chiefly distinguishes the self-employed (bound as they are by the directives and instructions of the subcontracting firms) from other waged workers is their lack of social protection. The onus is on them to contribute to social security schemes and pay their subscriptions for accident insurance, and invariably this does not always happen. They are responsible for their safety training, and for the provision and use of personal protective equipment, responsibilities that employers would have if people performing similar or identical tasks were legally their employees.

Subcontracting work is not the only form of labour division practised by building firms. There are also "labour-only subcontractors". This practice, prohibited in certain countries, consists of one firm recruiting and putting at the disposal of another firm, for an overall payment, a given number of workers responsible for carrying out one or several operations within a fixed time. In many Asian countries, it has been observed that the main firms in the building industry have no permanent employees, apart from a small technical staff to supervise work in progress. Subcontractors employ most operative workers (such as bricklayers, carpenters and drivers), and the majority of construction jobs are carried out in this way. In addition, there are the problems of: casual seasonal workers recruited for short periods and unfamiliar with the plant, processes or people; migrant workers living in makeshift quarters and often unfamiliar with the local language; and clandestine workers, who are particularly vulnerable to accidents and exploitation. In some countries, children are still employed in this industry, often in forms of bonded labour bordering on slavery, and subject to particularly high (fatal) accident rates.

The effect of subcontracting on working conditions

The tendency for small enterprises to proliferate militates against the development of safe working practices in a variety of ways. Self-employed workers have no access to in-house training programmes provided by larger construction firms for their employees. The financial resources of many small firms are meagre and their managerial knowledge, while based on experience, often lacks a theoretical background. Small contractors are unable to provide in-house training or employ professional safety advisers, and frequently have neither the time nor the inclination to keep abreast of legal requirements or technological developments in safety and health. Moreover, the growth of smaller enterprises clearly makes the role of national labour inspectorates more difficult, in that there are significantly more contacts to make for inspection, enforcement and advice than if there were fewer enterprises with a higher average number of workers.

While this multiplicity of firms enables their workforces to be easily dispersed in an increased number of worksites, the concurrent presence of a number of small firms working separately on the same site creates problems in the coordination of occupational safety and health measures, in inequalities between workers and in the allocation of multiple responsibilities. Hazards should be recognized by common consent, not assessed separately to varying standards by individual workers or enterprises. In most cases, however, reactions to a common risk are divergent. On the occasion of each visit, labour inspectors have to unravel the tangle of each enterprise's responsibilities – not necessarily obvious at first glance – and determine which workers belong to which enterprise. On these sites, workers and their supervisors often find themselves working in close proximity with employees of other enterprises whom they do not even know. This fragmentation of the construction industry is regularly a source of concern for the public authorities responsible for the supervision of labour protection regulations and standards compliance.

Some labour inspectorates are concerned about the consequences of the extension of self-employment and subcontracting in the building industry, from the point of view of industrial accidents. While in many countries the number of fatal accidents occurring to wage earners tends to be stable, or is even on the decrease, it has tended to rise sharply among self-employed workers. The tendency is towards fewer accidents overall, with the number of accidents involving major injuries on the increase. And while there is no radical difference between accidents in the construction industry and those occurring in other sectors, it is the working environment where they occur that distinguishes them and increases hazards in so marked a fashion.

Poor general working conditions

Activity in the building industry is subject to the vagaries of the weather and the constraints of climate. Bad weather, apart from the interruptions it causes to the work in hand, also accentuates its arduous character and affects workers' health. The rigours of climate – heat or cold, according to region and time of the year – cause fatigue, aggravate existing hazards and sometimes make brutal inroads on the workers' health (heat stroke or dehydration). This accounts for the fact that workers in the construction industry suffer more often than other workers from a poor state of general health, especially from problems such as bronchitis, back pains or nervous tension, brought on by heavy manual work, often performed in an awkward posture and without protection against bad weather.

Hard, dangerous or unhealthy work is frequently found in the building industry. Workers responsible for carrying out such work are frequently compensated by way of cash bonuses. For certain kinds of work carried out in unhealthy regions, the working day is either reduced or frequent rest periods are allowed in the course of work. The seasonal character of the employment means that many workers recruited on the job have been working for a certain length of time in some other sector (agriculture), are in poor physical condition and have forgotten the hazards to which they are to be exposed.

Working hours in the construction industry vary to a notable extent, but on average they are higher than in other branches of industry. This is due to factors already enumerated such as the nature of the work, its urgency (frequently with fixed time limits for completion and heavy penalties for failure to meet the deadline), large numbers of workers of different trades operating simultane-ously on the same site and dependence on climatic conditions. Working hours are rarely spread out in a regular fashion throughout the year, and in some seasonal periods, excessive hours are not uncommon. Regulations and collective agreements, when they exist, often confine themselves to fixing the length of the working day. They set limits to the number of overtime hours and prescribe limitations, circumstances and restrictions (with prior authorization by the labour inspectorate) to which enterprises wishing to recover hours lost because of bad weather are required to observe. In practice, these rules are often infringed, as are those regulating weekly rest periods and annual paid holidays.

The fact that construction sites are frequently temporary, mobile and situated in remote areas has repercussions on essential matters such as housing, meals arrangements at the worksite, access to basic necessities, and reliable means of transport between living quarters and construction sites. Other services that need to be provided are decent sanitary facilities and the welfare services that the location and duration of the worksite may require. Whilst the situation in this respect has improved in most industrialized countries, developing countries often have a long way to go in the provision of these welfare services.

Employment in the construction trade is high risk compared to most other employment. Fatal accidents, falls, noise, vibrations, chemical exposure and dust are well-known hazards in the traditional working environment of con-struction workers.

Occupational ill health

In the past, risks to health encountered in construction have not generally been given priority attention, their importance being often masked by the frequency and gravity of occupational accidents. In addition, it is difficult to identify the causes and trace the evolution of occupational diseases in this industry, given the geographical mobility of the workforce, its turnover and structural composition, and the high proportion of temporary and migrant workers. The main occupa-tional diseases are those affecting the respiratory systems, in particular pneumoconiosis produced by inhaling dust and fibres. The risk of contracting silicosis is one to which bricklayers and workers employed in drilling concrete, the machine cutting of various materials and the polishing of marble and other stones are particularly exposed. The number of cases of silicosis is on the decline in some countries, but this is not a general tendency in developing countries.

As a result of the draconian measures taken to prohibit the use of asbestos as an insulating material and in the manufacture of fibro-cement products, the dangers of asbestosis and asbestos-induced cancer have been reduced in a growing number of countries, but have by no means disappeared altogether. Although new insulating work using materials including asbestos has been practically eliminatcd, the demolition of buildings where it was used in the form of asbestos cement or fibre-board still presents a very high risk. This applies not only to those engaged in demolition, but also maintenance workers, such as electricians and plumbers, who may unknowingly disturb asbestos material in their work. Because the symptoms only manifest themselves some 15 to 20 years after exposure, asbestosis, lung cancer and mesothelioma continue to figure in the list of occupational diseases typical of the building industry. In developing countries, a substantial information campaign on these risks is a priority if these diseases are to be prevented.

Skin diseases, especially forms of dermatitis caused by contact, make up an important proportion of the total number of occupational diseases in the construction industry. They are linked to the growing use of irritant or toxic chemical substances such as solvents in paints, adhesives, sealants and the products used for the protective treatment of wood, the oils used in shuttering work, soluble chromes and other substances used in the making and application of concrete. Cement dust affects large numbers of workers. The nature of the work on site in continually changing locations makes it much more difficult to use normal protective measures such as local exhaust ventilation. More reliance has to be placed on personal protective equipment, with all the problems involved in ensuring – let alone enforcing – its correct use.

Noise-induced hearing loss affects many drivers, drillers and demolition workers. Those working with vibrating tools, such as pneumatic chisels, drills and compactors, are exposed to the risk of vibration-induced white finger or hand–arm vibration syndrome (HAVS).

The heavy physical effort involved in heavy lifting and awkward handling contributes to a variety of spinal injuries and deterioration. This not only affects the workers' quality of life, but may also compel their early retirement, with all the adverse social and financial consequences. Finally, in recent years there has been increasing concern about levels of stress in construction workers, as well as bullying.

26.2 Special international labour standards

General remarks

From more than 180 Conventions and 190 Recommendations adopted by the International Labour Organization, almost half either concern or cover the construction industry. At national levels, coverage presupposes ratification.

While Labour Inspection Convention, 1947 (No. 81), which clearly covers the building and construction industry, has been ratified by 128 ILO member States, the record is less positive for other standards with a direct impact on the sector. The Occupational Safety and Health Convention, 1981 (No. 155), had had only 37 ratifications, and the Safety Provisions (Building) Convention, 1937 (No. 62), and the Safety and Health in Construction Convention, 1988 (No. 167), have been ratified by 30 and 15 member States respectively. Convention No. 167, adopted 50 years after Convention No. 62, has been revised and thus largely supersedes the first international standard specific to the building industry. It is perhaps useful to recall some of its main provisions.

Convention No. 167

The Convention applies to all construction activities, building, civil engineering, and erection and dismantling work, including any process, operation or transport on a construction site, from the preparation of the site to the completion of the project, and applies also to self-employed persons.

It contains general provisions, where the most representative organizations of employers and workers concerned shall be consulted on the measures to be taken to give effect to the provisions of the Convention.

Whenever two or more employers undertake activities simultaneously at one construction site:

- the principal contractor, or other person or body with actual control over or primary responsibility for overall construction site activities, should be responsible for coordinating the prescribed safety and health measures and, in so far as is compatible with national laws and regulations, for ensuring compliance with such measures;
- each employer should remain responsible for the application of the prescribed measures for the workers placed under his or her authority.

Furthermore, those concerned with the design and planning of a construction project should take into account the safety and health of the construction workers in accordance with national laws, regulations and practice.

National laws or regulations should provide workers with the right and the duty, at any workplace, to participate in ensuring safe working conditions concerning their control over the equipment and methods of work, and to express views on the working procedures adopted that may affect safety and health.

National laws or regulations should ensure that workers are obliged to:

- cooperate as closely as possible with their employer in the application of the prescribed safety and health measures;
- take reasonable care for their own safety and health and that of other people who may be affected by their acts or omissions at work;
- use facilities placed at their disposal and not misuse anything provided for their own protection or the protection of others;
- report immediately to their direct supervisor, and to the workers' safety representative where one exists, any situation which they believe could present a risk, and which they cannot properly deal with themselves;
- comply with the prescribed safety and health measures.

Finally, national laws or regulations should provide workers with the right to remove themselves from danger when they have good reason to believe that there is an imminent and serious danger to their safety or health, and with the duty to inform the supervisor immediately. Where there is an imminent danger to the safety of workers, the employer shall take immediate steps to stop the operation and evacuate workers as appropriate.

The Convention contains further provisions on:

- the safety of workplaces;
- scaffolds and ladders;
- lifting appliances and gear;
- transport, earth-moving and materials-handling equipment;
- plant, machinery, equipment and hand tools;
- work at heights, including roof work;
- excavations, shafts, earthworks, underground works and tunnels;
- cofferdams and caissons;
- work in compressed air;
- structural frames and formwork;
- work over water;
- demolition;
- lighting;
- electricity; and
- explosives.

On health hazards, the Convention states that:

- Where a worker is liable to be exposed to any chemical, physical or biological hazard to such an extent that it is liable to be dangerous to health, appropriate preventive measures should be taken against such exposure.
- The preventive measures referred to above should comprise:

- the replacement of hazardous substances by harmless or less hazardous substances wherever possible;
- technical measures applied to the plant, machinery, equipment or process; or
- where it is not possible to comply with the abovementioned measures, other effective measures including the use of personal protective equipment and protective clothing.

- Where workers are required to enter an area in which a toxic or harmful substance may be present, or in which there may be an oxygen deficiency, or a flammable atmosphere, adequate measures should be taken to guard against danger.
- Waste should not be destroyed or otherwise disposed of on a construction site in a manner liable to be injurious to health.

Furthermore, there are provisions on:

- fire precautions;
- personal protective equipment and protective clothing;
- first aid;
- welfare;
- information and training; and
- reporting of accidents and diseases.

Finally, on implementation, Convention No. 167 prescribes that each member State shall:

- take all necessary measures, including the provision of appropriate penalties and corrective measures, to ensure the effective enforcement of the provisions of the Convention;
- provide appropriate inspection services to supervise the application of the measures to be taken in pursuance of the Convention and provide these services with the resources necessary for the accomplishment of their task, or satisfy itself that appropriate inspection is carried out.

Recommendation No. 175

Convention No. 167 is accompanied by the Safety and Health in Construction Recommendation, 1988 (No. 175), which amplifies it by a set of general provisions:

- National laws or regulations should require that employers and self-employed persons have a general duty to provide a safe and healthy workplace and to comply with the prescribed safety and health measures.

- The measures to be taken to ensure that there is organized cooperation between employers and workers to promote safety and health at construction sites should be prescribed by national laws or regulations or by the competent authority.

Such measures should include the:

- establishment of safety and health committees representative of employers and workers with such powers and duties as may be prescribed;
- election or appointment of workers' safety delegates with such powers and duties as may be prescribed;
- appointment by the employer of suitably qualified and experienced persons to promote safety and health; and
- the training of safety delegates and safety committee members.

This Recommendation contains provisions on preventive and protective measures, safety at workplaces, scaffolds, transport, health hazards and welfare, but in a non-binding manner, giving guidance for ILO member States wishing to go beyond the (minimum) standards of Convention No. 167, and orientation for all those who have not yet ratified it.

Other international labour standards

As already briefly mentioned, there are a considerable number of other Conventions, both "solitary" and with an accompanying Recommendation, with a direct impact on the construction industry. Although all international labour standards have their own specific importance, perhaps the most important Conventions in this context, besides the fundamental rights embodied in the ILO "core" Conventions, are:

- the Guarding of Machinery Convention, 1963 (No. 119);
- the Occupational Cancer Convention, 1974 (No. 139);
- the Working Environment (Air Pollution, Noise and Vibration) Convention, 1977 (No. 148);
- the Occupational Health Services Convention, 1985 (No. 161);
- the Asbestos Convention, 1986 (No. 162).

Lastly, two core Conventions should be specifically mentioned, as the construction industry in a number of developing and even developed countries is particularly prone to violating them, namely the two ILO standards on child labour: the Minimum Age Convention, 1973 (No. 138), and the Worst Forms of Child Labour Convention, 1999 (No. 182), which specifically forbids children and young people to work in high-hazard workplaces.

26.3 Labour inspection systems

Non-specialized or specialized?

Different inspection systems handle labour problems in the construction industry in different ways. Nevertheless, the prevailing tendency is for the labour inspectorate to be generalists and for inspectors' visits to building firms and sites to be just one part of a wide range of duties, covering either all major labour inspection functions or specifically occupational safety and health matters, plus the whole range of activities in this and all other industrial sectors. Some countries, however, have a specialist labour inspectorate service for the building and construction industry.

In non-specialized systems, the labour inspectorate officials may be generalists, with no special technical competence regarding activities in the building industry, or they may be officials with some technical training, including professional knowledge corresponding to the technical requirements of the construction sector. In some countries, the labour inspectors responsible for visiting building sites are generally recruited as a result of a competition based on knowledge of law and economics, and are not, at the outset, trained to work in this branch of industry. Sometimes engineers are recruited for inspection duties, but this is not a dominant characteristic of labour inspectorate recruitment. Other countries strengthen the technical elements in their labour inspectorates by recruiting inspectors with high technical qualifications, even if there are no specialist labour inspectorate services to which they can be assigned. Generally, in countries where there is no specialized labour inspectorate for the building industry, there are technical support services on which inspectors can call to deal with a problem that goes beyond their personal competence.

In specialized systems, inspectors trained in the techniques of building and construction are exclusively assigned to supervisory duties in that industry. This indicates an awareness on the part of the countries concerned (in their overall policies for workers' protection and the prevention of occupational risks) of the special hazards encountered in this sector. It is a solution which appears to offer the advantage of enabling these inspectors to develop and enhance their knowledge of the questions and problems to be found within the confines of this sector of activity. This built-in technical specialization allows for greater concentration of administrative resources, and better follow-up of waged employment on worksites by visits, which in principle occur more frequently and are in greater depth. In most cases, this specialization results in labour inspectors dealing essentially with questions of a technical character concerning industrial safety and health. The problems encountered by workers and employers in the field of industrial relations (conflicts, complaints, dispute settlements) and of working conditions other than those affecting safety and health (negotiations, wages, working hours, holidays and trade union rights) are usually dealt with by other bodies.

Advantages and disadvantages

Generalist integrated systems present some obvious advantages. Their organization is fairly simple and homogeneous, as in each geographical area every kind of activity and enterprise is subject to the control of a single official, whose responsibilities cover activities in the building and construction industry and all other branches of industry. This official's knowledge and competence usually extend to all the questions and problems relating to safety and health, working conditions, working hours, trade union rights, and collective and individual trade disputes. When employees or their representatives approach the labour inspectorate, they can deal with a single interlocutor who is empowered to attend to all their difficulties in every aspect of employment. The inspectors must be well trained, as they have to simultaneously tackle a wide variety of issues, ranging from technical to medical to legal. Therefore, insufficient means, especially financial, do not always allow generalist systems to function to their full capacity.

In most English-speaking countries in Africa, Asia and the Caribbean, the generalist system (in terms of inspection of the construction industry) is still characterized by a dichotomy between labour and factory inspectorates. This split, more often than not, results in a waste of resources, administrative overlaps, competitive friction, and ensuing loss of efficiency and diminishing overall labour protection. Visits to workplaces will always be few and far between, and this is even more true of the construction industry with its numerous small, mobile and temporary worksites. As and when an inspector does visit a site, there seems to be little justification to limit his or her responsibilities and interventions only to some labour protection problems. Workers rarely understand such a fragmented and limited approach. Indeed, the experience in many countries shows that dual inspectorates serve mainly the needs of the bureaucracy and not those of the workforce.

Labour inspectors specializing in the building industry have the equally obvious task, especially when recruited from former members of the trade, of enabling inspection visits to be conducted in greater technical depth. Qualified staff, generally trained technicians and engineers, have no difficulty in dealing with technical problems and are respected by architects, main contractors, builders and research departments. These specialized inspectors combine a level of knowledge which enables them to deal quickly with difficult problems of safety and health with an "insider's view" of accepted trade practices on the spot. They know the part played by each actor on a construction site, how relationships are worked out between those who design the project and those who carry it out, and the operational methods in use. However, this type of inspection, although it may be more effective in ensuring compliance with safety and health regulations, has its limitations with regard to compliance with other areas of labour legislation. The inspectors' competence is limited to their technical field, and more often than not excludes other subjects dealt with by a country's labour protection legislation. The result is that several inspectors from different services may have to be called in to deal with questions relating to the same worksite. Workers as well as employers are reluctant to accept this separation of services and the plurality of competent intervening authorities it involves. Another point to note is that if the labour inspectorate is to preserve the effectiveness of its supervisory system, it must ensure that the activities of its different services are well coordinated. Finally, developing countries encounter difficulties in adopting these inspection systems, as they are expensive in terms of the technical training required, and there are often no engineering or technical schools to train inspectors.

The role of the social partners

The role of workers' and employers' organizations is crucial in regard to safety and health in construction, as in all other sectors, and Articles 3, 10 and 11 of Convention No. 167, as well as para. 6 of Recommendation No. 175, clearly give due consideration to this fact. However, it is necessary to note the particular difficulties in establishing effective safety committees and attracting competent safety representatives in the construction industry.

Many countries have legislation providing for safety committees where more than a certain number of workers are employed. In construction work the only answer is to have a site committee. However, with a multiplicity of small employers and sometimes a main contractor who has few direct employees but merely coordinates the work of subcontractors, special provisions must be made. One approach has been to make the main contractor responsible for organizing safety measures. Similarly, with the decline in trade union membership and numerous self-employed or casual workers, it is difficult to identify potential safety representatives or constitute safety and health committees. Whilst they could be particularly helpful in a potentially hazardous and continually changing worksite, few people feel any commitment to this role.

26.4 New legislative strategies

The need for a new approach

With a fixed industrial establishment, one body is in clear control; the physical and legal and operational boundaries are well demarcated; physical conditions and workforce provisions (particularly supervision) are relatively permanent; and the public is almost always remote from the workplace. On construction sites, however, the situation is quite the reverse. In many cases there will be a multiplicity of employers with responsibilities depending upon the contractual chain. The client will determine the funds available and the timetable; the workforce will be largely casual; and special efforts will be required to exclude the public from the site after and during working hours.

When these difficulties are considered, it is small wonder that routine controls of good management, which alone reduce the toll of accidents and ill health, are not as effective as in other sectors. Indeed, given the withdrawal from direct employment by so many larger firms, the tide has turned on the improvements needed.

An example of one difficulty is where the law requires the employer of the workforce to substitute safe or less dangerous substances for dangerous ones in, say, surface coatings. Yet employers, themselves bound under civil law to perform specifications drawn up by others, are not in apparent violation of "safety and health at work" legislation.

Various strategies have therefore been developed over the past decade. The approach of the EU, in its Temporary or Mobile Construction Sites Directive (92/57/EEC),[1] has been to favour the statutory appointment of a manager carrying ultimate on-site safety and health responsibility.

The German approach

The German Ordinance for Construction Sites 1998 is primarily addressed to the clients or customers for whom the building is being constructed. They are the principal contact for all contractors on site. Their most important duty consists of appointing "coordinators of safety and health". The essential task of coordinators, as authorized experts, is to ensure that "safety and health organization is part of the management system of a building project". They are responsible for developing a concept for safety and health policy for managers responsible for the execution of construction. It is of great importance that the preparation of the policy, based on legal principles, takes place at the planning stage of a building project. During project execution, the coordination task consists of keeping the safety and health concept alive. To achieve this, the coordinators deliver their concept to the contractors by handing out a safety and health protection plan (SHP). This "schedule" should contain essential information making it easier for individual civil engineers (contract supervisors), responsible for the construction of the building, to fulfil their management obligations.

Both client and contractor are responsible for safety and health, the customer as duty holder of the Ordinance and the contractor as an independent organizational unit. In creating effective management, which must include safety and health, they both fulfil their general legal duty to ensure that "third parties" are safe at all times, as well as the welfare and safety obligations for the contractors' own employees. Put simply, this involves organization, staff selection and supervisory tasks with their corresponding responsibilities. Managers, employed by client and contractor, are responsible for performing their management duties correctly. They are "guarantors" for safety and health. The coordinators have to support them with their organizational input.

Before starting construction, the customer must make sure that the (outside) contractor is instructed on local and operational risks. These instructions are addressed to every contractor, who is responsible for ensuring that the information is passed on to employees. Contractors must guarantee that their own competent supervisor is acquainted with the local risks and is available on site. Furthermore, contractors may only deploy staff who have first been instructed by them or by their management on safe behaviour, as well as on any particular risks.

Both customer and contractor have a basic obligation to employ staff with sufficient knowledge, experience and reliability. Furthermore, the customer has to select a qualified contractor who is able to fulfil the obligations, but may not necessarily be the cheapest. Similarly, the contractor has the same obligations towards subcontractors: the contractor is responsible for contractual partners, even if the customer has given consent to hire them.

Apart from the supervision of their own employees, both customer and contractor have to ensure that their contractors (or subcontractors) perform their particular duties correctly. They have an obligation to the independent outside company to provide "additional safety surveillance". Irrespective of the overriding responsibility of the contractor/subcontractor for its own employees, the customer/hiring contractor must also intervene in cases of "obvious" safety violations. The customer/hiring contractor is obliged to stop any ongoing dangerous work, especially if third parties are involved.

The United Kingdom approach

Since 1994, United Kingdom legislation has placed specific requirements on clients, or their agents, to appoint a planning supervisor and a principal contractor for each project. They may be the same person but must be competent in both roles. The planning supervisor must give due notice of the project to the inspectorate. Anyone appointing designers must ascertain their competence, resources and knowledge of construction processes, and safety and health requirements. Similarly, the person making the appointment must check the competency of contractors and subcontractors.

Construction may not start until the planning supervisor has ensured that a safety and health plan has been prepared, which includes arrangements for managing the project and monitoring compliance with legislation. The designer must also adhere to specific requirements to avoid foreseeable risks during the construction phase and after the structure is completed. Finally, the planning supervisor must ensure that the client is provided with a safety and health file with all the necessary information to ensure safety and health during or after onstruction.

A separate voluntary initiative is the development of a "construction safety passport", which details the training received by individual workers and gives them a preferential position in obtaining employment.

26.5 Inspection, enforcement and persuasion

Notification

In most countries legislation requires notification of sites likely to last a certain period of time or of contracts over a certain value. Many countries also require pre-notification of particular processes, especially the stripping of asbestos. In view of the risks and the need for stringent precautions, this enables the inspector to visit and check compliance. Nevertheless, even in countries where workplace management information systems have been highly developed, it is not easy to achieve systematic and complete follow-up of information received about building sites, because of their short-lived and shifting character. Whereas it is easy to classify and list details of an enterprise whose headquarters and structures are known and to build up information through multiple visits by labour inspectors, the "fleeting" nature of a building site is an impediment to the communication and exploitation of information concerning it. The inspectorate must therefore be vigilant and cooperate with planning authorities to ensure that it is aware of new sites.

Planning inspection

Clear guidance should be given to field units on priorities for the year. This may include sites of a particular size, projects of a particular character, the use of particular plant or processes (such as tunneling or demolition), which may have caused problems in the past, or sites likely to be particularly hazardous to health (for example, asbestos stripping).

Many countries have found it effective to target a particular area or town and deploy extra inspectors for "blanket coverage". Letters to all local contractors may precede such campaigns, and advertising in the press can attract the attention of the local media, particularly if widespread punitive measures are found necessary.

It is important that "generalist" inspectorates allocate specific time to oversee safety and health in construction, otherwise time will be allocated to more immediate industrial relations issues or more easily identified industrial enterprises.

Balancing advice and enforcement

Convention No. 81 gives the labour inspectors the principal task of ensuring compliance with legal provisions, and this entails providing advice and recommendations or taking enforcement action to repress infringements of the law in the enterprises inspected. The Convention, in fact, requires the labour inspectorate to ensure that all provisions relating to workers' protection and working conditions are complied with, and to supply technical information and advice to employers and workers on the most effective means of complying with any legal requirements. For three reason, the supervisory and advisory functions of compliance enforcement are, in practice, inseparable.

First, in the course of visits to enterprises and worksites the technically highly equipped inspectorate is naturally requested by employers' and workers' representatives or members of safety committees to suggest solutions to problems, propose a choice of plant to be installed, or give advice on protective or safety equipment. In these cases, the inspector can help to put a series of preventive measures into effect.

Second, inspectors are aware that they will achieve compliance with the legal requirement in question more quickly through advice or warning than by using other measures. The kind of relationship between the labour inspector and the enterprise or worksite manager tends to influence the choice of an inspection follow-up. The prospect of a slow and cumbersome court procedure, with a doubtful outcome or with fines considered derisory, frequently deters labour inspectors from initiating legal action against the employer, especially if the work is to be of short duration. The effect of all this is to minimize recourse to legal action.

The third reason may be the expressed preference of lawmakers or public authorities for using the advisory as distinct from the "policing" function in law enforcement.

However, contractors who do not comply, for whatever reason, must not be allowed to gain a competitive advantage over those who do provide proper scaffolding, adequate and safe equipment and health protection. This is in the interest of both the workers and of law-abiding employers. The progressive stages of coercive actions vary from country to country but may include a variety of measures. Warning notices constitute the first stage and, although they are the least severe, they are perhaps the most compelling for the enterprise. They enable the inspecting official to assure that the irregularities noted in the course of visits to worksites will have been eliminated within a given period of time, as required by the law.

Many countries have formal "enforcement" or improvement notices requiring the employer to comply with the law within a given stated period. Within the time limit allowed, employers may generally appeal against such a notice. Failure to comply may well lead to prosecution. It can be argued, however, that such notices are of limited value on construction sites where matters need to be rectified quickly.

More effective in many countries is the power to stop a particular unsafe tool, machine (ladder, crane and so on) or process on the whole site, but this power can generally only be invoked only where there is an immediate risk of serious bodily injury.

In some countries, the labour inspection service can impose administrative fines on enterprises. On the one hand, this is a questionable option in so far as the administration then has the power to supervise the application of the law and to penalize its violation. It saps the principle of the separation of the administrative and judicial powers. On the other hand, it has the advantage of both de-penalizing the sanctions procedure and being much more swift, and therefore more effective.

Finally, almost all labour inspection systems have the right to initiate or undertake legal action. Recourse to this right varies from one country to another according to professional practice and the relative seriousness of the infringements observed. In general, however, it seems to be exercised more severely in the building and construction industry than elsewhere in the economy. This is probably due to the more serious consequences of breaches of the law on safety levels, occupational hazards and the physical integrity of the workers. Given the changing nature of work situations on the same site, the frequency and repetition of breaches of regulations are likely to be higher; for example, as a building rises in height from one floor to another and the problem of the absence of guard-rails is renewed at every stage of the work. This is not the same as the safety considerations affecting a worker in a fixed post in industry whose exposure is relatively easy to assess on the spot. Prosecution, particularly if heavy fines are imposed, can sometimes be the only way to change the attitude and policies of uncooperative contractors. The resulting publicity can also adversely affect the public image of the company, and this can have a highly preventive impact.

Influencing other players

Developments in EC and national laws have made it necessary to alert manufacturers and suppliers, designers and architects, customers and clients, as well as contractors, to their new obligations.

Conferences and seminars, high-level discussions with professional institutions, reports and guidance publications, and the use of professional journals and the media, are all means of influencing the attitudes and practices that can affect the safety and health of those who work in and benefit from the construction industry.

Note

[1] Council Directive 92/57/EEC of 24 June 1992 on the implementation of minimum safety and health requirements at temporary or mobile construction sites.

LABOUR INSPECTION AND MAJOR HAZARDS PREVENTION 27

27.1 Special considerations

Fires, explosions and the release of toxic gases can cause death and injuries to workers and to the public, resulting in the evacuation of communities and adversely affecting the environment as a whole. Past disasters, known collo-quially as "Basel", "Bhopal", "Flixborough", "Mexico City" and "Seveso", gave rise to the terms "major hazards" and "major hazard control", which have become a pressing global issue. The potential for major accidents caused by increased production, storage and use of dangerous substances requires a well-defined and systematic approach to prevent resultant disasters. Typical accidents involve the leakage of flammable material that mixes with air to form a flammable vapour cloud, with the cloud drifting to a source of ignition causing a fire or explosion. Alternatively, the leakage of toxic material results in the formation of a toxic vapour cloud, which then drifts. In both cases the sites and populated areas may be affected.

In the case of the release of flammable materials, the greatest danger arises from the sudden massive escape of volatile liquids or gases producing a large cloud of flammable and possibly explosive vapour. If ignited, the effects of combustion could lead to a large number of casualties, and wholesale damage on site and beyond its boundaries. The sudden release of very large quantities of toxic material has the potential to cause deaths and severe injuries at a much greater distance, but the actual number of casualties would depend on the population density in the path of the cloud and the effectiveness of emergency arrangements. Some installations or groups of installations pose both types of threat, which could cause an escalation of the disaster, sometimes referred to as the "domino effect".

International legislation

In response to these concerns, the Council of the European Communities (EC) in 1982 issued a Directive on major accidents hazards of certain industrial activities ("the Seveso Directive"), subsequently revised by the EU and published as Council Directive 96/82/EC of 9 December 1996 on the control of major-accident hazards involving dangerous substances.

After extensive consultation, the ILO's International Labour Conference adopted the Prevention of Major Industrial Accidents Convention, 1993 (No. 174), and Recommendation, 1993 (No. 181). Earlier, in 1988, the ILO had published a practical manual, *Major hazard control*,[1] giving comprehensive and authoritative guidance on this issue and followed up in 1991 with a code of practice, *Prevention of major industrial accidents*.[2]

The purpose of this chapter is not to provide guidance on the mechanisms and processes used to control major hazards, but to alert senior labour inspection managers and others to the special problems presented to labour inspectorates by the control of major hazards, and to describe some ways in which various countries have attempted to solve them. The processes of oversight and enforcement in such installations require new knowledge, new contacts and new skills, in addition to those involved in the normal process of labour inspection.

Articles 18 and 19 of Convention No. 174 are worth quoting in full.

Article 18

The competent authority shall have properly qualified and trained staff with the appropriate skills, and sufficient technical and professional support, to inspect, investigate, assess, and advise on the matters dealt with in this Convention and to ensure compliance with national laws and regulations.

Representatives of the employer and representatives of the workers of a major hazard installation shall have the opportunity to accompany inspectors supervising the application of the measures prescribed in pursuance of this Convention, unless the inspectors consider, in the light of the general instructions of the competent authority, that this may be prejudicial to the performance of their duties.

Article 19

The competent authority shall have the right to suspend any operation which poses an imminent threat of a major accident.

The scale of potentially disastrous consequences and the evident failure of traditional inspection methods to prevent disasters in the past justify a different approach. This requires a great degree of expertise to effectively comprehend the hazards and their possible interaction, to systematically and comprehensively identify possible causes of failure, to assess the risks and consequences of failure occurring, and to have confidence in the preventive and precautionary measures adopted.

The potential risk to the public necessitates that the inspector become involved in the provision of information outside the installation; ensuring cooperation between the various emergency authorities; planning their response strategy; and collaborating with planning authorities in the design of special controls in respect of developments within and in the vicinity of the enterprise.

The scale of the hazards and the seriousness of the consequences of any failure in preventive measures render it inappropriate for a labour inspectorate to treat these installations in a conventional manner by inspecting them from time to time. The approach adopted in some extremely high-hazard plants, such as nuclear installations, has been to institute a licensing regime. This is extremely resource intensive for the inspectorate and, because a positive decision has to be taken to approve the plant and its procedures, inevitably results in the inspectorate, to some extent, sharing responsibility for safety with the plant management.

Because of the number of major hazard installations in nuclear plants, competent authorities have adopted a "half-way" procedure requiring management to provide safety reports or safety cases for both existing and proposed plants. The inspectorate then selectively examines the safety report, and assesses its credibility and the adequacy of the plant and procedures described. Approval is only implied when the inspectorate does not require further action.

In short, the international approach to the control of major hazards involves:

- the identification of installations presenting, or liable to present, a major hazard, the recognition of this fact by the operator concerned and its notification to the relevant authorities;
- measures of prevention and control achieved by operators assessing their processes in order to determine the hazards and risks, and then using this information to ensure that appropriate precautions are taken to secure safe operations; and
- mitigation measures, including separating vulnerable populations from hazardous installations through land-use planning controls, on-and-off-site emergency plans to provide for effective responses to major accidents, and warnings to the general public about the potential hazards and action to be taken in an emergency.

Consequences for the labour inspectorate

A different legislative approach requires a different process of inspection, involving:

- an in-depth understanding of the technicalities of the hazards and the requisite precautions, in assessing the safety report;
- a support team of specialists or consultants;
- clear guidance from senior inspectorate management on the approach to the assessment of the safety report; and
- appropriate audit and inspection on the ground.

The implications for the inspectorate are discussed in sections 27.3 and 27.4.

27.2 Key elements of major hazard control

Legislation

Convention No. 174, together with its associated Recommendation No. 181, represent not only highly practical documents but also a summation of the experience of many countries which have sought to legislate on this subject. They provide a ready template for use by any national administration wishing to do the same.

Within the EU, Council Directive 96/82/EC on the control of major-accidents hazards involving dangerous substances is transposed into national legislation. In both the Convention and the Directive, the key element is the obligation of the employer or operator to submit a safety report.

Identifying major hazard installations

The national legislation will have defined, by substance, size, quantity, throughput, process and/or location, installations that fall within the definition of major hazards, as well as a system for identifying them and requiring their notification. Labour inspectorates will need to remain alert to the possibility that installations, previously below the threshold of limits, may gradually increase production or storage, or that there may be processes or storages below the limits which, in the event of failure, could interact and thus call for a specialist assessment and, possibly, exceptional treatment.

The safety report

The safety report is the key element in the control of major hazards. The employer or operator must demonstrate that they have identified and assessed all relevant risks and have taken all the necessary steps to reduce these risks to a level as low as reasonably practicable. Common features of all safety regimes include the following:

- The operator of the installation, in other words, the person responsible for its safe operation, must produce the safety report. Only the operator has the in-depth knowledge required to analyse what could go wrong and to put in place the appropriate controls, both hardware and managerial.
- The safety report must identify the safety-critical aspects of the installation, both technical (in terms of design, construction, operation and maintenance) and managerial (in terms of training, supervision and procedures).
- Appropriate performance standards expressed in qualitative or quantitative terms must be established. These should cover the performance required of a system, an item of equipment, a person or procedure, so that both the operator and regulator can effectively assess the performance of both the technical and managerial systems.

The safety report is then scrutinized by a competent and independent regulator, usually the labour inspectorate.

Benefits to the operator

In practice, it has been found that the process of preparing a safety report enhances the operators' own understanding of the hazards and risks, and their knowledge of the technical and managerial controls required to manage them. Sometimes the preparation of the safety report is the first time that an operator has systematically analysed how the installation is designed, built and operated, and often the process of preparing the document has led to improvements being identified and implemented before it is even submitted.

Consequently, the operator may be able to reduce the quantity of hazardous substances on site and the inspector may be to instruct the operator to improve and formalize its safety management system. The process of preparing and reviewing safety reports provides both the driving force and framework to identify and to assess areas of improvement, and to prepare and agree on programmes of action.

Accident reporting

National legislation usually requires the submission of a detailed report following a significant accident or incident. In the event of an escape of toxic gases, the labour inspectorate may be the only external agency suitably equipped and resourced to carry out the requisite tests. The inspectorate will have a crucial involvement in the aftermath of an accident, ensuring that affected areas are rehabilitated safely.

Information for the public

Uniquely in the case of major hazards, the public in the vicinity of a designated installation must receive certain information. This obligation is normally placed on the employer or operator, but there may be a certain reluctance to explain the scale of the potential hazards and the vital importance of complying with guidance on how to behave in the event of an emergency. The labour inspectorate will therefore have to check that the information is presented fairly and clearly.

However, the experience of some countries is that the public in the vicinity of an established plant are already familiar, perhaps through employees in the family, with some of the risks and respond calmly if they perceive management as honest and open. Some companies make public presentations and invite people living nearby to "open days" at the plant to demonstrate their competence and commitment to safety.

27.3 The inspectorate's response to the safety report

The safety report

The fact that the inspectorate is presented with a detailed report describing the plant, processes and procedures presents the inspector with a task, indeed a challenge, quite different from the processing of a conventional inspection in which the inspector observes, questions and listens. While inspectors usually ask about various stages of processes and procedures, their knowledge, experience and prior observation, as well as their assessment of the competence and commitment of management, essentially govern the content of such questioning.

The appraisal of a major hazard safety report differs considerably from a conventional inspection, in that the safety report should already have identified the critical safety issues and the inspector can concentrate on these. One of the problems with safety reports is getting the level of detail right. There is the temptation to require excessive detail, so that the inspector may judge whether the case for safety has been made adequately in order for enforcement action to be taken if the operator does not do as required. The more general the statement, the more difficult it can be to make this judgement and to use it for enforcement. However, the more detail the case contains, the larger the documents become, thus running the risk of being less useful to the operator's own staff. In practice a balance has to be struck between the needs of the regulator and the needs of the operator and staff.

The process of assessment

It is common practice for some assessment to be made of the safety report, but the nature and extent of the assessment must be proportionate to the risk. Typically the process involves a group of specialists who have particular skills and knowledge of the technology involved, and its management, and who are familiar with the particular installation. Depending on the circumstances, there may be some verification in the form of inspection and audit to ensure that what actually happens on the installation concurs with the safety report.

The report on a new installation will generally require more verification before the case for safety is accepted. Where minor modifications are required, the report may be accepted, provided it is reasonable and consistent with what is known about the installation. Verification is then carried out during the normal inspection programme.

The process of assessment and the need to come to a judgement within a defined deadline require a project management approach. This enables proper arrangements be made to coordinate teamwork and bring together the whole range of skills and knowledge needed. The process can be further strengthened by the introduction of peer review and independent audit of the process.

The inspectorate must be on its guard against the operator's "stretching" probabilistic risk assessment methods such as quantitative risk assessment (QRA) beyond reasonable usefulness and validity. For example, while there may be substantial data available on the failure rates of valves, it is not necessarily the case that these are valid for very large and individually designed valves used at gas terminals and elsewhere.

QRA is a valuable tool, but it cannot be used in isolation, or replace the use of good engineering judgement. Both approaches are important.

Verification on the ground

As every inspector knows, what is said to exist or be done, and indeed what management actually believes is in place, is often not consistent with reality. It is not unusual therefore to find that the reality of an installation does not always match what was intended or stated in the safety report. This may be because a well-managed installation submits a poor report, which does not do justice to the reality, or because poor installations submit reports suggesting that conditions are better than they actually are.

Either way, verification on the ground is essential and this must involve questioning workers. Their involvement, both at the preparation stage and during verification, is essential: they know what actually happens in practice and why. It is also important to check that operators are familiar with the safety aspects of the plant, both hardware and software, and have clear operating instructions, including, for example, the actions required of them in the event of process deviation.

Apart from verifying the safety report, the inspection of a major hazard plant is like any other, in that the inspector is making an adequate check in order to be satisfied with management's competence to operate the plant safely and to maintain control in the event of an incident.

Although inspectorates do not normally have the resources to inspect every item of the plant and every operational procedure, they will need to adopt a sampling technique by selecting a typical item of plant, representing a number of similar components, and inspecting that sample in depth. Careful records should be kept so that, as the years pass and inspectors change, new incoming inspectors will be inspecting different parts of plants or samples over time.

Public confidence in the inspector

An inspectorate faces two problems operating a safety report regime for major hazard installations. First, there is relatively little visible formal enforcement. A safety report regime can create a false impression of a low level of enforcement because the public and the media only see the final product of the process, usually an accepted safety case. The public (and the media) do not see the extensive series of interactions between the inspectorate and the operator, during which critical aspects of the safety report are vigorously challenged and resultant improvements are made to the risk control arrangements. This challenge-based dialogue is a robust enforcement process, but it needs to be explained to the public and made more transparent.

The second difficulty for an inspectorate is that the public and the media may see it as part of the problem when things go wrong. It is unrealistic to think that safety reports can protect operators and society from every major disaster, but if the inspectorate has accepted or in some way approved the safety report, then it may likewise be seen to have failed in the event of a major incident. While this would be correct if the hazard accident happened because one of the "accepted" control systems was deficient, the general experience is that accidents happen because operators fail to meet the standards they themselves set in their safety reports. This will generally be a clear breach of the law and attract appropriate penalties.

27.4 Other inspectorate responsibilities

Off-site emergency preparedness

The section "Information for the public", above, referred to the labour inspectorate's role in seeing that full and accurate information is given to the public on
what to do in an emergency. The control of major hazards also puts unique
responsibilities on the labour inspectorate to ensure that emergency plans and
procedures for the protection of the public and the environment are established,
updated at appropriate intervals and coordinated with the relevant authorities and
bodies. This will almost certainly involve the inspectorate establishing new
relationships with the police, fire services, and health and local authorities.
Each of these bodies will have already considered their responsibilities individually; the labour inspectorate's role is to ensure that these emergency plans and
procedures are in place, coordinated and revised as necessary, focusing on the
particular characteristics and location of the installation.

The labour inspectorate will also want to see that there have been "table-
top" exercises and full-scale rehearsals to test the emergency procedures,
including the response to any escalation in the degree of emergency. Essential
in any trial is full testing of all communication links, and especially those with
the emergency control centre.

Siting policies

Article 17 of Convention No. 174 requires the competent authority to establish
a comprehensive siting policy for the appropriate separation of proposed major
hazard installations from residential areas and public facilities, and to establish
appropriate measures for existing installations. This brings the labour
inspectorate into direct involvement with local planning authorities, one of
their major responsibilities, and with local elected representatives, because of
the political sensitivity of some issues. Deciding a policy on the application of
Article 17 to a proposed installation will depend on the characteristics and
quantities of the substances concerned, the processes carried out, and local
topographical and climatic conditions. There is an abundant supply of expertise
and research worldwide to guide policy development.

It can be much more difficult to apply appropriate measures in the case of
established installations. Careful analysis of the safety report and inspection of
the plant will provide the basis for the labour inspectorate's proposals to the
planning authorities for ensuring appropriate separation from, or limitation on
the development of, residential areas and public facilities within certain radii of

the installation. The inspectorate must be prepared to justify its case in terms of scientific and technical considerations, and its judgement of the residual risk even when best precautions have been taken.

Conversely, where there are existing public facilities unacceptably close to the installation, the planning authorities may be advised to prevent further development of the installation in that area. These negotiations present labour inspectorates with a new and challenging task, to deploy and coordinate the presentation of scientific and technical considerations and at the same time use their political sensitivity and negotiating skills.

Workers' rights and duties

Article 20 of Convention No. 174 requires workers and their representatives to be informed about hazards and their likely consequences, as well as the orders, instructions and recommendations made by the inspectorate, and to be consulted in the preparation of the safety report, the emergency plans, access to them and any incident reports. Reference has already been made to the need to involve workers in the verification process, but in view of these special provisions, the labour inspectorate would do well to establish close relations with key workers' representatives. They may be the first to learn of workers' concerns about a particular plant or process and, while clearly their first duty is to discuss these with management, they have the right to notify the competent authority of potential hazards.

The appropriate reaction of the labour inspectorate may be to reassure, or alternatively to react rapidly, but either way inspectors will make better judgements if they already know the workers' representatives involved.

Notes

[1] ILO: *Major hazard control: A practical manual* (Geneva, 1994).
[2] idem: *Prevention of major industrial accidents*, An ILO code of practice (Geneva, 1991).

LABOUR INSPECTION AND "NEW HAZARDS"   28

28.1 Dimensions of the problem[1]

In the mid-1960s, long before "stress" and "psychosocial factors" became common expressions, a special report entitled *Protecting the health of eighty million workers – A national goal for occupational health*[2] was issued by the United States Department of Health. The report noted that psychological stress was increasingly apparent in workplaces, presenting "new threats to mental health", and possible risk of somatic disorders. Technological change and increasing psychological demands on workers were noted as contributing factors. The report concluded with a list of urgent problems requiring priority attention, including occupational mental health and contributing workplace factors.

Almost 40 years later, this report has proved remarkably prophetic. Job stress has become a leading source of worker disability in industrialized countries and elsewhere. In 1990, 13 per cent of all worker disability cases handled by one major American workers' compensation insurer were due to job stress-related disorders. A 1985 study by the United States National Council on Compensation Insurance found that one type of claim, involving psychological disability due to "gradual mental stress" at work, had grown to 11 per cent of all occupational disease claims.

These developments reflect the pressures of modern work. A survey of the European Foundation for the Improvement of Living and Working Conditions (Dublin, 1992) found that the proportion of workers complaining of organizational constraints leading to stress was higher than the proportion complaining of physical constraints. A more recent study of workers in the Netherlands found that half of those reviewed reported a fast work pace, three-quarters reported little opportunity for promotion, and one-third reported a poor match between education and job. The impact of these problems in terms of lost productivity, disease and reduced quality of life is formidable, although difficult to estimate reliably.

Another recent survey by the European Foundation (Dublin, 2000)[3] indicates that out of the roughly 159 million workers in the EU, 2 million annually are victims of violence; 3 million are subject to sexual harassment, as – increasingly – defined and sanctioned in national legislation; and some 14 million are victims of psychological harassment and stress.

At the national level, some data (e.g. from France and Germany) reveal similar trends and underline the seriousness of the problem. In Germany, between 1995 and 2000, the number of absences from work for more than three days due to stress, violence and harassment stands continuously at around 5,000. More than 150 people annually are permanently incapacitated for the same reasons, and some 15 to 20 fatal accidents are recorded each year in this respect. In France, partly because of different ways of recording the data, the annual figures are even higher: between 7,000 and 8,000 cases of work absence of more than three days for the same reasons; 600–700 cases of permanent incapacity; and up to 20 fatal accidents.[4]

Conditions leading to stress at work and associated safety and health problems are commonly referred to as "psychosocial factors". They include aspects of the job and work environment such as enterprise climate or culture, work roles, relationships at work, and the design and content of tasks (variety, meaning, scope and repetitiveness, among others). The concept also extends to the external environment (e.g. domestic demands) and aspects of the individual (e.g. personality and attitudes) that may influence the development of stress at work. Frequently, the expressions "work organization" or "organizational factors" are used interchangeably with "psychosocial factors" in reference to working conditions that may lead to stress and result in work-related mental health problems.

Today, it is clear that a number of psychosocial problems are interrelated, sometimes as the cause, sometimes as the result, and sometimes contributing to the result by increasing its severity. A recent ILO training programme, *Managing emerging health-related problems at work*,[5] examines five work-related psychosocial issues from a policy point of view. Known as SOLVE, it explores the interrelations among stress, violence, the use of alcohol, drugs and tobacco, and HIV/AIDS. The programme also examines these problems from the perspective of the worker, the task, the enterprise and the community.

A recent WHO/ILO publication, *Mental health at work: Impact, issues and good practice*,[6] points out that this field is still very much "under-researched". This is certainly true with regard to the role of labour inspection in this context. For the very large majority of labour inspectorates worldwide, these problems are no doubt new and unfamiliar (hence the term "new hazards", even though the above-cited scientific evidence is already a generation old). Indeed, even in the majority of ILO member States that have ratified the Labour Inspection Convention, 1947 (No. 81) – 130 as of 1 December 2001 – the notion that inspectors should address these new hazards would be considered unusual, so much so that the author of this book hesitated to include with any sense of urgency – or at all – a chapter on the subject for fear of being thought esoteric.

Yet these hazards are permeating the world of work and, under the many aspects of globalization, their effects and their consequences are likely to grow exponentially. The same is true of the costs related to them and thus the lack of preventive action (including that of labour inspection) in dealing with them.

The above-mentioned WHO/ILO publication on mental health and work reports that there are as yet few evaluations of the costs involved, but it gives some alarming facts and figures, pointing out that there is growing evidence of the global impact of mental illness. Mental health problems are among the most important contributors to the burden of disease and disability worldwide; five of the ten leading causes of disability worldwide are related to mental health.[7] They are as relevant in low-income countries as they are in high-income ones, cutting across age, sex and social strata. Furthermore, all predictions indicate that the future will see a dramatic increase in work-related mental health problems.

The burden of mental health disorders on health and productivity has long been underestimated. Recently, however, the United Kingdom's Department of Health and the Confederation of British Industry have estimated that 15–30 per cent of workers will experience some form of mental health problem during their working lives. The EU's European Mental Health Agenda has recognized the prevalence and impact of mental health disorders in workplaces in EU countries. It has been estimated that 20 per cent of the adult working population has some type of mental health problem at any given time. In the United States, estimates indicate that more than 40 million people have some type of mental health disorder and, of that number, 4–5 million adults are considered seriously mentally ill. Depressive disorders represent one of the most common health problems of adults in the United States workforce.

The impact of mental health problems in the workplace has serious consequences for the individual and the productivity of the enterprise. Employee performance, rates of illness, absenteeism, accidents and staff turnover are all affected by employees' mental health status. In the United Kingdom, 80 million days are lost every year due to mental illnesses, costing employers £1–2 billion each year; over and above absenteeism, this has an impact on reduced productivity, poor timekeeping and accidents. In the United States, estimates for national spending on depression alone are US$30–40 billion, with an estimated 200 million workdays lost each year. Even in a relatively small country such as Switzerland, according to a recent government study, these costs amount to

4.2 billion Swiss francs (approximately US$3 billion), or 1.2 per of GNP. To this must be added the costs of stress-induced accidents, which account for another 3.8 billion Swiss francs. Overall, some 8 billion Swiss francs (approximately US$5 billion) or 2.3 per cent of GNP are lost annually in Switzerland. Clearly, these facts must concern any labour inspectorate with prevention as its primary mission.

28.2 Stress

In the language of engineering, stress is "a force which deforms bodies". In biology and medicine, the term usually refers to the human body's general plan for adapting to all the influences, changes, demands and strains to which it is exposed, for example, when a person is assaulted on the street, but also when someone is exposed to toxic substances or to extreme heat or cold. However, physical exposure to stress will activate this response, as will mental and social exposure to stress.

The ILO's *Encyclopaedia of occupational health and safety* (which contains several excellent articles on the subject in Volume IV) lists some of the most important situational factors that can give rise to work-related stress:

- **Quantitative overload.** Too much to do, time pressure and repetitive work flow. This is to a great extent typical of mass-production technology and routinized office work.
- **Qualitative underload.** Too narrow and one-sided job content, lack of stimulus and variation, no demands on creativity or problem solving, and low opportunities for social interaction. These situations seem to be more common with poorly designed automation and increased use of computers in both offices and manufacturing (even though there are examples of the opposite).
- **Role conflicts.** When people occupy several roles concurrently, as superiors of some people and subordinates of others, conflicts arise easily and are often stress evoking, as when demands at work clash with private ones, or when someone is divided between loyalty to superiors and to fellow workers and subordinates.
- **Lack of control over one's own situation.** When others decide what to do, and when and how, for example, in relation to workplace and working methods; when the worker concerned has no influence or control; and when there is uncertainty, or lack of any clear structure in the work situation.
- **Lack of social support.** This can occur at home and with superiors or fellow workers.

- **Physical stress factors.** These can influence the worker both physically and chemically, as for example, through organic solvents that directly affect the brain. Secondary psychosocial effects can also originate from distress caused by odours, glare, noise, extremes of air temperature or humidity. These effects can also be due to the worker's awareness, suspicion or fear of exposure to life-threatening chemical hazards or to accident risks.
- **Real-life conditions at work and outside work.** These usually imply a combination of various types of exposure, which might become super-imposed on each other in a cumulative way. A rather trivial environmental factor, but one that comes on top of a very considerable, pre-existing environmental load, may trigger the determining incident, making it difficult to establish a direct cause–effect relationship.

The Labour Inspectorate of the Netherlands (a country formerly affected by above-average absenteeism by EU standards, and worker incapacity – mainly for mental health reasons – leading to politically and economically unaccept-ably high early retirement rates in the 1990s[8]) has recently undertaken major steps to ensure that its inspectors deal with these "new" hazards effectively. It has published a document entitled *Inspection and enforcement of labour risks*,[9] which provides internal instructions for its inspectors. This document deals with a range of issues such as: repetitive-action work and static working positions; pressures of work; work with computers; work sitting and standing; aggression and violence; and sexual harassment.

With regard to stress, a useful questionnaire has been developed for inspectors to assess whether specific jobs involve excessive pressure. This questionnaire, which can be modified to accommodate particular working situations investigated during inspection visits, contains a mix of questions pertaining to the worker and to the work. Where possible, the questions should be presented to a variety of people occupying the same job so as to reduce the influence of a single individual on the assessment.

The results can be assessed as follows:

- In the event that all questions are answered in the negative, there are probably no problems.
- In the event that more than three questions are answered in the affirmative, there may be problems that need further investigation by the inspector.

The questionnaire on difficulties in the performance of duties is as follows:

- Do you often encounter problems with the amount of work you are required to do?

- Do you often have to make an extra effort to complete something?
- Do you often have problems with the content of the work?
- Do you often have problems with the pace of the work?
- Do you often have difficulty taking a break?
- Does taking leave often lead to problems?
- Do you often have to work overtime?
- Do you often work unusual hours (evenings, weekends, nights)?
- Do you often have problems with contacts (with your supervisor, colleagues or others)?

During an inspection (proactive or reactive) focusing on stress, inspectors are instructed to:

- use the questionnaire to determine whether excessive work pressure is a problem;
- in the event of potential problems, proceed by determining whether the company safety policy and plan of action (PoA) required of all enterprises, irrespective of their size, by Dutch law, devote proper attention to this problem; and
- in the event of problems with stress, check what kind of remedial action can be taken during working hours.

Should the inspection reveal that problems of stress and pressures of work are inadequately addressed in the PoA, then a requirement would be imposed pursuant to the Netherlands Working Conditions Act 1980 (as revised in 1998) in the form of a notice. This requirement is accompanied by the reasons why the PoA is incomplete, together with an indication as to what standards must be met for the Inspectorate to consider them complete. A further investigation would subsequently be carried out by a private occupational safety and health service at a later stage.

28.3 Aggression and violence

Work-related aggression and violence are understood as occurrences in which employees are either psychologically or physically harassed, threatened or attacked under circumstances that are directly related to the execution of their work. The source of violence can come from within (internal) or outside (external) the enterprise where the victim is working. The labour inspectorate in a growing number of countries has a duty to ensure compliance with legislation concerning employers' obligations in instances of this nature. Physical violence against employees in shops and supermarkets has advanced to become the single most important cause of occupational fatalities in the

United States, for example. (The police and the judicial authorities would, however, be expected to take the lead in the event of criminal offences.)

Instances of the deliberate use of physical aggression and violence in situations involving dealings with cash or other valuable goods are considered to have a criminal purpose. Aggression and violence are also likely to occur in the services sector: where there is direct contact between employees and customers; in situations involving an unequal balance of power between employees and customers; in situations where employees adopt a customer-unfriendly attitude; or in situations involving coercion such as, for example, an apprehension or an arrest.

Enterprises, institutions and their employees can also be confronted with psychological aggression and violence that are not primarily motivated by material gain, tangible disputes or conflicts of interest. In these situations the enterprise or employee primarily serves as a scapegoat that others can use to vent their dissatisfaction. Mobbing is an example of this kind of situation.

Acts of aggression or violence can also occur more frequently during the execution of work at unusual hours (early in the morning or late at night, and at weekends) and the execution of work by specific groups (such as young people, women or foreign workers).

Aggression and violence have different effects on employees. These effects can be classified according to their nature into physical, material, emotional and organizational effects. Examples include physical injury, damage to goods or property, disruption of everyday work, reduced motivation to continue with the performance of the (same) work, the presence or increase of stress at work and post-traumatic stress disorders. Other typical examples of these effects are an increase in absenteeism due to illness and the concomitant rise in insurance premiums to be paid by the enterprise, an increase in staff turnover and greater problems with the recruitment of new personnel. It should be noted that the victims of violence may, in the future, become the perpetrators of physical and psychological violence.

Both aggression and violence can often be traced to alcohol and drug abuse, increasing levels of negative stress, and discrimination due to various factors.

The following summary (once again from the Dutch instruction manual) contains an indicative list of sectors or situations where employees may be confronted with aggression and violence:

- **retailing**: shops, department stores (cash-desk staff), jewellery shops, video shops, service stations;
- **public transport:** trams, scheduled bus services and trains (drivers and conductors), taxi drivers;

- **catering:** snack-bars, restaurants, cafes and bars;
- **sport and recreation:** swimming pools, football stadiums and sports halls;
- **banks:** banks, post offices and exchange offices (counter staff), cash transports;
- **social services:** housing associations (counter staff), hostels, psychiatric institutions (nursing and care staff);
- **municipal services:** counter staff, public works departments;
- **prisons:** staff of penal institutions;
- **education:** teachers, teachers' aides and maintenance staff;
- **health care:** emergency departments, institutions for mental welfare (nursing staff);
- **security services:** private security companies and security services;
- **investigation departments:** police, safety and health inspectorate;
- **governmental departments:** tax authorities, bailiffs and even labour inspectors.

Employers can be said to conduct an adequate policy to protect staff from (the consequences of) aggression and violence if:

- measures have been implemented to provide information and instruction to staff;
- protocols have been drawn up for work with a risk of aggression and violence;
- procedures have been implemented for the notification of incidents involving aggression or violence;
- incidents of aggression and/or violence are discussed in enterprise meetings or bipartite committees;
- procedures have been implemented for the caring and counselling of employees confronted with aggression or violence;
- material, structural and/or organizational measures have been implemented, where feasible and where necessary;
- any risks of aggression or violence have been addressed in the enterprise occupational safety and health policy (statement) and tangible measures have been incorporated in a subsequent plan of action, where relevant, stating the time frame within which the intended measures are to be implemented.

During an inspection focusing on aggression and violence, inspectors in the Netherlands are instructed to investigate:

- whether incidents have occurred, or have taken place in the past, which are indicative of an existing problem, through:
    - discussions with the employees and the employer;

- examinations of the list of industrial accidents, to determine whether there are incidents that could have a relationship with aggression or violence;
- whether effective measures have been implemented, where necessary, by:
  - examining workplaces eligible for such measures, and discussing the issues with the people involved;
- examining whether the (written) enterprise OSH policy or statement mentions measures to be implemented (of importance, for example, after incidents[10]);
- whether any policy to counter aggression and violence is implemented by:
  - checking if there is a notification procedure and if records of notifications are kept;
  - examining whether the abovementioned OSH policy devotes attention to this issue and, if so, reviewing the documents with respect to the adequacy of technical and (structural) organizational measures and facilities.

Should an investigation of these aspects reveal that no, or insufficient, attention is devoted by the employer to the protection of the enterprise's employees from aggression and violence, then the inspector is instructed to enforce the law under established procedures for offences pursuant to the Working Conditions Act. As with stress (referred to earlier), an improvement notice is issued, accompanied by a statement of the reasons why the required labour protection policy is incomplete (or absent), together with an indication of what the inspector considers to be adequate.

More severe measures, including legal sanctions, may be taken, depending on the nature and possible consequences of the contravention.

28.4 Sexual harassment

A form of psychological and at times physical violence is sexual harassment. The Dutch Working Conditions Act 1980 (as revised in 1998), contains the following formal definition:

Undesired sexual approaches, requests for sexual favours or other verbal, non-verbal or physical conduct of a sexual nature that exhibits one or more of the following elements:
- submission to conduct of this nature explicitly or implicitly forms a condition for the employment of a person;
- subjection to, or rejection of, conduct of this nature by a person serves as the basis for decisions affecting the work of that person;

- conduct of this nature is intended to impair the work performance of a person and/or to create an intimidating, hostile or unpleasant working environment, or results in the impairment of the work performance of a person and/or an intimidating, hostile or unpleasant working environment.

Well-known forms of sexual harassment exhibited in everyday life include:

- **verbal conduct:** remarks and jokes of a sexual nature, remarks about women and femininity, teasing with a sexual undertone, sexual advances, appointments with an ulterior motive;
- **non-verbal conduct:** staring, leering, standing close by, obtrusiveness;
- **physical conduct:** physical contact (touching, blocking the way, taking hold of the person, an arm over the shoulder), indecent assault and rape.

Sexual harassment is relatively frequent in situations where people of the opposite sex join groups of workers of the same sex. When a change occurs in the traditional composition of a group of employees, the newcomers are often "tried out" and/or have to prove themselves more than necessary. Clients can also exhibit sexual harassment towards employees, especially those working in care professions or other services involving direct contact with customers, flight personnel among others.

In relative terms, sexual harassment is more common in certain business sectors where (young) women frequently work in individual, isolated or unsupervised situations, for example; hotels and catering; business services (such as office staff and cleaners); health care and welfare (such as nursing staff, home helps, maternity nurses and district nurses); industry (such as staff in packaging departments); construction; and the wholesale trade.

Employers can make use of a large number of potential measures in the implementation of a policy to counter sexual harassment. The following examples are not "mandatory" elements of OSH enterprise policy; in many cases, a tailor-made package of measures will be required:

- **Prevention.** Sexual harassment can be prevented by devoting attention to the working environment and the workplace layout; good lighting; ready accessibility; avoiding one-worker isolated workplaces as far as possible; and the prevalent culture at work (zero tolerance vis-à-vis remarks of a sexual nature, pin-ups and so forth).
- **Sanctions.** The imposition of sanctions against perpetrators of sexual harassment can have a preventive and corrective effect. Sanctions can consist of measures such as a reprimand, an unfavourable note in the personnel file, transfer and, in serious instances, suspension or dismissal.

- **Provision of information.** Workers can be informed of the employer's views on sexual harassment. They can be told that it is not an acceptable form of conduct within the organization; that measures have been implemented to prevent sexual intimidation; and that victims are provided with means of dealing with instances of sexual harassment.
- **Counsellors.** In practice, people find it difficult to reveal that they suffer from sexual harassment. It is recommended that employers, in consultation with the workers' representative body (e.g. shop stewards, works council, OSH committee), appoint one or more counsellors (preferably women). Employers can also collaborate with other employers, for example, within the branch or sector, in the appointment of one or more counsellors.
- **Mediation.** Studies and experience show that the majority of persons exhibiting conduct considered to be sexual harassment desist once they have been called to account by an independent mediator. An important precondition for this approach is the acceptance of the mediator's role by both "parties".
- **Employer's complaints procedure.** An official complaints procedure can offer a solution to problems that cannot be resolved in an informal manner. It is recommended that the counsellor appointed by the enterprise should also be a member of the committee dealing with complaints and should also advise the employer about settlements.

The Netherlands procedure for complaints of sexual harassment is dealt with by the labour inspectorate as follows:

- On notification, the complainant is informed that she or he will be contacted by a "counsellor-inspector". The complainant is requested to indicate when this will be convenient, and the manner in which he or she can be contacted (by telephone or in person, and where). The complainant can opt for a male or a female counsellor-inspector.
- The counsellor-inspector discusses further particulars with the complainant and, should the complainant be someone other than the victim, decides whether a discussion with the victim is required.
- The counsellor-inspector informs the complainant and/or victim about the possible means of enforcement in matters pertaining to sexual harassment. The counsellor-inspector can also be of assistance in informing the complainant or victim of other persons or institutions that can offer advice or assistance.
- An inspection of the enterprise takes place only when the complainant has been informed of the possible consequences of a specific inspection of this nature, and has agreed to it.

- The counsellor-inspector uses the results from the inspection to form an opinion about the employer's policy to counter sexual harassment. This opinion is discussed with the complainant and with the employer.

During an inspection focusing on sexual harassment, the inspector will investigate whether:

- incidents occur or have occurred that are indicative of a possible problem, by interviewing workers and the complainant;
- appropriate measures have been or are being implemented, where necessary, by means of:
  - investigation at the relevant workplaces, and with the persons involved (accessibility, visibility, provision of information, etc.);
  - investigating whether the OSH plan of action refers to measures that must be implemented (of importance, for example, subsequent to incidents);
- a policy to counter sexual harassment is conducted within the enterprise or institution, by means of investigating whether:
  - the enterprise has a complaints procedure and keeps records of complaints;
  - the plan of action devotes attention to the subject, and is regularly reviewed to incorporate preventive and corrective measures. A checklist has been developed which can be used for this purpose.

Should an investigation reveal that no, or insufficient, attention is devoted by the employer to the protection of employees from (the consequences of) sexual harassment, then the inspector will enforce the law as follows: if the enterprise does not conduct a policy, or only an inadequate policy against sexual harassment, an improvement notice, calling for compliance, is issued. This requirement is accompanied by a statement outlining the reasons why the policy is inadequate (or absent) and an indication of how to comply. Again, further measures (*procès-verbaux*, legal proceedings, sanctions) may be taken by the inspector, depending on the degree of violation.

28.5 Conclusions

New and emerging hazards – and there will undoubtedly be more of them – will increasingly preoccupy labour inspectorates' attention and place greater demands on their competence, resources, and professional and institutional capacity. This final chapter endeavours to draw the reader's attention to those not-so-new issues and attempts to use good practice, already introduced in one high-performance system, as a benchmark. Other labour inspectorates, notably in the Nordic countries, have also pioneered work in this field, setting new priorities, developing new methodologies and adopting new recruitment procedures to meet new competency requirements. Thus, in Sweden, the OSH inspectorate recruits more than 50 per cent of its professional staff from non-technical faculties (sociologists, psychologists, etc.). The role of occupational health services is significantly increasing in this context – and so is the need for labour inspection to cooperate more closely with these and others, such as national institutes of safety and health.

The SOLVE programme, mentioned above, is being used in a number of developing countries to explore the interrelationships among these psycho-social problems and provide management with policy-level elements to address strategies for action. The comprehensive policy, developed through SOLVE, is holistic. It takes into account day-to-day enterprise activities such as purchasing, human resources development, finance and public relations. It addresses occupational safety and health, and provides a high-level framework for action. Included in the policy are statements addressing prevention, treatment, rehabilitation, non-discrimination, confidentiality, workers' involvement, personal growth through knowledge acquisition, enterprise survival, productivity, and a supportive working environment and culture.

As a result of the policy, concepts and strategies will develop and will be transformed into sustained action at the enterprise level.

A final example comes from Finland, where a long-term pilot programme to improve cooperation between some 1,200 people working in occupational health services with some 650 labour inspectors (both covering a working population of some 2.2 million – an almost ideal ratio) is under way with a view to creating OSH synergies, mainly in the SME sector. The measures most commonly taken at Finnish workplaces aim to:

- improve the work environment (enhancing occupational safety and ergonomics, communication, clear goals and independence at work);
- provide further training and learning opportunities (improving occupational skills and teamwork or promoting independent study);
- promote health (promoting physical activities and a healthy lifestyle, offering rehabilitation and preventing substance abuse).

The Finnish Institute of Occupational Health (which has some 850 employees) recommends the following methods of promoting mental health in work situations:

- implement models of good workplace practices and disseminate this information in the community;

- increase the cooperation of mental health and occupational health professionals in promoting mental health activities at the workplace;
- train occupational health-care professionals in mental health issues and mental health professionals in work–life issues;
- increase the general knowledge of the entire population regarding the preconditions for and value of good mental health in working life and develop self-help skills for creating satisfactory working conditions.

These points illustrate a close-to-optimal coverage of old and new labour protection issues, and also in terms of available resources. As such, they could serve as a benchmark for every labour inspection system that wishes to strengthen its impact on the world of work. For labour inspection professionals in many other countries, these approaches and solutions to common problems, and the resources devoted to them, are likely to remain a dream for years to come. In Finland, the Netherlands and other countries with high-performance inspection systems, the evident, sustainable success of their respective economies in the context of globalization is also attributed to the high priority that their societies give to labour and social protection. In the long run, this will be the way forward for labour inspection the world over.

Notes

[1] Unless otherwise stated, all the data in this section are taken from ILO: *Encyclopaedia of occupational health and safety*, edited by J. M. Stellman, 4-volume print version and CD-ROM (Geneva, 4th edition, 1998), Vol. IV.

[2] US Department of Health: *Protecting the health of eighty million workers – A national goal for occupational health* (Washington, DC, 1996).

[3] The third in a series on working conditions in the EU: first study (30 questions), 1990; second study (60 questions), 1995; third study, 2000 (results not yet fully published).

[4] Data are taken from annual reports of the Hauptverband der Gewerblichen Berufsgenossenschaften (HVBG), Germany; and Caisse nationale d'assurance maladie (CNAM), France.

[5] V. Di Martino, D. Gold and A. Schaap: *Managing emerging health-related problems at work* (Geneva, ILO, 2002).

[6] WHO/ILO: *Mental health at work: Impact, issues and good practice* (Geneva, 2000).

[7] Ibid.

[8] The average retirement age for male workers was around 51 years.

[9] Netherlands Labour Inspectorate: *Inspection and enforcement of labour risks* (The Hague, 2000).

[10] An incident is defined as "an unsafe occurrence arising out of or in the course of work where no personal injury is caused" (ILO: *Guidelines on occupational safety and health management systems, ILO-OSH 2001* (Geneva, 2001)).

MAJOR INTERNATIONAL LABOUR STANDARDS ON LABOUR INSPECTION

The Labour Inspection Convention, 1947 (No. 81)

Excerpts, Articles 1 to 24

PART I. LABOUR INSPECTION IN INDUSTRY

Article 1

Each Member of the International Labour Organization for which this Convention is in force shall maintain a system of labour inspection in industrial workplaces.

Article 2

1. The system of labour inspection in industrial workplaces shall apply to all workplaces in respect of which legal provisions relating to conditions of work and the protection of workers while engaged in their work are enforceable by labour inspectors.

2. National laws or regulations may exempt mining and transport undertakings or parts of such undertakings from the application of this Convention.

Article 3

1. The functions of the system of labour inspection shall be:

(a) to secure the enforcement of the legal provisions relating to conditions of work and the protection of workers while engaged in their work, such as provisions relating to hours, wages, safety, health and welfare, the employment of children and young persons, and other connected matters, in so far as such provisions are enforceable by labour inspectors;

(b) to supply technical information and advice to employers and workers concerning the most effective means of complying with the legal provisions;

(c) to bring to the notice of the competent authority defects or abuses not specifically covered by existing legal provisions.

2. Any further duties which may be entrusted to labour inspectors shall not be such as to interfere with the effective discharge of their primary duties or to prejudice in any way the authority and impartiality which are necessary to inspectors in their relations with employers and workers.

Article 4

1. So far as is compatible with the administrative practice of the Member, labour inspection shall be placed under the supervision and control of a central authority.

2. In the case of a federal State, the term "central authority" may mean either a federal authority or a central authority of a federated unit.

Article 5

The competent authority shall make appropriate arrangements to promote:

(a) effective cooperation between the inspection services and other government services and public or private institutions engaged in similar activities; and

(b) collaboration between officials of the labour inspectorate and employers and workers or their organizations.

Article 6

The inspection staff shall be composed of public officials whose status and conditions of service are such that they are assured of stability of employment and are independent of changes of government and of improper external influences.

Article 7

1. Subject to any conditions for recruitment to the public service which may be prescribed by national laws or regulations, labour inspectors shall be recruited with sole regard to their qualifications for the performance of their duties.

2. The means of ascertaining such qualifications shall be determined by the competent authority.

3. Labour inspectors shall be adequately trained for the performance of their duties.

Article 8

Both men and women shall be eligible for appointment to the inspection staff; where necessary, special duties may be assigned to men and women inspectors.

Article 9

Each Member shall take the necessary measures to ensure that duly qualified technical experts and specialists, including specialists in medicine, engineering, electricity and chemistry, are associated in the work of inspection, in such manner as may be deemed most appropriate under national conditions, for the purpose of securing the enforcement of the legal provisions relating to the protection of the health and safety of workers while engaged in their work and of investigating the effects of processes, materials and methods of work on the health and safety of workers.

Article 10

The number of labour inspectors shall be sufficient to secure the effective discharge of the duties of the inspectorate and shall be determined with due regard for:

(a) the importance of the duties which inspectors have to perform, in particular:

    (i)   the number, nature, size and situation of the workplaces liable to inspection;

    (ii) the number and classes of workers employed in such workplaces; and

    (iii) the number and complexity of the legal provisions to be enforced;

(b) the material means placed at the disposal of the inspectors; and

(c) the practical conditions under which visits of inspection must be carried out in order to be effective.

Article 11

1. The competent authority shall make the necessary arrangements to furnish labour inspectors with--

(a) local offices, suitably equipped in accordance with the requirements of the service, and accessible to all persons concerned;

(b) the transport facilities necessary for the performance of their duties in cases where suitable public facilities do not exist.

2. The competent authority shall make the necessary arrangements to reimburse to labour inspectors any travelling and incidental expenses necessary for the performance of their duties.

Article 12

1. Labour inspectors provided with proper credentials shall be empowered:

(a) to enter freely and without previous notice at any hour of the day or night any workplace liable to inspection;

(b) to enter by day any premises which they may have reasonable cause to believe to be liable to inspection; and

(c) to carry out any examination, test or enquiry which they may consider necessary in order to satisfy themselves that the legal provisions are being strictly observed, and in particular:

    (i)   to interrogate, alone or in the presence of witnesses, the employer or the staff of the undertaking on any matters concerning the application of the legal provisions;

    (ii)   to require the production of any books, registers or other documents the keeping of which is prescribed by national laws or regulations relating to conditions of work, in order to see that they are in conformity with the legal provisions, and to copy such documents or make extracts from them;

    (iii) to enforce the posting of notices required by the legal provisions;

    (iv) to take or remove for purposes of analysis samples of materials and substances used or handled, subject to the employer or his representative being notified of any samples or substances taken or removed for such purpose.

2. On the occasion of an inspection visit, inspectors shall notify the employer or his representative of their presence, unless they consider that such a notification may be prejudicial to the performance of their duties.

Article 13

1. Labour inspectors shall be empowered to take steps with a view to remedying defects observed in plant, layout or working methods which they may have reasonable cause to believe constitute a threat to the health or safety of the workers.

2. In order to enable inspectors to take such steps they shall be empowered, subject to any right of appeal to a judicial or administrative authority which may be provided by law, to make or to have made orders requiring –

(a) such alterations to the installation or plant, to be carried out within a specified time limit, as may be necessary to secure compliance with the legal provisions relating to the health or safety of the workers; or

(b) measures with immediate executory force in the event of imminent danger to the health or safety of the workers.

3. Where the procedure prescribed in paragraph 2 is not compatible with the administrative or judicial practice of the Member, inspectors shall have the right to apply to the competent authority for the issue of orders or for the initiation of measures with immediate executory force.

Article 14

The labour inspectorate shall be notified of industrial accidents and cases of occupational disease in such cases and in such manner as may be prescribed by national laws or regulations.

Article 15

Subject to such exceptions as may be made by national laws or regulations, labour inspectors:

(a) shall be prohibited from having any direct or indirect interest in the undertakings under their supervision;

(b) shall be bound on pain of appropriate penalties or disciplinary measures not to reveal, even after leaving the service, any manufacturing or commercial secrets or working processes which may come to their knowledge in the course of their duties; and

(c) shall treat as absolutely confidential the source of any complaint bringing to their notice a defect or breach of legal provisions and shall give no intimation to the employer or his representative that a visit of inspection was made in consequence of the receipt of such a complaint.

Article 16

Workplaces shall be inspected as often and as thoroughly as is necessary to ensure the effective application of the relevant legal provisions.

Article 17

1. Persons who violate or neglect to observe legal provisions enforceable by labour inspectors shall be liable to prompt legal proceedings without previous warning: Provided that exceptions may be made by national laws or regulations in respect of cases in which previous notice to carry out remedial or preventive measures is to be given.

2. It shall be left to the discretion of labour inspectors to give warning and advice instead of instituting or recommending proceedings.

Article 18

Adequate penalties for violations of the legal provisions enforceable by labour inspectors and for obstructing labour inspectors in the performance of their duties shall be provided for by national laws or regulations and effectively enforced.

Article 19

1. Labour inspectors or local inspection offices, as the case may be, shall be required to submit to the central inspection authority periodical reports on the results of their inspection activities.

2. These reports shall be drawn up in such manner and deal with such subjects as may from time to time be prescribed by the central authority; they shall be submitted at least as frequently as may be prescribed by that authority and in any case not less frequently than once a year.

Article 20

1. The central inspection authority shall publish an annual general report on the work of the inspection services under its control.

2. Such annual reports shall be published within a reasonable time after the end of the year to which they relate and in any case within twelve months.

3. Copies of the annual reports shall be transmitted to the Director-General of the International Labour Office within a reasonable period after their publication and in any case within three months.

Article 21

The annual report published by the central inspection authority shall deal with the following and other relevant subjects in so far as they are under the control of the said authority:

(a) laws and regulations relevant to the work of the inspection service;

(b) staff of the labour inspection service;

(c) statistics of workplaces liable to inspection and the number of workers employed therein;

(d) statistics of inspection visits;

(e) statistics of violations and penalties imposed;

(f) statistics of industrial accidents;

(g) statistics of occupational diseases.

PART II. LABOUR INSPECTION IN COMMERCE

Article 22

Each Member of the International Labour Organization for which this Part of this Convention is in force shall maintain a system of labour inspection in commercial workplaces.

Article 23

The system of labour inspection in commercial workplaces shall apply to workplaces in respect of which legal provisions relating to conditions of work and the protection of workers while engaged in their work are enforceable by labour inspectors.

Article 24

The system of labour inspection in commercial workplaces shall comply with the requirements of Articles 3 to 21 of this Convention in so far as they are applicable.

Protocol of 1995 to the Labour Inspection Convention, 1947 (No. 81)

Excerpts, Articles 1 to 6

The General Conference of the International Labour Organization,

Having been convened at Geneva by the Governing Body of the International Labour Office, and having met in its Eighty-Second Session on 6 June 1995, and

Noting that the provisions of the Labour Inspection Convention, 1947, apply only to industrial and commercial workplaces, and

Noting that the provisions of the Labour Inspection (Agriculture) Convention, 1969, apply to workplaces in commercial and non-commercial agricultural undertakings, and

Noting that the provisions of the Occupational Safety and Health Convention, 1981, apply to all branches of economic activity, including the public service, and

Having regard to all the risks to which workers in the non-commercial services sector may be exposed, and the need to ensure that this sector is subject to the same or an equally effective and impartial system of labour inspection as that provided in the Labour Inspection Convention, 1947, and

Having decided upon the adoption of certain proposals with regard to activities in the non-commercial services sector, which is the sixth item on the agenda of the session, and

Having determined that these proposals shall take the form of a Protocol to the Labour Inspection Convention, 1947,

adopts this twenty-second day of June of the year one thousand nine hundred and ninety-five the following Protocol, which may be cited as the Protocol of 1995 to the Labour Inspection Convention, 1947:

PART I. SCOPE, DEFINITION AND APPLICATION

Article 1

1. Each Member which ratifies this Protocol shall extend the application of the provisions of the Labour Inspection Convention, 1947 (hereunder referred to as " the Convention"), to activities in the non-commercial services sector.

2. The term activities in the non-commercial services sector refers to activities in all categories of workplaces that are not considered as industrial or commercial for the purposes of the Convention.

3. This Protocol applies to all workplaces that do not already fall within the scope of the Convention.

Article 2

1. A Member which ratifies this Protocol may, by a declaration appended to its instrument of ratification, exclude wholly or partly from its scope the following categories:

(a) essential national (federal) government administration;

(b) the armed services, whether military or civilian personnel;

(c) the police and other public security services;

(d) prison services, whether prison staff or prisoners when performing work,

1. if the application of the Convention to any of these categories would raise special problems of a substantial nature.

2. Before the Member avails itself of the possibility afforded in paragraph 1, it shall consult the most representative organizations of employers and workers or, in the absence of such organizations, the representatives of the employers and workers concerned.

3. A Member which has made a declaration as referred to in paragraph 1 shall, following ratification of this Protocol, indicate in its next report on the application of the Convention under article 22 of the Constitution of the International Labour Organization the reasons for the exclusion and, to the extent possible, provide for alternative inspection arrangements for any categories of workplaces thus excluded. It shall describe in subsequent reports and measures it may have taken with a view to extending the provisions of the Protocol to them.

4. A Member which has made a declaration referred to in paragraph 1 may at any time modify or cancel that declaration by a subsequent declaration in accordance with the provisions of this Article.

Article 3

1. The provisions of this Protocol shall be implemented by means of national laws or regulations, or by other means that are in accordance with national practice.

2. Measures taken to give effect to this Protocol shall be drawn up in consultation with the most representative organizations of employers and workers or, in the absence of such organizations, the representatives of the employers and workers concerned.

PART II. SPECIAL ARRANGEMENTS

Article 4

1. A Member may make special arrangements for the inspection of workplaces of essential national (federal) government administration, the armed services, the police and other public security services, and the prison services, so as to regulate the powers of labour inspectors as provided in Article 12 of the Convention in regard to:

(a) inspectors having appropriate security clearance before entering;

(b) inspection by appointment;

(c) the power to require the production of confidential documents;

(d) the removal of confidential documents from the premises;

(e) the taking and analysis of samples of materials and substances.

2. The Member may also make special arrangements for the inspection of workplaces of the armed services and the police and other public security services so as to permit any of the following limitations on the powers of labour inspectors:

(a) restriction of inspection during manoeuvres or exercises;

(b) restriction or prohibition of inspection of front-line or active service units;

(c) restriction or prohibition of inspection during declared periods of tension;

(d) limitation of inspection in respect of the transport of explosives and armaments for military purposes.

3. The Member may also make special arrangements for the inspection of workplaces of prison services to permit restriction of inspection during declared periods of tension.

4. Before a Member avails itself of any of the special arrangements afforded in paragraphs (1), (2) and (3), it shall consult the most representative organizations of employers and workers or, in the absence of such organizations, the representatives of the employers and workers concerned.

Article 5

The Member may make special arrangements for the inspection of workplaces of fire brigades and other rescue services to permit the restriction of inspection during the fighting of a fire or during rescue or other emergency operations. In such cases, the labour inspectorate shall review such operations periodically and after any significant incident.

Article 6

The labour inspectorate shall be able to advise on the formulation of effective measures to minimize risks during training for potentially hazardous work and to participate in monitoring the implementation of such measures.

The Labour Inspection (Agriculture) Convention, 1969 (No. 129)

Excerpts, Articles 1 to 27

Article 1

1. In this Convention the term "agricultural undertaking" means undertakings and parts of undertakings engaged in cultivation, animal husbandry including livestock production and care, forestry, horticulture, the primary processing of agricultural products by the operator of the holding or any other form of agricultural activity.

2. Where necessary, the competent authority shall, after consultation with the most representative organizations of employers and workers concerned, where such exist, define the line which separates agriculture from industry and commerce in such a manner as not to exclude any agricultural undertaking from the national system of labour inspection.

3. In any case in which it is doubtful whether an undertaking or part of an undertaking is one to which this Convention applies, the question shall be settled by the competent authority.

Article 2

In this Convention the term "legal provisions" includes, in addition to laws and regulations, arbitration awards and collective agreements upon which the force of law is conferred and which are enforceable by labour inspectors.

Article 3

Each Member of the International Labour Organization for which this Convention is in force shall maintain a system of labour inspection in agriculture.

Article 4

The system of labour inspection in agriculture shall apply to agricultural undertakings in which work employees or apprentices, however they may be remunerated and whatever the type, form or duration of their contract.

Article 5

1. Any Member ratifying this Convention may, in a declaration accompanying its ratification, undertake also to cover by labour inspection in agriculture one or more of the following categories of persons working in agricultural undertakings:

(a) tenants who do not engage outside help, sharecroppers and similar categories of agricultural workers;

(b) persons participating in a collective economic enterprise, such as members of a co-operative;

(c) members of the family of the operator of the undertaking, as defined by national laws or regulations.

2. Any Member which has ratified this Convention may subsequently communicate to the Director-General of the International Labour Office a declaration undertaking to cover one or more of the categories of persons referred to in the preceding paragraph which are not already covered in virtue of a previous declaration.

3. Each Member which has ratified this Convention shall indicate in its reports under article 22 of the Constitution of the International Labour Organization to what extent effect has been given or is proposed to be given to the provisions of the Convention in respect of such of the categories of persons referred to in paragraph 1 of this Article as are not covered in virtue of a declaration.

Article 6

1. The functions of the system of labour inspection in agriculture shall be:

(a) to secure the enforcement of the legal provisions relating to conditions of work and the protection of workers while engaged in their work, such as provisions relating to hours, wages, weekly rest and holidays, safety, health and welfare, the employment of women, children and young persons, and other connected matters, in so far as such provisions are enforceable by labour inspectors;

(b) to supply technical information and advice to employers and workers concerning the most effective means of complying with the legal provisions;

(c) to bring to the notice of the competent authority defects or abuses not specifically covered by existing legal provisions and to submit to it proposals on the improvement of laws and regulations.

2. National laws or regulations may give labour inspectors in agriculture advisory or enforcement functions regarding legal provisions relating to conditions of life of workers and their families.

3. Any further duties which may be entrusted to labour inspectors in agriculture shall not be such as to interfere with the effective discharge of their primary duties or to prejudice in any way the authority and impartiality which are necessary to inspectors in their relations with employers and workers.

Article 7

1. So far as is compatible with the administrative practice of the Member, labour inspection in agriculture shall be placed under the supervision and control of a central body.

2. In the case of a federal State, the term "central body" may mean either one at federal level or one at the level of a federated unit.

3. Labour inspection in agriculture might be carried out for example –

(a) by a single labour inspection department responsible for all sectors of economic activity;

(b) by a single labour inspection department, which would arrange for internal functional specialisation through the appropriate training of inspectors called upon to exercise their functions in agriculture;

(c) by a single labour inspection department, which would arrange for internal institutional specialisation by creating a technically qualified service, the officers of which would perform their functions in agriculture; or

(d) by a specialised agricultural inspection service, the activity of which would be supervised by a central body vested with the same prerogatives in respect of labour inspection in other fields, such as industry, transport and commerce.

Article 8

1. The labour inspection staff in agriculture shall be composed of public officials whose status and conditions of service are such that they are assured of stability of employment and are independent of changes of government and of improper external influences.

2. So far as is compatible with national laws or regulations or with national practice, Members may include in their system of labour inspection in agriculture officials or representatives of occupational organizations, whose activities would supplement those of the public inspection staff; the persons concerned shall be assured of stability of tenure and be independent of improper external influences.

Article 9

1. Subject to any conditions for recruitment to the public service which may be prescribed by national laws or regulations, labour inspectors in agriculture shall be recruited with sole regard to their qualifications for the performance of their duties.

2. The means of ascertaining such qualifications shall be determined by the competent authority.

3. Labour inspectors in agriculture shall be adequately trained for the per-formance of their duties and measures shall be taken to give them appropriate further training in the course of their employment.

Article 10

Both men and women shall be eligible for appointment to the labour inspections staff in agriculture; where necessary, special duties may be assigned to men and women inspectors.

Article 11

Each Member shall take the necessary measures to ensure that duly qualified technical experts and specialists, who might help to solve problems demanding technical knowledge, are associated in the work of labour inspection in agriculture in such manner as may be deemed most appropriate under national conditions.

Article 12

1. The competent authority shall make appropriate arrangements to promote effective cooperation between the inspection services in agriculture and government services and public or approved institutions which may be engaged in similar activities.

2. Where necessary, the competent authority may either entrust certain inspection functions at the regional or local level on an auxiliary basis to appropriate government services or public institutions or associate these services or institutions with the exercise of the functions in question, on condition that this does not prejudice the application of the principles of this Convention.

Article 13

The competent authority shall make appropriate arrangements to promote collaboration between officials of the labour inspectorate in agriculture and employers and workers, or their organizations where such exist.

Article 14

Arrangements shall be made to ensure that the number of labour inspectors in agriculture is sufficient to secure the effective discharge of the duties of the inspectorate and is determined with due regard for:

a) the importance of the duties which inspectors have to perform, in particular:

   (i)   the number, nature, size and situation of the agricultural undertakings liable to inspection;

   (ii) the number and classes of persons working in such undertakings; and

   (iii) the number and complexity of the legal provisions to be enforced;

(b) the material means placed at the disposal of the inspectors; and

(c) the practical conditions under which visits of inspection must be carried out in order to be effective.

Article 15

1. The competent authority shall make the necessary arrangements to furnish labour inspectors in agriculture with:

(a) local offices so located as to take account of the geographical situation of the agricultural undertakings and of the means of communication, suitably equipped in accordance with the requirements of the service, and, in so far as possible, accessible to the persons concerned;

(b) the transport facilities necessary for the performance of their duties in cases where suitable public facilities do not exist.

2. The competent authority shall make the necessary arrangements to reimburse to labour inspectors in agriculture any travelling and incidental expenses which may be necessary for the performance of their duties.

Article 16

1. Labour inspectors in agriculture provided with proper credentials shall be empowered:

(a) to enter freely and without previous notice at any hour of the day or night any workplace liable to inspection;

(b) to enter by day any premises which they may have reasonable cause to believe to be liable to inspection;

(c) to carry out any examination, test or inquiry which they may consider necessary in order to satisfy themselves that the legal provisions are being strictly observed, and in particular:

    (i) to interview, alone or in the presence of witnesses, the employer, the staff of the undertaking or any other person in the undertaking on any matters concerning the application of the legal provisions;

    (ii) to require, in such manner as national laws or regulations may prescribe, the production of any books, registers or other documents the keeping of which is prescribed by national laws or regulations relating to conditions of life and work, in order to see that they are in conformity with the legal provisions, and to copy such documents or make extracts from them;

    (iii) to take or remove for purposes of analysis samples of products, materials and substances used or handled, subject to the employer or his representative being notified of any products, materials or substances taken or removed for such purposes.

2. Labour inspectors shall not enter the private home of the operator of the undertaking in pursuance of subparagraph (a) or (b) of paragraph 1 of this Article except with the consent of the operator or with a special authorization issued by the competent authority.

3. On the occasion of an inspection visit, inspectors shall notify the employer or his representative, and the workers or their representatives, of their presence, unless they consider that such a notification may be prejudicial to the performance of their duties.

Article 17

The labour inspection services in agriculture shall be associated, in such cases and in such manner as may be determined by the competent authority, in the preventive control of new plant, new materials or substances and new methods of handling or processing products which appear likely to constitute a threat to health or safety.

Article 18

1. Labour inspectors in agriculture shall be empowered to take steps with a view to remedying defects observed in plant, layout or working methods in agricultural undertakings, including the use of dangerous materials or substances, which they may have reasonable cause to believe constitute a threat to health or safety.

2. In order to enable inspectors to take such steps they shall be empowered, subject to any right of appeal to a legal or administrative authority which may be provided by law, to make or have made orders requiring:

(a) such alterations to the installation, plant, premises, tools, equipment or machines, to be carried out within a specified time limit, as may be necessary to secure compliance with the legal provisions relating to health or safety; or

(b) measures with immediate executory force, which can go as far as halting the work, in the event of imminent danger to health or safety.

3. Where the procedure described in paragraph 2 is not compatible with the administrative or judicial practice of the Member, inspectors shall have the right to apply to the competent authority for the issue of orders or for the initiation of measures with immediate executory force.

4. The defects noted by the inspector when visiting an undertaking and the orders he is making or having made in pursuance of paragraph 2 or for which he intends to apply in pursuance of paragraph 3 shall be immediately made known to the employer and the representatives of the workers.

Article 19

1. The labour inspectorate in agriculture shall be notified of occupational accidents and cases of occupational disease occurring in the agricultural sector in such cases and in such manner as may be prescribed by national laws or regulations.

2. As far as possible, inspectors shall be associated with any inquiry on the spot into the causes of the most serious occupational accidents or occupational diseases, particularly of those which affect a number of workers or have fatal consequences.

Article 20

Subject to such exceptions as may be made by national laws or regulations, labour inspectors in agriculture:

(a) shall be prohibited from having any direct or indirect interest in the undertakings under their supervision;

(b) shall be bound on pain of appropriate penalties or disciplinary measures not to reveal, even after leaving the service, any manufacturing or commercial secrets or working processes which may come to their knowledge in the course of their duties; and

(c) shall treat as absolutely confidential the source of any complaint bringing to their notice a defect, a danger in working processes or a breach of legal provisions and shall give no intimation to the employer or his representative that a visit of inspection was made in consequence of the receipt of such a complaint.

Article 21

Agricultural undertakings shall be inspected as often and as thoroughly as is necessary to ensure the effective application of the relevant legal provisions.

Article 22

1. Persons who violate or neglect to observe legal provisions enforceable by labour inspectors in agriculture shall be liable to prompt legal or administrative proceedings without previous warning: Provided that exceptions may be made by national laws or regulations in respect of cases in which previous notice to carry out remedial or preventive measures is to be given.

2. It shall be left to the discretion of labour inspectors to give warning and advice instead of instituting or recommending proceedings.

Article 23

If labour inspectors in agriculture are not themselves authorised to institute proceedings, they shall be empowered to refer reports of infringements of the legal provisions directly to an authority competent to institute such proceedings.

Article 24

Adequate penalties for violations of the legal provisions enforceable by labour inspectors in agriculture and for obstructing labour inspectors in the performance of their duties shall be provided for by national laws or regulations and effectively enforced.

Article 25

1. Labour inspectors or local inspection offices, as the case may be, shall be required to submit to the central inspection authority periodical reports on the results of their activities in agriculture.

2. These reports shall be drawn up in such manner and deal with such subjects as may from time to time be prescribed by the central inspection authority; they shall be submitted at least as frequently as may be prescribed by that authority and in any case not less frequently than once a year.

Article 26

1. The central inspection authority shall publish an annual report on the work of the inspection services in agriculture, either as a separate report or as part of its general annual report.

2. Such annual reports shall be published within a reasonable time after the end of the year to which they relate and in any case within twelve months.

3. Copies of the annual reports shall be transmitted to the Director-General of the International Labour Office within three months after their publication.

Article 27

The annual report published by the central inspection authority shall deal in particular with the following subjects, in so far as they are under the control of the said authority:

(a) laws and regulations relevant to the work of labour inspection in agriculture;

(b) staff of the labour inspection service in agriculture;

(c) statistics of agricultural undertakings liable to inspection and the number of persons working therein;

(d) statistics of inspection visits;

(e) statistics of violations and penalties imposed;

(f) statistics of occupational accidents, including their causes;

(g) statistics of occupational diseases, including their causes.

The Labour Inspection Recommendation, 1923 (No. 20)

Excerpts

...

Whereas the Constitution of the International Labour Organization includes among the methods and principles of special and urgent importance for the physical, moral and intellectual welfare of the workers the principle that each State should make provision for a system of inspection in which women should take part, in order to ensure the enforcement of the laws and regulations for the protection of the workers;

Whereas the resolutions adopted at the First Session of the International Labour Conference concerning certain countries where special conditions prevail involve the creation by these countries of an inspection system if they do not already possess such a system;

Whereas the necessity of organising a system of inspection becomes especially urgent when Conventions adopted at sessions of the Conference are being ratified by Members of the Organization and put into force;

Whereas while the institution of an inspection system is undoubtedly to be recommended as one of the most effective means of ensuring the enforcement of Conventions and other engagements for the regulation of labour conditions, each Member is solely responsible for the execution of Conventions to which it is a party in the territory under its sovereignty or its authority and must accordingly itself determine in accordance with local conditions what measures of supervision may enable it to assume such a responsibility;

Whereas, in order to put the experience already gained at the disposal of the Members with a view to assisting them in the institution or reorganization of their inspection system, it is desirable to indicate the general principles which practice shows to be the best calculated to ensure uniform, thorough and effective enforcement of Conventions and more generally of all measures for the protection of workers; and

Having decided to leave to each country the determination of how far these general principles should be applied to certain spheres of activity;

And taking as a guide the long experience already acquired in factory inspection;

The General Conference recommends that each Member of the International Labour Organization should take the following principles and rules into consideration:

I. SPHERE OF INSPECTION

1. That it should be the principal function of the system of inspection which should be instituted by each Member in accordance with the ninth principle of article 41 of the Constitution of the International Labour Organization to secure the enforcement of the laws and regulations relating to the conditions of work and the protection of the workers while engaged in their work (hours of work and rest; night work; prohibition of the employment of certain persons on dangerous, unhealthy or physically unsuitable work; health and safety, etc.). (Note: This Paragraph refers to the Constitution of the International Labour Organization prior to its amendment in 1946. The Constitution as amended in 1946 contains no specific reference to the setting up of a system of labour inspection. See, however, the provisions of the Labour Inspection Convention, 1947 (No. 81).)

2. That, in so far as it may be considered possible and desirable, either for reasons of convenience in the matter of supervision or by reason of the experience which they gain in carrying out their principal duties, to assign to inspectors additional duties which may vary according to the conceptions, traditions and customs prevailing in the different countries, such duties may be assigned, provided:

(a) that they do not in any way interfere with the inspectors' principal duties;

(b) that in themselves they are closely related to the primary object of ensuring the protection of the health and safety of the workers;

(c) that they shall not prejudice in any way the authority and impartiality which are necessary to inspectors in their relations with employers and workers.

II. NATURE OF THE FUNCTIONS AND POWERS OF INSPECTORS

A. General

1. That inspectors provided with credentials should be empowered by law:

(a) to visit and inspect, at any hour of the day or night, places where they may have reasonable cause to believe that persons under the protection of the law are employed, and to enter by day any place which they may have reasonable cause to believe to be an establishment, or part thereof, subject to their supervision; provided that, before leaving, inspectors should, if possible, notify the employer or some representative of the employer of their visit;

(b) to question, without witnesses, the staff belonging to the establishment, and, for the purpose of carrying out their duties, to apply for information to any other persons whose evidence they may consider necessary, and to require to be shown any registers or documents which the laws regulating conditions of work require to be kept.

2. That inspectors should be bound by oath, or by any method which conforms with the administrative practice or customs in each country, not to disclose, on pain of legal penalties or suitable disciplinary measures, manufacturing secrets, and working processes in general, which may come to their knowledge in the course of their duties.

3. That, regard being had to the administrative and judicial systems of each country, and subject to such reference to superior authority as may be considered necessary, inspectors should be empowered to bring breaches of the laws, which they ascertain, directly before the competent judicial authorities; - That in countries where it is not incompatible with their system and principles of law, the reports drawn up by the inspectors shall be considered to establish the facts stated therein in default of proof to the contrary.

4. That the inspectors should be empowered, in cases where immediate action is necessary to bring installation or plant into conformity with laws and regulations, to make an order (or, if that procedure should not be in accordance with the administrative or judicial systems of the country, to apply to the competent authorities for an order) requiring such alterations to the installation or plant to be carried out within a fixed time as may be necessary for securing full and exact observance of the laws and regulations relating to the health and safety of the workers; - That in countries where the inspector's order has executive force of itself, its execution should be suspended only by appeal to a higher administrative or judicial authority, but in no circumstances should provisions intended to protect employers against arbitrary action prejudice the taking of measures with a view to the prevention of imminent danger which has been duly shown to exist.

B. Safety

5. Having regard to the fact that, while it is essential that the inspectorate should be invested with all the legal powers necessary for the performance of its duties, it is equally important, in order that inspection may progressively become more

effective, that, in accordance with the tendency manifested in the oldest and most experienced countries, inspection should be increasingly directed towards securing the adoption of the most suitable safety methods for preventing accidents and diseases with a view to rendering work less dangerous, more healthy, and even less exhausting, by the intelligent understanding, education, and cooperation of all concerned, it would appear that the following methods are calculated to promote this development in all countries:

(a) that all accidents should be notified to the competent authorities, and that one of the essential duties of the inspectors should be to investigate accidents, and more especially those of a serious or recurring character, with a view to ascertaining by what measures they can be prevented;

(b) that inspectors should inform and advise employers respecting the best standards of health and safety;

(c) that inspectors should encourage the collaboration of employers, managing staff and workers for the promotion of personal caution, safety methods, and the perfecting of safety equipment;

(d) that inspectors should endeavour to promote the improvement and perfecting of measures of health and safety, by the systematic study of technical methods for the internal equipment of undertakings, by special investigations into problems of health and safety, and by any other means;

(e) that in countries where it is considered preferable to have a special organization for accident insurance and prevention completely independent of the inspectorate, the special officers of such organizations should be guided by the foregoing principles.

III. ORGANIZATION OF INSPECTION

A. Organization of the Staff

6. That, in order that the inspectors may be as closely as possible in touch with the establishments which they inspect and with the employers and workers, and in order that as much as possible of the inspectors' time may be devoted to the actual visiting of establishments, they should be localised, when the circumstances of the country permit, in the industrial districts.

7. That, in countries, which for the purposes of inspection are divided into districts, in order to secure uniformity in the application of the law as between district and district and to promote a high standard of efficiency of inspection, the inspectors in the districts should be placed under the general supervision of an inspector of high qualifications and experience. Where the importance of the industries of the country is such as to require the appointment of more than one supervising inspector, the supervising inspectors should meet from time to time to confer on questions arising in the divisions under their control in connection with the application of the law and the improvement of industrial conditions.

8. That the inspectorate should be placed under the direct and exclusive control of a central State authority and should not be under the control of or in any way responsible to any local authority in connection with the execution of any of their duties.

9. That, in view of the difficult scientific and technical questions which arise under the conditions of modern industry in connection with processes involving the use of dangerous materials, the removal of injurious dust and gases, the use of electrical plant and other matters, it is essential that experts having competent medical, engineering, electrical or other scientific training and experience should be employed by the State for dealing with such problems.

10. That, in conformity with the principle contained in Article 41 of the Constitution of the International Labour Organization, the inspectorate should include women as well as men inspectors; that, while it is evident that with regard to certain matters and certain classes of work, inspection can be more suitably carried out by men, as in the case of other matters and other classes of work inspection can be more suitably carried out by women, the women inspectors should in general have the same powers and duties and exercise the same authority as the men inspectors, subject to their having had the necessary training and experience, and should have equal opportunity of promotion to the higher ranks. (Note: This Paragraph refers to the Constitution of the International Labour Organization prior to its amendment in 1946. The Constitution as amended in 1946 contains no specific reference to the participation of women inspectors in the work of the inspectorate. See, however, Article 8 of the Labour Inspection Convention, 1947 (No. 81).)

B. Qualifications and Training of Inspectors

11. That, in view of the complexity of modern industrial processes and machinery, of the character of the executive and administrative functions entrusted to the inspectors in connection with the application of the law and of the importance of their relations to employers and workers and employers' and workers' organizations and to the judicial and local authorities, it is essential that the inspectors should in general possess a high standard of technical training and experience, should be persons of good general education, and by their character and abilities be capable of acquiring the confidence of all parties.

12. That the inspectorate should be on a permanent basis and should be independent of changes of Government; that the inspectors should be given such a status and standard of remuneration as to secure their freedom from any improper external influences and that they should be prohibited from having any interest in any establishment which is placed under their inspection.

13. That inspectors on appointment should undergo a period of probation for the purpose of testing their qualifications and training them in their duties, and that their appointment should only be confirmed at the end of that period if they have shown themselves fully qualified for the duties of an inspector.

14. That, where countries are divided for the purposes of inspection into districts, and especially where the industries of the country are of a varied character, it is

desirable that inspectors, more particularly during the early years of their service, should be transferred from district to district at appropriate intervals in order to obtain a full experience of the work of inspection.

C. Standards and Methods of Inspection

15. That, as under a system of State inspection the visits of the inspectors to any individual establishment must necessarily be more or less infrequent, it is essential:

(1) (a) That the principle should be laid down and maintained that the employer and the officials of the establishment are responsible for the observance of the law, and are liable to be proceeded against in the event of deliberate violation of or serious negligence in observing the law, without previous warning from the inspector; it is understood that the foregoing principle does not apply in special cases where the law provides that notice shall be given in the first instance to the employer to carry out certain measures.

(b) That, as a general rule, the visits of the inspectors should be made without any previous notice to the employer.

(2) It is desirable that adequate measures should be taken by the State to ensure that employers, officials and workers are acquainted with the provisions of the law and the measures to be taken for the protection of the health and safety of the workers, as, for example, by requiring the employer to post in his establishment an abstract of the requirements of the law.

16. That, while it is recognised that very wide differences exist between the size and importance of one establishment and another, and that there may be special difficulties in countries or areas of a rural character where factories are widely scattered, it is desirable that, as far as possible, every establishment should be visited by an inspector for the purposes of general inspection not less frequently than once a year, in addition to any special visits that may be made for the purpose of investigating a particular complaint or for other purposes; and that large establishments and establishments of which the management is unsatisfactory from the point of view of the protection of the health and safety of the workers, and establishments in which dangerous or unhealthy processes are carried on, should be visited much more frequently. It is desirable that, when any serious irregularity has been discovered in an establishment, it should be revisited by the inspector at an early date with a view to ascertaining whether the irregularity has been remedied.

D. Cooperation of Employers and Workers

17. That it is essential that the workers and their representatives should be afforded every facility for communicating freely with the inspectors as to any defect or breach of the law in the establishment in which they are employed; that every such complaint should as far as possible be investigated promptly by the inspector; that the complaint should be treated as absolutely confidential by the inspector and that no intimation even should be given to the employer or his officials that the visit made for the purpose of investigation is being made in consequence of the receipt of a complaint.

18. That, with a view to securing full cooperation of the employers and workers and their respective organizations in promoting a high standard in regard to the conditions affecting the health and safety of the workers, it is desirable that the inspectorate should confer from time to time with the representatives of the employers' and workers' organizations as to the best measures to be taken for this purpose.

IV. INSPECTORS' REPORTS

19. That inspectors should regularly submit to their central authority reports framed on uniform lines dealing with their work and its results, and that the said authority should publish an annual report as soon as possible and in any case within one year after the end of the year to which it relates, containing a general survey of the information furnished by the inspectors; that the calendar year should be uniformly adopted for these reports.

20. That the annual general report should contain a list of the laws and regulations relating to conditions of work made during the year which it covers.

21. That this annual report should also give the statistical tables necessary in order to provide all information on the organization and work of the inspectorate and on the results obtained. The information supplied should as far as possible state:

(a) the strength and organization of the staff of the inspectorate;

(b) the number of establishments covered by the laws and regulations, classified by industries and indicating the number of workers employed (men, women, young persons, children);

(c) the number of visits of inspection made for each class of establishment with an indication of the number of workers employed in the establishments inspected (the number of workers being taken to be the number employed at the time of the first visit of the year), and the number of establishments inspected more than once during the year;

(d) the number of and nature of breaches of the laws and regulations brought before the competent authorities and the number and nature of the convictions by the competent authority;

(e) the number, nature and the cause of accidents and occupational diseases notified, tabulated according to class of establishment.

The Labour Inspection Recommendation, 1947 (No. 81)

Excerpts

...

Whereas the Labour Inspection Recommendation, 1923, and the Labour Inspection Convention, 1947, provide for organization of systems of labour inspection and it is desirable to supplement the provisions thereof by further recommendations:

The Conference recommends that each Member should apply the following provisions as rapidly as national conditions allow and report to the International Labour Office as requested by the Governing Body concerning the measures taken to give effect thereto.

I. PREVENTIVE DUTIES OF LABOUR INSPECTORATES

1. Any person who proposes to open an industrial or commercial establishment, or to take over such an establishment, or to commence in such an establishment the carrying on of a class of activity specified by a competent authority as materially affecting the application of legal provisions enforceable by labour inspectors, should be required to give notice in advance to the competent labour inspectorate either directly or through another designated authority.

2. Members should make arrangements under which plans for new establishments, plant, or processes of production may be submitted to the appropriate labour inspection service for an opinion as to whether the said plans would render difficult or impossible compliance with the laws and regulations concerning industrial health and safety or would be likely to constitute a threat to the health or safety of the workers.

3. Subject to any right of appeal which may be provided by law, the execution of plans for new establishments, plant and processes of production deemed under national laws or regulations to be dangerous or unhealthy should be conditional upon the carrying out of any alterations ordered by the inspectorate for the purpose of securing the health and safety of the workers.

II. COLLABORATION OF EMPLOYERS AND WORKERS IN REGARD TO HEALTH AND SAFETY

4. (1) Arrangements for collaboration between employers and workers for the purpose of improving conditions affecting the health and safety of the workers should be encouraged.

(2) Such arrangements might take the form of safety committees or similar bodies set up within each undertaking or establishment and including representatives of the employers and the workers.

5. Representatives of the workers and the management, and more particularly members of works safety committees or similar bodies where such exist, should be authorised to collaborate directly with officials of the labour inspectorate, in a manner and within limits fixed by the competent authority, when investigations and, in particular, enquiries into industrial accidents or occupational diseases are carried out.

6. The promotion of collaboration between officials of the labour inspectorate and organizations of employers and workers should be facilitated by the organization of conferences or joint committees, or similar bodies, in which representatives of the labour inspectorate discuss with representatives of organizations of employers and workers questions concerning the enforcement of labour legislation and the health and safety of the workers.

7. Appropriate steps should be taken to ensure that employers and workers are given advice and instruction in labour legislation and questions of industrial hygiene and safety by such measures as:

(a) lectures, radio talks, posters, pamphlets and films explaining the provisions of labour legislation and suggesting methods for their application and measures for preventing industrial accidents and occupational diseases;

(b) health and safety exhibitions; and

(c) instruction in industrial hygiene and safety in technical schools.

III. LABOUR DISPUTES

8. The functions of labour inspectors should not include that of acting as conciliator or arbitrator in proceedings concerning labour disputes.

IV. ANNUAL REPORTS ON INSPECTION

9. The published annual reports on the work of inspection services should, in so far as possible, supply the following detailed information:

(a) a list of the laws and regulations bearing on the work of the inspection system not mentioned in previous reports;

(b) particulars of the staff of the labour inspection system, including:

   (i)   the aggregate number of inspectors;

   (ii)   the numbers of inspectors of different categories;

   (iii)   the number of women inspectors; and

   (iv)   particulars of the geographical distribution of inspection services;

(c) statistics of workplaces liable to inspection and of the number of persons therein employed, including:

   (i)   the number of workplaces liable to inspection;

   (ii)   the average number of persons employed in such workplaces during the year;

   (iii)   particulars of the classification of persons employed under the following headings: men, women, young persons, and children;

(d) statistics of inspection visits, including:

   (i)   the number of workplaces visited;

   (ii)   the number of inspection visits made, classified according to whether they were made by day or by night;

   (iii)   the number of persons employed in the workplaces visited;

   (iv)   the number of workplaces visited more than once during the year;

(e) statistics of violations and penalties, including:

   (i)   the number of infringements reported to the competent authorities;

    (ii)   particulars of the classification of such infringements according to the legal provisions to which they relate;

    (iii) the number of convictions;

    (iv) particulars of the nature of the penalties imposed by the competent authorities in the various cases (fines, imprisonment, etc.);

(f) statistics of industrial accidents, including the number of industrial accidents notified and particulars of the classification of such accidents:

    (i)   by industry and occupation;

    (ii) according to cause;

    (iii) according to whether fatal or non-fatal;

(g) statistics of occupational diseases, including:

    (i)   the number of cases of occupational disease notified;

    (ii) particulars of the classification of such cases according to industry and occupation;

    (iii) particulars of the classification of such cases according to their cause or character, such as the nature of the disease, poisonous substance or unhealthy process to which the disease is due.

The Labour Inspection (Agriculture) Recommendation, 1969 (No. 133)

Excerpts

...

1. Where national conditions permit, the functions of the labour inspectorate in agriculture should be enlarged so as to include collaboration with the competent technical services with a view to helping the agricultural producer, whatever his status, to improve his holding and the conditions of life and work of the persons working on it.

2. Subject to the provisions of Article 6, paragraph 3, of the Labour Inspection (Agriculture) Convention, 1969, the labour inspectorate in agriculture might be associated in the enforcement of legal provisions on such matters as:

(a) training of workers;

(b) social services in agriculture;

(c) cooperatives;

(d) compulsory school attendance.

3. (1) Normally, the functions of labour inspectors in agriculture should not include that of acting as conciliator or arbitrator in proceedings concerning labour disputes.

(2) Where no special bodies for this purpose exist in agriculture, labour inspectors in agriculture may be called upon as a temporary measure to act as conciliators.

(3) In the case provided for by subparagraph (2) of this Paragraph, the competent authority should take measures in harmony with national law and compatible with the resources of the labour department of the country concerned with a view to relieving labour inspectors progressively of such functions, so that they are able to devote themselves to a greater extent to the actual inspection of undertakings.

4. Labour inspectors in agriculture should become familiar with conditions of life and work in agriculture and have knowledge of the economic and technical aspects of work in agriculture.

5. Candidates for senior positions in the labour inspectorate in agriculture should be in possession of appropriate professional or academic qualifications or have acquired thorough practical experience in labour administration.

6. Candidates for other positions in the labour inspectorate in agriculture (such as assistant inspectors and junior staff) should, if the level of education in the country allows, have completed secondary general education, supplemented, if possible, by appropriate technical training, or have acquired adequate administrative or practical experience in labour matters.

7. In countries where education is not sufficiently developed, persons appointed as labour inspectors in agriculture should at least have some practical experience in agriculture or show an interest in and have capacity for this type of work; they should be given adequate training on the job as rapidly as possible.

8. The central labour inspection authority should give labour inspectors in agriculture guidelines so as to ensure that they perform their duties throughout the country in a uniform manner.

9. The activity of labour inspectors in agriculture during the night should be limited to those matters which cannot be effectively controlled during the day.

10. The use in agriculture of committees for hygiene and safety which include representatives of employers and of workers might be one of the means of collaboration between officials of the labour inspectorate in agriculture and employers and workers, or their organizations where such exist.

11. The association of the labour inspectorate in agriculture in the preventive control of new plant, new materials or substances and new methods of handling or processing products which appear likely to constitute a threat to health or safety, provided for in Article 17 of the Labour Inspection (Agriculture) Convention, 1969, should include prior consultation with the labour inspectorate on:

(a) the putting into operation of such plant, materials or substances, and methods; and

(b) the plans of any plant in which dangerous machines or unhealthy or dangerous work processes are to be used.

12. Employers should provide the necessary facilities to labour inspectors in agriculture, including, where appropriate, the use of a room for interviews with persons working in the undertaking.

13. The annual report published by the central inspection authority might, in addition to the subjects listed in Article 27 of the Labour Inspection (Agriculture) Convention, 1969, deal with the following matters in so far as they are within the competence of the said authority:

(a) statistics of labour disputes in agriculture;

(b) identification of problems regarding application of the legal provisions, and progress made in solving them; and

(c) suggestions for improving the conditions of life and work in agriculture.

14. (1) Members should undertake or promote education campaigns intended to inform the parties concerned, by all appropriate means, of the applicable legal provisions and the need to apply them strictly as well as of the dangers to the life or health of persons working in agricultural undertakings and of the most appropriate means of avoiding them.

(2) Such campaigns might, in the light of national conditions, include:

(a) use of the services of rural promoters or instructors;

(b) distribution of posters, pamphlets, periodicals and newspapers;

(c) organization of film shows, and radio and television broadcasts;

(d) arrangements for exhibitions and practical demonstrations on hygiene and safety;

(e) inclusion of hygiene and safety and other appropriate subjects in the teaching programmes of rural schools and agricultural schools;

(f) organization of conferences for persons working in agriculture who are affected by the introduction of new working methods or of new materials or substances;

(g) participation of labour inspectors in agriculture in workers' education programmes; and

(h) arrangements of lectures, debates, seminars and competitions with prizes.

BIBLIOGRAPHY

I. ILO codes of practice, guides and manuals*

Accident prevention, A workers' education manual (2nd edition, 1983).

Accident prevention on board ship at sea and in port, An ILO code of practice (2nd edition, 1996).

Alli, B. *Fundamental principles of occupational health and safety* (2001).

Ambient factors at the workplace, An ILO code of practice (1999).

Bakar Che Man, A.; Gold, D. *Safety and health in the use of chemicals at work: A training manual* (1993).

Di Martino V.; Gold, D.; Schaap, A. *Managing emerging health-related problems at work*, Modular series, Training Centre, SafeWork (2002).

Ergonomic checkpoints: Practical and easy-to-implement solutions for improving safety, health and working conditions (1996).

Guidelines for the radiation protection of workers in industry (ionising radiations), Occupational Safety and Health Series No. 62 (1987).

Guidelines on inspection in chemical factories, especially major accident hazard installations, International Occupational Safety and Health Information Centre (CIS), Series No. 2 (1992).

Guidelines on occupational safety and health management systems, ILO-OSH 2001 (2001).

HIV/AIDS and the world of work, An ILO code of practice (2001).

Human stress, work and job satisfaction: A critical approach, Occupational Safety and Health Series No. 50 (1982).

Inspection of labour conditions on board ship: Guidelines for procedure (1990).

Labour inspection, A workers' education manual (revised edition, 1986).

Labour inspection and the adoption of a policy on child labour: A training guide, Labour Administration Branch, Series No. 36 (1994).

Major hazard control: A practical manual (1994).

*The place of publication is Geneva unless otherwise stated. Some of these publications are out of print, but may be consulted in libraries.

Management of alcohol- and drug-related issues in the workplace, An ILO code of practice (1996).

Managing emerging health-related problems at work: Stress, tobacco, alcohol and drugs, HIV/AIDS, violence (SOLVE), training package, SafeWork (2002).

Occupational exposure to airborne substances harmful to health, An ILO code of practice (1991).

Occupational safety and health in the iron and steel industry, An ILO code of practice (1983).

Occupational safety in high mountains for construction and engineering works, An ILO code of practice (1985).

Prevention of accidents due to underground explosions in coal mines, An ILO code of practice (1974).

Prevention of major industrial accidents, An ILO code of practice (1991).

Protection of workers against noise and vibration in the working environment, An ILO code of practice (1984).

Recording and notification of occupational accidents and diseases, An ILO code of practice (1996).

Safe construction and installation of electric passenger, goods and service lifts, An ILO code of practice (1972).

Safety and health in agricultural work, An ILO code of practice (1965).

Safety and health in building and civil engineering work, An ILO code of practice (2nd edition, 1985).

Safety and health in coal mines, An ILO code of practice (1986).

Safety and health in construction, An ILO code of practice (1992).

Safety and health in dock work, An ILO code of practice (2nd edition, 1992).

Safety and health in forestry work, An ILO code of practice (2nd edition, 1998).

Safety and health in opencast mines, An ILO code of practice (1991).

Safety and health in shipbuilding and ship repairing, An ILO code of practice (1984).

Safety and health in the use of agrochemicals: A guide (1990).

Safety, health and welfare on construction sites: A training manual (Geneva, 1995).

Safety in the use of asbestos, An ILO code of practice (1990).

Safety in the use of chemicals at work, An ILO code of practice (1993).

Safety in the use of synthetic vitreous fibre insulation wools (glass wool, rock wool, slag wool), An ILO code of practice (2001).

Safety, health and working conditions in the transfer of technology to developing countries, An ILO code of practice (1988).

Technical and ethical guidelines for workers' health surveillance, Occupational Safety and Health Series, No. 72 (1998).

II. ILO Labour Administration Branch documents

No. 6 *L'efficacité de l'inspection du travail* [The effectiveness of labour inspection] (1987) ; in French only.

No. 8 *Labour inspection in the construction industry* (1989).

No. 10 *La inspección del trabajo en la agricultura para países de América Central y Panamá* [Labour inspection in agriculture for countries in Central America and Panama], (1988); in Spanish only.

No. 12 *Staff training and development units in labour ministries* (1989).

No. 14 *Les méthodes de l'inspection du travail pour promouvoir la sécurité et la santé des travailleurs* [Methods of labour inspection to promote workers' safety and health], Guide de formation de formateurs (1990); in French only.

No. 17 *Factory inspection in the Caribbean,* Report on a workshop on effective labour in the field of working conditions and environment, Jamaica (1988).

No. 18 *The use of computers in labour inspection,* Report of a symposium, Vienna (1989).

No. 20 *Informe final sobre la Reunión subregional sobre la inspección del trabajo* [Report on the subregional meeting on labour inspection], Montevideo, Uruguay (1989); in Spanish only.

No. 22 *Labour inspection and chemical hazards: A spectral analysis of systems of labour inspection* (1992).

No. 27 *L'intervention de l'inspection du travail dans le secteur de la construction en Afrique* [Labour inspection intervention in the construction sector in Africa], Rapport sur deux séminaires (1991); in French only.

No. 30 *Labour inspection in the non-commercial services sector* (1991).

No. 31 *Labour inspection and child labour* (1992).

No. 33 *Labour inspection in the oil refining and large-scale petrochemical industries* (1992).

No. 34 *Labour inspection systems and labour inspectors' training policies* (1993).

No. 35 *Productivity in labour administration* (1993).

No. 36 *Labour inspection and the adoption of a policy on child labour. Training guide* (1994).

No. 37 *Labour inspection in the public sector* (1993).

No. 42 *Labour inspection and the adoption of a policy on child labour. The working child: A psychosociological approach* (1994).

No. 43 *Etude sur l'inspection du travail et le travail précaire dans l'agriculture et les industries agro-alimentaires en Amérique latine* [Study on labour inspection and precarious work in agriculture and agricultural food industries in Latin America](1994); in French only.

No. 48 *The role of labour inspection in transition* (1996).

No. 56 *New prevention strategies for labour inspection* (1998).

III. Other ILO publications

Bryant, M. *Success with occupational safety programmes,* Occupational Safety and Health Series No. 52 (Geneva, 3rd edition, 1984).

Encyclopaedia of occupational health and safety, edited by Jeanne Mager Stellman, 4-volume print version and CD-ROM (Geneva, 4th edition, 1998).

Decent work, Report of the Director-General to the 87th session of the International Labour Conference, Geneva, 1999.

Declaration on Fundamental Principles and Rights at Work and its Follow-up (Geneva, 1998).

Developing inspection services: The changing role of factory inspection, CIS, Report No. 5 (CIS), 1994.

Factory inspection: Selected technical papers (Harare, ILO/ARLAC, 1991).

Forastieri, V. *Children at work: Health and safety risks* (Geneva, 2nd edition, 2002).

International labour standards concerned with labour inspection: Main provisions (Geneva, 1990).

Labour inspection. General Survey of the Committee of Experts on the Application of Conventions and Recommendations, International Labour Conference, Report III (Part 4B), 71st Session, 1985 (Geneva).

Labour inspection and child labour (1999).
    I. Report for an International High-Level Tripartite Meeting of Experts, Geneva
    II. Report of the Meeting

Labour inspection: Purposes and practice (Geneva, 1972).

Labour inspection in agriculture in South Asia (Bangkok, 1988).

Labour inspection in agriculture in South East Asia (Bangkok, 1983).

Labour inspection skills in the petroleum industry, Labour administration training material. (Bangkok, ILO/EASMAT, 1991).

Labour statistics based on administrative records: Guidelines for compilation and presentation (Bangkok, ILO/EASMAT, 1997).

Mental health in the workplace: Situation analyses for Poland, Finland and Germany (Geneva, 2000).

Report of the meeting organized by the International Labour Office and the Commission of the European Communities on labour inspection in Europe, Geneva, 1992.

Stopping forced labour, Global Report under the Follow-up to the ILO Declaration on Fundamental Principles and Rights at Work (Geneva, 2001).

IV. ILO Conventions, Recommendations and Protocols

Web address http://ilolex.ilo.ch:1567/english/index.htm

Conventions

No. 62   Safety Provisions (Building) Convention, 1937

No. 81   Labour Inspection Convention, 1947 and Protocol of 1995 to the Labour Inspection Convention, 1947

No. 110   Plantations Convention, 1958

No. 119   Guarding of Machinery Convention, 1963

No. 129   Labour Inspection (Agriculture) Convention, 1969

No. 138   Minimum Age Convention, 1973

No. 139   Occupational Cancer Convention, 1974

No. 144   Tripartite Consultation (International Labour Standards) Convention, 1976

No. 148   Working Environment (Air Pollution, Noise and Vibration) Convention, 1977

No. 150   Labour Administration Convention, 1978

No. 155   Occupational Safety and Health Convention, 1981

No. 161   Occupational Health Services Convention, 1985

No. 162   Asbestos Convention, 1986

No. 167   Safety and Health in Construction Convention, 1988

No. 174   Prevention of Major Industrial Accidents Convention, 1993

No. 182   Worst Forms of Child Labour Convention, 1999

No. 184   Safety and Health in Agriculture Convention, 2001

Recommendations

No. 5   Labour Inspection (Health Services) Recommendation, 1919

No. 20   Labour Inspection Recommendation, 1923

No. 81   Labour Inspection Recommendation, 1947

No. 82   Labour Inspection (Mining and Transport) Recommendation, 1947

No. 85   Protection of Wages Recommendation, 1949

No. 158   Labour Administration (Public Service) Recommendation, 1978

No. 174   Prevention of Major Industrial Accidents Recommendation, 1993

No. 175   Safety and Health in Construction, Recommendation, 1988

No. 90   Worst Forms of Child Labour Recommendation, 1999

No. 92   Safety and Health in Agriculture Recommendation, 2001

V. Other publications

Bundesanstalt für Arbeitsschutz und Arbeitsmedizin (BAuA). *Managementsysteme in Arbeitsschutz* [Management systems in the protection of industrial health and safety standards] (Dortmund, Germany, 1999).

Commission of the European Union (DGV). *Common principles for labour inspectorates regarding inspection of safety and health at the workplace*, and "Questionnaire for evaluating the policies and practices in occupational health and safety inspection" (Luxembourg, 1997).

European Agency for Safety and Health at Work. *Economic impact of occupational safety and health in the Member States of the European Union* (Bilboa, 1999).

European Foundation for the Improvement of Living and Working Conditions. *Design for sustainable development: Environmental management and safety and health* (Luxembourg, Office for Official Publications of the European Communities, 2000).

Finnish Ministry of Social Affairs and Health. *Economics of the Working Environment 1997* (Tampere, Finland, 1997).

Glendon, I. "Risk management in the 1990s: Safety auditing" in *Journal of Occupational Health and Safety Australia and New Zealand*, Vol. 11, No 6, 1995, pp.507–510.

Gunningham, N. "Towards effective and efficient enforcement of occupational health and safety: Two paths to enlightenment", in *Comparative Labour Law and Policy Journal*, Vol. 19 No. 4, 1998, pp.547-583.

__; Johnstone, R. *Regulating workplace safety-systems and safety* (Oxford, Oxford University Press, 1999).

Her Majesty's Stationery Office (HMSO), United Kingdom. *Safety and health at work*, Robens Report of the Parliamentary Committee 1970-72, Cmnd. 5034 (London, 1972).

Hopkins, A.; Hogan, L. "Influencing small business to attend to occupational health and safety", in *Journal of Occupational Health and Safety*, Vol.14 No.3, 1998, pp.237-244.

Selected publications of the Health and Safety Executive (HSE), HSE Books UK, PO Box 1999, Sudbury, CO10 2WA, United Kingdom

Enforcement policy statement (1995).

Farmwise. Your essential guide to health and safety in agriculture (1999).

Preventing accidents to children in agriculture, Approved code of practice (2nd edition, 1999).

Successful health and safety management (2nd edition, 1997).

The costs of accidents at work (1993).

The costs to Britain of workplace accidents and work-related ill-health (1995/96).

Selected publications of the International Association of Labour Inspection (IALI), PO Box 3974, 1211 Geneva 3, Switzerland

Report on the International Symposium, "Hazardous substances and labour inspection", Wiesbaden, 1991.

Report on the international technical symposium,"Labour inspection strategies for vulnerable groups", Tunis, 1994.

Report on the international conference, "Inspection for health", London, 1996.

Report on the international symposium, "Modern management systems in labour inspection", Lyons, 1997.

Report on the international symposium, "The SME approach", Bergen, 1998.

Report on the international symposium, "Labour inspection: roles and practical solutions beyond 2000", Nicosia, 1998.

Report on an ILO/IALI seminar, "Labour and inspection prevention in agriculture", Malawi, 1991 (Geneva, 2001).

Report on the international conference "Labour inspection priorities in the new millennium", Dubrovnik, 2000.

Report on an ILO/IALI symposium, "Labour inspection and occupational safety and health management systems and standards", Dusseldorf, 2001.

Netherlands Labour Inspectorate (Arbeidsinspectie). *Inspection and enforcement of (new) labour risks* (The Hague, 2000).

Occupational health and safety management systems. Guidelines for the implementation of OHSAS 18001 (Hitchin, Herts., 2000).

Senior Labour Inspectors Committee (SLIC), European Union. *Common principles for labour inspectorates regarding inspection of health and safety at the workplace* (Brussels, 1997).

US Department of Health. *Protecting the health of eighty million workers – A national goal for occupational health* (Washington, DC, 1996).

World Health Organization (WHO). *Towards good practice in health, environment and safety management in industrial and other enterprises* (Copenhagen, Regional Office for Europe, 1999).

__/ILO. *Mental health and work: Impact, issues and good practices* (Geneva, 2000).

__. 2001. *Ministerial round tables: Mental health, 54th World Health Assembly*, Geneva, April 2001 (A54/DIV/4).

VI. Selected periodicals containing relevant articles

International Labour Review (Geneva, ILO).

African Newsletter on Occupational Health and Safety (Helsinki, ILO/CIS + FINNIDA).

American Industrial Hygiene Association Journal.

American Journal of Industrial Medicine.

Annals of Occupational Hygiene.

Asian-Pacific Newsletter on Occupational Health and Safety (Helsinki, ILO/CIS + FINNIDA).

Health and Safety.

IALI Forum (Wiesbaden, Germany, International Association of Labour Inspection).

Industrial Health.

International Journal of Industrial Ergonomics.

International Journal of Occupational Safety and Ergonomics.

Journal of Safety Research.

News (Newsletter of the European Agency for Safety and Health at Work).

Occupational Hygiene.

Safety and Health at Work (Geneva, ILO/CIS).

Safety and Health Practitioner.

Useful websites

1) ILO general: www.ilo.org

2) ILO programmes directly relevant to labour inspection:

   – Bureau of Library and Information Services (BIBL): www.ilo.org/bibl

   – Conditions of Work Branch (CONDI/T): www.ilo.org/condi/t

   – InFocus Programme on Promoting the Declaration on Fundamental Principles and Rights at Work (DECLARATION): www.ilo.org/declaration

   – Gender Promotion Programme (GENPROM): www.ilo.org/genprom

   – Department for Government and Labour Law and Administration (GLLAD): www.ilo.org/gllad

- International Programme on the Elimination of Child Labour (IPEC): www.ilo.org/ipec
- SafeWork – InFocus Programme on Occupational Safety and Health and the Environment: www.ilo.org/safework
- International Occupational Safety and Health Information Centre (SafeWork/CIS): www.ilo.org/cis

3) African Regional Labour Administration Center (ARLAC) (Harare, Zimbabwe): www.africaonline.co.zw/arlac.org

4) Arbetslivsinstitutet (Sweden): http://www.niwl.se/

5) Bundesanstalt für Arbeitsschutz und Arbeitsmedizin (BAuA) (Germany): http://www.baua.de/

6) Canadian Centre for Occupational Health and Safety (CCOHS): http://www.ccohs.ca/

7) European Agency for Occupational Safety and Health (Bilbao, Spain): www.europe.osha.int

8) European Foundation for the Improvement of Living and Working Conditions (Dublin, Ireland): www.eurofound.ie

9) European Union, Senior Labour Inspectors' Committee (SLIC) (Luxembourg): www.europa.eu.int/comm/dg05/hands/committ/insp.htm

10) Finnish Institute of Occupational Health: http://www.occuphealth.fi/e/

11) Health and Safety Executive (HSE) (United Kingdom): http://www.hse.gov.uk/hsehome.htm

12) International Association of Labour Inspection (IALI) (Geneva, Switzerland): www.iali.org.

13) Iberoamerican Confederation of Labour Inspectors (CIIT) (Montevideo, Uruguay, email only): ciit.@multi.com.uy

14) International Social Security Association (ISSA) (Geneva, Switzerland): www.issa.int

15) National Institute for Occupational Safety and Health (NIOSH) (United States): http://www.cdc.gov/niosh/homepage.html

16) National Institute for Safety at Work (INRS) (France): http://www.inrs.fr/index_fla.html

17) National Occupational Health and Safety Commission (Australia): http://www.nohsc.gov.au/

18) Occupational Safety and Health Administration (OSHA) (United States): http://www.osha.gov/

19) Schweizerische Versicherungsanstalt; Caisse national suisse d'assurance (SUVA)[Switzerland]: http://www.suva.ch/scripts/suva/index_f.asp

20) The XVI World Congress on Safety and Health at Work (Vienna, Austria): www.safety2002.at

INDEX

audit process 177
challenges to 2–3, 4–5, 20, 53–4, 61
consultative role of 30–1, 33–4, 71–2, 85–6,
    89–90
cooperation with government authorities
    48–50, 154–6
cooperation with social security authorities
    156–7, 223
external evaluation 178–80, 182, 261
functions of 41–2, 86
implications of OSHMS to 205–8
information management policies 112–16
internal evaluation 180–2, 183
and major hazard control 289–292, 294–6
management of 72–4, 161–2, 182
organization 89, 107–9
performance measures 73, 106, 180
pressure on resources 31–2, 72–3, 102–3,
    146–7, 180
promotional activities 180, 182
relations with workers 46–7
specialist 40–1, 69–70, 159–62, 280, 281–2
staffing and recruitment 69, 109, 172–3,
    181, 209–10
strategic partnerships 74–5, 140
systems management 105–7
technical expertise in 30, 89
training policies 109–11, 210
and wider client system 50–1
labour inspectors 15, 38, 118–19
additional duties 31–2, 36
advice on economics of OSH 124–5,
    126–7
as advisors 29–30, 36, 45, 100–3, 205
authority and status of 218–20, 226, 296
discretionary powers 99, 102, 104, 118, 210
enforcement role 29, 45, 100–3
and major hazard safety reports 294–6
monitoring and evaluation of 119, 178–83
and new hazards 301
organization of 153–4
powers of 11–12, 34, 71
problems in agriculture 245, 248–9
as public officials 38, 68, 106
relations with employers 47–8
relations with workers 46–7
role in internal control process 206–7
use of time 146–7, 180
see also cooperation; training
labour legislation
alternative regulatory approaches 234–5

bureaucratic burden of 94, 229, 232–4
and child labour 216–17
and framework of labour inspection 22–3
growth and complexity of 19, 20, 53, 58–9
inflexible application of 57, 229
inspectorates' input into 30–1, 33–4, 71–2,
    85–6, 89–90
regulatory impact statements 30–1, 124
labour market
fragmentation 2–3, 19, 20, 59–60
inspection 93
labour protection policy 85–6, 87–9
holistic approach 146
as statutory requirement 107
see also IPDS
Latin America 32, 81, 156, 160
enforcement 29
multi-function labour inspection system 25,
    41
law courts, collaboration with 158, 223
Le Grand, Daniel 10
legislation, national 14, 22–3, 31
on construction industry 276–7, 278–9
and IC systems 201
international labour Conventions and 81
policing of 33–4
see also labour legislation
legislative review 23, 70–2, 108, 234
livestock hazards, agriculture 247, 248
local authorities 158
enforcement functions delegated to 39, 67
Luxembourg 150

machine operators 57
agriculture 246–7, 253
management oversight and risk tree (MORT)
analysis 129
management standards see standards
manufacturers, responsibilities of 88, 118, 253,
    288
manufacturing sector (secondary) 3, 54
major industrial accidents 55–6
market-testing 20
Mauritius 41
media, relations with 89, 119, 180
mental health
cost of problems 301–2
problems 57–8, 300
protection 66, 311–12
see also psychological problems; stress and
    stress-related conditions

Publications on labour issues and labour law

ILOLEX: A database of International Labour Standards and Fundamental Principles and Rights at Work

A complete, definitive collection of international labour standards on CD-ROM.

In the course of its 80-year history, the International Labour Organization has developed an extensive body of instruments in the field of international labour law and fundamental principles and rights at work.

ILOLEX brings together over 80,000 official documents on international labour standards in a single full-text trilingual database (English/French/Spanish) equipped with sophisticated search and retrieval software. The ILOLEX interface allows users to search numerous categories of documents by various criteria, or to perform free text searches across documents using words or expressions. ILOLEX is an indispensable information source for government officials, employers' and workers' organizations, non-governmental organizations, libraries, academic and professional institutions, and individuals interested in the latest developments in international labour standards and related human rights.

"ILOLEX is an efficiently arranged and user-friendly resource. It provides valuable immediate access to vast arrays of comparative and international data on labour-related subjects and topics relevant to the International Labour Organization. It represents nothing less than a revolution in information retrieval for scholars and practitioners from all fields and endeavours concerned with labour and the employment relationship."
-Prof. Edward Weisband, Edward S. Diggs Chair, Virginia Tech, USA

ISBN 92-2-011302-3   Windows version
2001 edition
New customers: 275 Sw.frs.; US$200; £125; 175 Euros

Decent Work

Report of the Director-General to the International Labour Conference, 87th Session 1999

ISBN 92-2-110804-X
1999   92 pages
20 Sw.fr. ; US$12.95; £10.80; 13 Euros
Also available in French, Spanish, German, Russian, Arabic and Chinese

Your Voice at Work

Global Report under the follow-up to the ILO Declaration on Fundamental Principles and Rights at Work

ISBN 92-2-111504-6
2000   88 pages
20 Sw.fr.; US$12.95; £7.95; 13 Euros
Also available in French, Spanish, German, Russian, Arabic and Chinese

Stopping Forced Labour

Global Report under the follow-up to the ILO Declaration on Fundamental Principles and Rights at Work

ISBN 92-2-111948-3
2001   128 pages
20 Sw.fr.; US$12.95; £7.95; 13 Euros
Also available in French, Spanish, German, Russian, Arabic and Chinese

Publications on labour issues and labour law

New forms of labour administration: Actors in development

Edited by Norman Lécuyer; General editor: Jean Courdouan

In the rapidly changing world of work, labour administrations face significant challenges. This comprehensive volume examines how they are coping with globalization, modernization, and political and financial constraints while also contributing to the economic and social development of their countries.

Providing valuable real-life examples of effective and innovative practice, this work includes 27 case studies from countries around the world covering labour, employment and vocational training, industrial relations, and evaluation. In all these fields, the book considers how labour administrations can better promote social democracy, the legal and social protection of workers, and stronger ties between the social partners.

It examines the management, organization and internal functioning of labour administration while identifying issues that require close and high-priority attention. It also focuses on the difficulties of managing change and discusses various methods to help organizations become more effective and efficient as they modernize. *New forms of labour administration* offers a wealth of ideas and suggestions administrators can incorporate or modify to fit their given situation.

ISBN 92-2-106480-8
2002   380 pages
45 Sw. Fr.; US$29.95; £19.95; 30 Euros
Also available in French

Publications on labour issues and labour law

Violence at work. Second edition

Duncan Chappell and Vittorio Di Martino

Emerging as one of the greatest concerns at the workplace today, violence at work has become a priority issue for many governments, trade unions and employers. This new edition of *Violence at work* mirrors the state of transition in the field. It offers new cases and examples of successful responses to the problem of violence at work, and examines the latest surveys and studies being carried out on the topic. Aggression, assault, sexual harassment, physical abuse and homicide cause widespread concern across occupational sectors worldwide. This book looks at the existing legislation, guidelines and practices and calls for a systematic approach to eliminating violence in the workplace.

ISBN 92-2-110840-6
2000   180 pages
25 Sw.fr.; US$14.95; £9.95; 16 Euros